PRAISE FOR THE UNFOLDING SELF

"*The Unfolding Self* is a classic in the fie........................ ...es and personal growth. It was published the sam........................ ...ounded and has become increasingly relevant over time."

— Rick Doblin, PhD, Founder and Executive Director of the Multidisciplinary
   Association for Psychedelic Studies

"Drawing on decades of study and practice, Ralph Metzner explores powerful metaphors for transformation and awakening. *The Unfolding Self* is a timeless and essential volume for the libraries of modern day mystics and everyday seekers alike!"

— Tara Brach, PhD, Author of *Trusting the Gold*

"Poring over *The Unfolding Self: Varieties of Transformative Experience* a quarter century after it first appeared, I am thrilled to find in its pages more relevance and significance than ever. Given the unprecedented challenges confronting humanity at this historical moment, we owe a debt of gratitude for the choice to republish this book and put it freshly in our hands. Ralph Metzner has an unparalleled capacity to evoke the wonders of human consciousness when it is nourished, trusted, and unleashed."

— Joanna Macy, Author of *World As Lover, World As Self*

"Welcome to the mind of Ralph Metzner: scholarly, curious, informed by personal exploration of many different states of human consciousness and a desire to mean-ingfully integrate their contents into everyday existence."

— William A. Richards, PhD, Author of *Sacred Knowledge: Psychedelics and
   Religious Experiences*

"Transformational experiences are as unique as they are profound, yet each portrays universal truths of human nature. In *The Unfolding Self*, Ralph Metzner uses a tapestry of myth, allegory, and historical context to fathom this neglected aspect of human behavior—one that is vital to science's understanding of humanity and where it might be heading."

— Stanley Krippner, PhD, Affiliated Distinguished Faculty, California Institute of
   Integral Studies; Co-editor, *Varieties of Anomalous Experience: Examining the
   Scientific Evidence*

"In *The Unfolding Self*, Ralph Metzer brings together discoveries shared between himself and his colleagues—some of the great pioneers of mystical transformation of our times—and extensive research into psychological and spiritual traditions throughout the world. This book remains one of his major masterpieces and a gift to humanity."

— Mariana Caplan, MFT, PhD, author of *Eyes Wide Open: Cultivating Discernment on the Spiritual Path*

"Ralph Metzner's finely-woven narrative is as relevant today as it was decades ago—a tribute and beacon illuminating the search for something deep and substantive that permeates the fabric of daily life."

— Glenn Hartelius, PhD, co-author of *The Ketamine Papers: Science, Therapy, and Transformation*

"*The Unfolding Self* is required reading for those interested in transformation—for themselves or for their work with others. If you are anything like me, this book will be one of those on your shelf that is dog-eared, highlighted, and underlined. I'm thrilled to replace my well-worn copy with this new edition—more relevant today than ever."

— Cassandra Vieten, PhD, Director of Research, Arthur C. Clarke Center for Human Imagination, University of California, and co-author of *Living Deeply: The Art and Science of Transformation in Everyday Life*

"In this book, Metzner introduces the reader to the signposts marking the journey of evolutionary growth, charted in story, scripture, psychology, and poetry by a multitude of ages and peoples. The extraordinary range of his engaged scholarship and active practice has allowed him to navigate a cartography of psychospiritual transformation through which a life in the foothills can be transformed by what has been seen at the summit."

— Mariavittoria Mangini, PhD, FNP

"*The Unfolding Self* is a bridge between the awakening of consciousness in California during the 1960s and the timeless awakening—the sacred legacy of planet earth—that has been waiting since the beginning of time."

— Manuel Almendro, clinical psychologist and Director of Oxigeme, Center for a Psychology of Consciousness

THE
UNFOLDING
SELF

THE UNFOLDING SELF

Varieties of Transformative Experience

RALPH METZNER

Foreword by Diane Haug

SYNERGETIC PRESS

SANTA FE • LONDON

Published by Synergetic Press | 1 Blue Bird Ct. Santa Fe, NM 87508
& 24 Old Gloucester St. London, WCIN 3AL, England

Library of Congress Control Number: 2022902258

ISBN 9780907791959 (paperback)
ISBN 9780907791966 (ebook)

Cover design by Amanda Müller
Book design by Brad Greene
Managing Editor: Amanda Müller
Project Editor: Noelle Armstrong
Printed in the USA

I dedicate this book to my son Ari Krishna Metzner,
who was born in 1966 and died in an accident in 1974,
and whose joyous and exuberant spirit graced my life;

and to Angeles Arrien,
Basque seeress and wise woman,
creative teacher,
inspirer of visions,
long great friend of many lifetimes.

CONTENTS

FOREWORD

Ralph Metzner died peacefully at home in his own bed on March 14, 2019. As friends gathered just hours after he made his transition, there was a sense that he left his body on an outbreath as light as a feather. His face remained soft and relaxed; his hands rested gently on his chest in a position that could only be described as a mudra. A Good Death.

I had watched Ralph, my teacher, guide, friend, colleague, and co-conspirator, move consciously toward that transition over the last two decades of his life. For those of us who had the good fortune to gather with Ralph in the spirit of deep inner exploration, we all had repeated opportunities to practice the art of letting go. His teaching and guided divinations were rich with metaphor, symbol, myth, archetype, poetry, and storytelling. The Ralph I knew best was not only a scholar but the creator of sacred space, the alchemist-magician, the shaman, and bard.

Two or three years before Ralph died, we had a personal conversation about how he might craft his own death. He could feel it coming. His guided divinations in group settings were much more focused on the end of life. For those of us who knew him well, it felt like a time of personal preparation—a rehearsal. From his wife Cathy's reporting, at the end of Ralph's life his worldly business was complete, his intention was clear, and the veil between the worlds very thin.

Ralph Metzner created a respectful, soulful bridge to archaic, time-honored, cross-cultural practices for visioning and healing. In journeying with him, our lives were enriched.

When I learned that Synergetic Press had plans to re-publish Ralph's classic, *The Unfolding Self: Varieties of Transformative Experience*, I was delighted (and I sense that he is too!). I consider

Ralph's books absolutely essential reading for those interested in the healing potential of expanded or extra-ordinary states of consciousness.

I am so grateful for the decades of exploring the inner landscape together—of *remembering* where we came from and where we are headed. I offer a deep bow of appreciation for time spent together in the great Spirit Canoe.

Diane Haug
Glorieta, New Mexico

PREFACE to the 2010 edition

Twelve years had elapsed since the publication of *The Unfolding Self*, when the print-run and resources were finally exhausted and the rights reverted to me. I'm grateful to Byron Belitsos, founder and president of Origin Press, for the superb production of that 1997 edition, and for keeping it in print that long.

The market of book publishing, like all other parts of the economy, has gone through wrenching upheavals in recent years, due to the advent of the new digital technologies. I'm deeply appreciative of Alden Bevington, of Pioneer Imprints, for shepherding this book into the world of digital print-on-demand and distribution.

My interest in the themes of psycho-spiritual transformation has remained. For several years before my retirement from the California Institute of Integral Studies in 2006, I taught courses using *The Unfolding Self* as a syllabus and outline. I was always delighted at seeing how the readings seemed to trigger new understandings of life-changing experiences that my students remembered.

Whereas *The Unfolding Self* is focused on personal transformation, my 1999 book Green Psychology deals with the transformations of collective consciousness, particularly in the tense and dissociative relationship between human culture and the Earth. Subsequently, I put together two edited collections of essays on the science and phenomenology of ayahuasca and the psilocybe mushrooms. A combination of public science knowledge (botany, mycology, ethnology) and subjective experience knowledge seems to me to be the appropriate format for the exploration and communication of these areas. In *The Unfolding Self*, psychedelic experiences (and other states of expanded consciousness) are one of the source-pools of observation and insight.

The processes and metaphors described in *The Unfolding Self* continue to be a fruitful source of inspiration for personal growth and creativity. It is my wish and hope that this new edition may serve that purpose as well in the reader.

Ralph Metzner
Sonoma, California
2010

PREFACE to the 1997 edition

It is said that human transformation was the only miracle the Buddha recognized as such. This book describes the variegated experiences of psychospiritual transformation in terms of certain key metaphors. I believe these descriptions can prove useful to those who are in a transformational phase in their lives and are searching for signposts and markers on the way. Further, these metaphoric markers may themselves stimulate and catalyze the inner transformations they describe. My experience in writing this book was itself transformative, as each of the metaphors I was writing about triggered corresponding inner experiences.

I first began to realize several years ago that whereas there are literally hundreds of specific methods of bringing about psychospiritual transformation (yogic and psychotherapeutic methods in particular), only about a dozen or so key metaphors describing the process itself seem to occur over and over in the world's literature. I presented this idea for the first time at the annual conference of the International Transpersonal Association in Boston in 1979 and wrote an article entitled "Ten Classical Metaphors of Self-Transformation" for the *Journal of Transpersonal Psychology* in 1980. I wanted to demonstrate that with some variations in language and emphasis, the essential human process of evolutionary growth is described in similar terms in all major cultures and sacred traditions the world over.

By elucidating the underlying metaphoric structures—which have been variously referred to as archetypes, deep structures, or primordial images—we are uncovering something of humanity's common language. The language of symbols is this common language. It is the language we still use and understand—in dreams, in poetry and art, in the visions and voices that tell us of the sacred and the mystery.

To bring out this universal language, the book draws on the writings of Eastern and Western spiritual traditions, comparative mythology, literature and poetry, the writings of philosophers and teachers in the esoteric, shamanic, yogic, and hermetic traditions, and the formulations of modern depth psychotherapy, anthropology, and transpersonal psychology. In reaching beyond psychology, the field in which I was formally trained, in order to illustrate and understand the patterns and metaphors of transformation, I have probably made mistakes and omissions. I beg the indulgence of scholars and experts in these areas and would appreciate having any errors corrected.

The experience of self-transformation apparently has similar basic features, regardless of historical period or cultural background. Thus, personal accounts of such experiences, drawn from published anthologies and from my own files of patients, clients, and students, are also cited as examples. They often reveal the same metaphoric deep structures as are found in the ancient texts. Based on this admittedly nonstatistical research, I feel confident in saying that very many transformation experiences do in fact occur as the metaphors in this book suggest. A number of the experiential accounts given are my own, and the aptness of the metaphors has been validated by me personally, as well as through the testimony of many individuals known to me.

Two disclaimers and their associated assumptions are appropriate here. First, this book does not deal with social or collective transformation, although this is a vast and complex question of burning interest to many. I am convinced that individual or personal transformation is an essential aspect of—perhaps even a prerequisite to—changes at the familial, organizational, societal, and global levels. However, I do not believe, as many in the transpersonal and New Age movement appear to believe, that one should focus only on self-transformation, one's personal spiritual practice, expecting changes in the collective consciousness to somehow take place automatically. This seems to me like an avoidance of responsibility.

I believe that positive transformation in groups, organizations, societies, and on the whole planet is a direct function of the number of individuals who are consciously attempting to evolve and transform themselves. It appears natural for individuals, after having liberated their own minds to some degree, to want to share their insights and learnings with others and to apply them in social, economic, and political relationships.

The second self-imposed limitation of this work is that it does not delineate linear developmental models showing sequential stages of evolution. This is not to say that development does not proceed in stages—only that agreement on mapping these stages seems quite elusive. Much of the literature on evolutionary stages seems to me to be overly abstract, highly subjective, and sometimes indicative of a kind of premature conceptual crystallization. Subtle judgments of spiritual superiority seem to slip too easily into discussions of levels and stages.

Perhaps it is a matter of personality type or cognitive style. I prefer a pluralistic model of the transformation experience, with emphasis on the fluid processes of change in their manifold variety and individual uniqueness. Others lean to a more uniform model, with emphasis on hierarchical structures, with levels and stages clearly defined and outlined. Each approach certainly has its value.

There are many people whom I wish to acknowledge for their benign and inspiring influence on this work, as well as their friendship. They include the late Alan Watts, Huston Smith, Stanislav and Christina Grof, the late Arthur Young, Frank Barr, Andrew Weil, June Singer, Elaine Pagels, the late Timothy Leary, Richard Alpert (Ram Dass), Michael Harner, the late Ronald Laing, the late Rolf von Eckartsberg, Paul Lee, Jill Purce, Susan Boulet, Rowena Pattee Kryder, Charles Tart, Stanley Krippner, John Lilly, Rupert Sheldrake, the late Lama Govinda, Terence McKenna, Frances Vaughan, Roger Walsh, Michael Murphy, the late Willis Harman, Will Schutz, Frank Barron, Claudio Naranjo, the late Russell Paul Schofield (my teacher of Agni

Yoga), Angeles Arrien, the late Marija Gimbutas, Shyam Bhatnagar, Ann Armstrong, James and Dorothy Fadiman, Bob and Laraine Boyll, Padma Catell, Gunther Weil, Cecil Burney, the late Jack Downing, the late Leo Zeff, Michael Flanagin, Dominie Cappadonna, Richard Baker-Roshi, and Seymour and Sylvia Boorstein. In addition, there are many others—teachers, colleagues, and students at the California Institute of Integral Studies—from whom I have learned a great deal, and who have allowed me to cite their experiences.

This book is a completely revised, expanded, and illustrated version of Opening to Inner Light: *The Transformation of Human Nature and Consciousness,* published in 1986 by Jeremy P. Tarcher, Inc. Although we had our disagreements, I want to express my appreciation to Jeremy Tarcher, who is a publisher with vision and a man with a generous heart. I am very grateful to Simon Warwick-Smith and to Byron Belitsos of Origin Press for agreeing to bring this work out again twelve years after its original publication. I am also grateful to Julie Donovan, Production Manager at Origin Press, for her meticulous attention to detail in the preparation and production of this book. This new edition has been completely updated, and two new chapters have been added: one on resolving the conflict between good and evil, and the other on the integration of human and animal consciousness.

In the years since the publication of *Opening to Inner Light* I have continued to work with these metaphors of transformation—in my classes, workshops, and individual psychotherapy practice. They continue to evoke and catalyze new levels of meaning, lending support to the notion that these are deep archetypal structures of thought with universal applicability.

In my next work I explored the shamanistic, animistic mythology of the pre-Christian Nordic-Germanic peoples. This was published as *The Well of Remembrance: Rediscovering the Earth Wisdom Mythology of Northern Europe* (Shambhala Publications, 1994). Some of the transformation themes explored in the present volume, particularly perceptions, sensations, images, impulses, intentions, and the like exist and occur—is transformed when any of the following occur: changes in thinking, worldview, beliefs, feelings, motives, impulses, and values, as well as altered perceptions, such as heightened seeing (clairvoyance) and sensing (clairsentience).

A further characteristic of this transformation of consciousness is the altered perception of time and space. When time seems to pass at a different rate and when the space around us seems different and unfamiliar, we might experience a giddy or fearful recognition that we are in a process of change with an unpredictable outcome. We might get a feeling that reality is somehow changing, but we can't necessarily tell whether it is around us or inside us.

When our sense of who we are, our self-concept, changes, we speak of personal, or self-, transformation. This kind of experience changes the way we feel about the world—our emotional attitude of basic trust or mistrust, faith or doubt, acceptance or rejection—and the way we feel about ourselves, our self-acceptance, self-esteem, self-love.

Whatever our definition of personality or self may be, it is clear that as self-concepts, self-feelings, and self-images change, the personality changes, too. We feel and sense ourselves to be different persons. Without entering at this point into the debates over whether the ego should be subdued (as in many spiritual traditions) or strengthened (as in Western psychotherapy), we can agree, I believe, that the ego or its function, role, and place is changed.

This book explores the possible meanings of human self-transformation. Other expressions signifying this realm of human experience also focus on the self-concept. *Self-actualization,* a term used in humanistic and existential psychology, implies a bringing into actuality of something that has been a latent potentiality. The term *self-realization* suggests a making real, or a seeing as real, something that has been only a dream or a vague intuition. Similarly, Jung's term *individuation* refers on the one hand to developing individual consciousness, as distinct from mass consciousness, and on the other hand to becoming "un-divided," or whole.

Although self-concept and self-image play a pivotal role in most accounts of psychospiritual transformation, this is not always the case. Buddhist psychology, which does not recognize the existence of any self or ego, explains the transformation simply as an altered mode of functioning of the five "complex aggregates" of consciousness (*skandhas*). These aggregates or patterns of consciousness—intention, perception, feeling/valuing, form awareness, comprehension—together constitute what we think of as personality, according to Buddhist teachings. In the process of psychospiritual transformation, their functions and aims are radically changed.[4]

Two other aspects of individual identity, or selfhood, may be affected in the kind of core transformation we have been discussing: *behavior* and *appearance*. Whether a person's actual *behavior* changes as a result of a deep transformative experience is an open question; obviously, it depends on the individual's prior behavior. We know of extreme cases, such as that of Saul, who became Paul and changed from an enemy to a defender of the Christian faith. Criminals have been known to become saints. Others may, after a transcendent vision, simply find themselves confirmed in their life path and their spiritual practice, with no outwardly observable change in behavior. After enlightenment, the Zen masters said, you may just go back to cutting wood and drawing water.

Bodily appearance also may or may not be altered when consciousness and self are transformed. The traditions of yoga, alchemy, and shamanism contain numerous examples of *psychophysical* transformation. In illness and healing recovery, physical form and appearance may change drastically. Anyone who has undergone the "spontaneous remission" of a tumor has brought about a kind of alchemical transformation of the physical elements of the body. Michael Murphy and his associates have accumulated a large body of documentation and evidence of unusual psychophysical changes occurring in sports and other situations involving extreme physical challenge.[5]

Attempts at describing the process of transformation of consciousness and personality in abstract psychological language are comparatively recent. In prior periods—in the religious and mystical literature of East and West, in the traditions of shamanism, alchemy, and yoga, and in the allegorical language of mythology—symbols and metaphors were used to convey essential information and guidelines for those who found themselves plunged into a transformative crisis or pursuing a disciplined path of development. People often find it helpful to turn to the old texts and stories for guidance and insight into the process they are undergoing. Historical accounts and images from other cultures often evoke a kind of echo or resonance in us. Maybe this is a recognition of our common humanity. Some may feel that they are experiencing traces of "another life."

Through the work of Freud, Jung, and the other psychologists and students of comparative mythology and religion, it has become apparent that myths still function as they did in the eras before psychological theories were invented: many myths seem to articulate deep, archetypal patterns of growth and transformation. While Freud proposed that all men live out the Oedipus myth, modern psychologists agree that there are many different myths that men and women have found themselves living, without realizing it. From the discovery of such deep, mythic undercurrents in one's life, and the revelation of unsuspected levels of meaning, comes support for healing and the self-reflection that leads to understanding.

Symbols and Metaphors of Transformation

In virtually all the traditional systems of human transformation, symbols, metaphors, analogies, parables, myths, and allegories play a central role. This is true of the modern transpersonal psychological approaches as well as the traditional religious, mystical, and esoteric ways. In shamanism, for example, the altered state of consciousness, or trance, that the shaman healer undergoes is symbolized as a journey or a flight through the air; and modern explorers of consciousness, whether using psychedelic drugs or not, have spontaneously adopted the metaphoric language of "the trip" or of "being high." Similarly, alchemy uses the description of chemical processes going on in a retort as metaphors for energetic processes going on in the psychophysical (body-mind) system of the practitioner. Psychotherapists, especially those of a Jungian persuasion, frequently hear dreams with alchemical symbolism from their patients who are in the midst of a transformation process. We need only recall the images of the chakras as lotus flowers that unfold or the kundalini as a serpent that rises to realize how extensive is the use of analogy and symbolism in the yogic traditions.

We can usefully compare the central transformative metaphors used by three of the pioneers of modern depth psychology, Sigmund Freud, Wilhelm Reich, and C. G. Jung. For Freud, the unconscious was a deep and dangerous unknown, like the ocean; and psychoanalysis—making the unconscious conscious—was like reclaiming land from the sea, as practiced in Holland. In Reich's theory, repressed unconscious factors have become congealed into a kind of invisible armor, impacted into the tissues of the body, especially the musculature; bioenergetic therapy aims at the melting, or dissolving, of this armor. In Jung's view, the unconscious, both personal and collective, is like the night sky, an unknown infinity studded with myriads of tiny sparks of light that can become sources of illumination, insight, and creativity for the person in the process of individuation.[6]

Consciousness itself has been thought of in terms of two analogies. One is as a kind of space, context, or field, as in Buddhist notions of "emptiness" or in such expressions as "state of consciousness." The other analogy is that of a river, as in the expressions "stream of consciousness" and "stream of thought." We have, then, a topographical metaphor and a historical one, which correspond to the two main dimensions of our experience of reality—space and time.

In mythology and literature, which may be regarded as the repositories of psychological teachings before there was a separate discipline of psychology (that is, prior to the late nineteenth century), we find two widely used analogies for the human life cycle: the cycle of the day and that of the year. In the diurnal analogy, we think of birth and youth as the sunrise and morning, adulthood as midday, maturity as the afternoon, and aging as the evening of our days. In the seasonal metaphor, we speak of the springtime of our youth, the summer of full adult power and expression, the autumnal maturity of our capacities through midlife, and the "winter of our discontent," of aging and dying.

As these examples make clear, the use of metaphor and symbolism spreads far beyond the realm of literature and the arts. It appears to be such a pervasive characteristic of human language that it may even be regarded as a built-in feature of all human thinking. George Lakoff and Mark Johnson, in their seminal book entitled *Metaphors We Live By,* have made just this point.[7] Adducing evidence from linguistics and philosophy, they show how our ordinary conceptual system—which governs how we think, how we talk, and how we act, both consciously and unconsciously—is fundamentally metaphorical in nature. For example, an unconsciously held, or implicit, metaphor in our culture is the idea that money is liquid, as expressed by such phrases as "cash flow" or "liquid assets."

Lakoff and Johnson argue that the implicit metaphors of ordinary language surely have an experiential basis. There is, among others, an interesting group of metaphors they call orientational, which are based on our experience of the up/down dimension of space. We relate this dimension to feelings of happiness ("my spirits rose," "I feel down"), consciousness ("waking up," "falling asleep"), health and life ("he's at the peak of health," "he dropped dead"), control and power ("the height of power," "being under control"), status ("high society"), time ("upcoming events") and moral and other kinds of evaluation ("high-quality work," "high-mindedness," "low character," "the depths of depravity"). Some of these metaphors we shall encounter again as we discuss the process of consciousness transformation. Most models of psychospiritual development, for instance, use metaphors of an upward progression—"raising" one's level of consciousness, bringing an unconscious complex "up into awareness," "climbing to the top" of the holy, or mystical, mountain, "ascending the ladder" of evolution or perfection, and many more.

A useful distinction can be drawn between symbol and metaphor. A *symbol* is more likely to be an object or thing, whereas a *metaphor* usually stands for a process that extends through time. Thus, the tree is a symbol of the human being, standing vertically between heaven and earth, linking the upper world of Spirit and the lower world of nature. On the other hand, the growth of the tree from seed to flowering maturity is a metaphor for the growth of the individual, the unfolding of a human life from seedconception to full creative expression. The path, or road, is a symbol of development of consciousness; traveling on the road is a metaphor for the process of expanding the horizons of awareness.

The word *symbol* comes from the Greek roots *sym* ("together") and *ballein* ("to throw"). Thus, a symbol is a throwing together, a linkage, connecting two disparate elements in our psyche. The word *metaphor* comes from the Greek roots *meta* ("beyond") and *pherein* ("to carry"). Thus, it is a carrying beyond, a transferring of meaning from one domain into another. *Analogy* comes from the Greek *analogos* ("proportionate"), which in turn is based on *ana* ("according to") and *legein* ("to collect" and "to speak"). Thus, by analogy we can gather (understand) and speak of a similarity in proportion. A clock is a good example of an analog device: it shows the same proportions and relationships as the passage of the sun in relationship to the horizon.

In the writings of the mystics we find detailed and comprehensive descriptions of experiences of transformation, couched in the metaphors and symbols of the particular religion that the mystic adhered to. Transcending the boundaries of culture and religion in their visions and their writings, mystics are pioneers of evolution, reporting back to the rest of humanity on what lies ahead for all of us. As Evelyn Underhill writes in her masterful book *Mysticism*, "The mystic cannot wholly do without symbol and image, inadequate to his vision though they must always be: for his experience must be expressed if it is to be communicated, and its actuality is inexpressible except in some hint or parallel which will stimulate the dormant intuition of the reader."[8] The Jesus of the New Testament used parables constantly, as we know. The phrase "the Kingdom of heaven is like...," which runs like a golden thread through the gospel narrative, can be seen as the story of a transformation of consciousness from human to divine, from personal to transpersonal.

Likewise, myths, legends, and folktales are important sources of transformational metaphors and symbols. They often contain metaphoric accounts of transformative experiences. They are like the stories told by explorers to would-be future voyagers, describing in symbolic form major features of the interior landscapes traversed by the consciousness voyager. Sometimes in a cautionary mode, sometimes in an inspirational mode, they allude metaphorically to the interior conflicts to be resolved, hardships to be endured, obstacles to be overcome, rewards to be won, tools to be used, allies to be found, visions to be seen.[9]

Symbols and metaphors, then, function in the psyche as connecting links between states and levels of consciousness, bridging different domains of reality. They serve to elucidate the structures and functions of consciousness while we are undergoing both ordinary and extraordinary transformations. Many of the deepest, most powerful archetypal symbols are not necessarily articulated verbally. They may be numbers, shapes, colors, natural phenomena, plants, or animals, and they may be expressed in a great variety of cultural forms, including painting, sculpture, architecture, song, dance, ritual, movement, gesture. These primordial, or archetypal, images are found in virtually all cultures and during all ages, thus representing a kind of universal language.[10]

Perhaps the most important function of symbols is to induce or catalyze changes in our perception, feeling, or thinking. For example, a Buddhist monk meditating on a symbolic figure will experience specific definite changes in his consciousness, intentionally induced or facilitated by that symbolic image. In Jungian psychotherapy the patient is often encouraged, in a process known as active imagination, to extend and develop the meanings associated with images encountered in dreams. Jung repeatedly emphasized the active, dynamic nature of symbols and their ability to work within us—even on us—without our conscious recognition.

While Freud postulated that the symbols in the unconscious function primarily to conceal the impulses and conflicts that they symbolize, for Jung the symbol was a bridge between conscious and unconscious, an element that "points beyond itself to a meaning that is darkly divined yet still beyond our grasp." Religious symbols in particular, according to Jung, have a distinctly revelatory and transformative character. "Even today we can see in individuals the spontaneous genesis of genuine and valid religious symbols, springing from the unconscious like flowers of a strange species, while consciousness stands by perplexed."[11] Jung is referring here to the dynamic, spontaneous activity of symbols in the psyche, an activity that brings symbolic visions to people in dreams, meditations, and other such states of consciousness. Such visions always "just come," they are not "made up," and they may surprise the individual in whom they arise.

In the following chapters we shall examine twelve key metaphors that are found in most of the world's great spiritual and philosophical traditions. Mystics, hermits, monks, yogis, saints, sages, magicians, shamans, physicians, wizards, teachers, warriors, scholars, artists, poets, philosophers, scientists, psychologists—all of those who have functioned as wayshowers on the evolutionary path—have found these metaphors and symbols indispensable for describing their experience, for awakening intuition, and for catalyzing transformation.

I invite the reader then to explore these central metaphors. A particular metaphor may trigger a memory of a deeply moving transformative experience the reader has had. Another may point dimly to some totally new, as yet unknown yet subtly sensed dimension of experience. There is no preestablished sequence, no predetermined goal. Each one finds his own path, each works out her own destiny. The myth of each life is a unique configuration of elements.

While it is widely believed and often asserted that "all roads lead to the same mountaintop," I find this to be an oversimplified and misleading analogy. I prefer the ancient symbolism of humans as radiating sources of light, as "walking stars" treading the earth path; or the image of giant trees rooted in the earth, with crown and branches reaching to the heavens; or that of caterpillars dimly sensing their potential as scintillating, liberated butterflies. The exploration of the psyche, of inner space, seems to me very analogous to the exploration of outer space: one can go in all directions for an infinite distance and length of time. As Buckminster Fuller pointed out, each individual exists at the center of a movable sphere of omnidirectional awareness, that moves, like a shadow, everywhere we move.[12]

The process of sharing these inexpressible experiences of transformation may bring us to a greater awareness of our interdependent, common humanity: whether we speak of union with God or with the Tao, of cosmic consciousness or of wholeness, there is a common core here in all of us. We are one in this—further, we are interconnected with the natural world and the cosmos in which we live. Everything is then seen as metaphor: reality itself throws symbols at us with an abundance of meaning. We seem to be designed for the comprehension and communication of meaning.

The phenomenal world is a mirror reflection of a basic ground reality unknowable by us, according to the ancient Indian sages. "All phenomena," said the philosopher-poet Goethe, "are merely metaphorical" ("Alles Vergängliche ist nur ein Gleichnis"). Or, as Gregory Bateson stated it, mind is metaphorical, and mind is "the pattern that connects." In this kind of vision, we are "carried across" metaphorically, across boundaries of culture, of historical era, of race and language. We find linkages, from self to world, from world to world, and from self to other selves.

Theories of Human Transformation

It may be useful to take a brief look at some of the theoretical approaches to the understanding of transformation that have been proposed by historians of religion, philosophers, evolutionary theorists, and psychologists. These theories, as we shall see, have often resorted to the same symbols, metaphors, and images we find in the accounts of the mystics and in the myths of ancient peoples, to explain their perspectives on transformation. Each of these theories and each of the metaphors contributes a valuable thread to the tapestry of our understanding.

William James, in his masterful classic work on religious experience, used the concept of *conversion*, literally a "turning around," to describe not only a person's change from one religion to another but also the process of attaining a sense of the religious dimension of life, a sense of the sacred. "To be converted, to be regenerated, to receive grace, to experience religion, to gain an assurance, are so many phrases which denote the process, gradual or sudden, by which a self hitherto divided, and consciously wrong, inferior and unhappy, becomes unified and consciously right, superior and happy, in consequence of its firmer hold upon religious realities."[13] Religious conversion then is one form that a transformative experience might take for contemporary men and women. The metaphors of awakening and of progressing from fragmentation to wholeness are related to this conversion model of transformation.

The historian of religion Mircea Eliade has emphasized the importance of the *discovery of the sacred*. This does not necessarily imply belief in God or gods or spirits; rather, awareness of the sacred is inherent in a person's mode of being in the world. "Through experience of the sacred the mind grasps the difference between what is revealed as real, potent, rich, and meaningful and that which is deficient in those qualities—in other words, the chaotic and perilous flux of things, their fortuitous and meaningless appearances and disappearances."[14] This kind of experience of a sacred quality of the world, of all life, and of our life in particular is often a significant element in the transformative experience of modern individuals, even those of an atheistic or agnostic orientation. The metaphor of lifting the veils of illusion to discover the real is felt to be a particularly appropriate one for this kind of experience. A person may echo the words of that wonderful spiritual *Amazing Grace*: "I was blind and now I see."

The language of *mysticism* speaks of the human transformation most directly, in language that is usually, though not necessarily, reflective of a specific set of religious beliefs concerning the nature of God or divinity. Hence we have Jewish mysticism, Christian mysticism, and so forth. The word *mystical* refers to an experience of which one cannot speak (it comes from the Greek *muein*, "to keep silent"). As William James wrote: "We pass into mystical states out of ordinary consciousness as from a lesser into a more, as from a smallness into a vastness, and at the same time as from an unrest to a rest. We feel them as reconciling, unifying states." And Evelyn Underhill speaks of mysticism as "an organic process which . . . involves the achievement here and now of the immortal heritage of man ... the art of establishing his conscious relation with the Absolute."[15] The mystical literature of both East and West provides lucid and detailed accounts of the phenomenology of transformative experiences. Mystics try to show us the ineffable, to point to visions of reality inexpressible in ordinary terms. They are the butterflies who try to awaken the human larval caterpillars to the "immortal heritage" that awaits them.

Several writers have outlined *stages of the mystic path.* Underhill states that in Christian mysticism the stages are (1) awakening or conversion to divine reality; (2) purgation and purification; (3) illumination, visions, ecstatic states; (4) death, "the dark night of the soul"; and (5) union with the divine. The teachings of the Gnostics distinguished three stages: (1) awakening, (2) revelation, and (3) anamnesis, or recollection. Many other models similarly outline a developmental sequence of stages in transformation. Each of these stages is associated with a metaphor, and without prejudging whether these experiences always occur exactly in this order, we will examine these metaphors.

Another concept that recurs again and again in this literature is *rebirth* and regeneration. The so-called mystery religions of ancient times preserved secret mythological teachings of rebirth, which were passed on to the initiates as dramatized ceremonies. Some native cultures still practice ancient rituals of rebirth and regeneration. As Jung pointed out in his essay "Concerning Rebirth," much of this literature is concerned with beliefs about reincarnation and resurrection into life after death. Rebirth (*renovatio*) within one lifetime, however, is "an essential transformation, that implies a change of essential nature."[16]

Those who went through the mysteries in these religions were provided an experience they were not allowed to speak about. Through hearing the mythic story recited and seeing it enacted, they were initiated or entered into the process, the way, as prescribed in that particular culture. In some instances, hallucinogenic plant derivatives may have been used, as has been suggested for the Eleusinian mysteries by Wasson, Ruck, and Hofmann.[17] This kind of initiation, clearly involving an altered state of consciousness, could be regarded as a preview or rehearsal for those who were preparing to experience the dying and regeneration in the domain of their own psyches.

From the merging of Hellenistic philosophy and early Christian thought, we have the concept of *metanoia,* which literally means "beyond (*meta*) the mind (*nous*)," a transcending of the rational mind. *Metanoia* was usually translated in the Christian writings as "repentance," which means "feeling sorry again"; it is more accurately rendered, as A. K. Coomaraswamy has said, as "change of mind," or intellectual metamorphosis. "Metanoia is a transformation of one's whole being, from human thinking to divine understanding."[18]

In modern psychology, the terms *spiritual development* and *personal development* have been used to describe this central human process. The work of developmental psychologists, such as Freud, Erikson, Piaget, Loevinger, Kohlberg, and others, has delineated sequences of human development from infancy to adulthood (and more recently into maturity and old age) in such areas as sexuality, social relationships, cognition, and moral values. Eastern philosophies, on the other hand, focus on development beyond the stage of normal, well-adjusted maturity into transpersonal, transrational levels of consciousness, variously called subtle, causal, mystical, spiritual, or unitive. The transpersonal theorist Ken Wilber has formulated an integration of these two traditions: in his approach, human development proceeds in a linear sequence through different levels, each of which transcends and includes the previous one.[19] The details of these linear models will not concern us in this work. It is my belief that the processes described by the metaphors occur at all levels or, one might say, at each transition from one level to another.

Other theorists of human development have suggested the concept of *transition:* William Bridges, for instance, has pointed to a basic

The transformation may be invisible or openly manifest. The healings and miracles performed by Jesus were the "signs" that were needed by the common people of his time to persuade them of his nature and mission. Yet the history of religion is filled with unrecognized saints who labored in selfless love and service, motivated by an inner vision or experience that transformed their being. Eastern texts describe the special physical and psychological features of an enlightened Buddha or the various psychic capacities (*siddhis*) that yogis acquire in the course of their practice. On the other hand, there is the Taoist tradition of the self-effacing sage, "tentative, as if fording a river in winter; hesitant, as if in fear of his neighbors; formal, like a guest." The mind of this Taoist sage is described as being like muddy water, which if left to settle gradually becomes clear.[26]

A transformation may be progressive, regressive, or digressive. This is probably the most important issue concerning the nature and value of a transformative experience, and the one least often discussed. *Progressive transformation* leads from limitation to freedom, from darkness to light, from fragmentation to wholeness, from separation to oneness, from sleeplike inertia to awakened awareness, from personality to spirit, from ego to Self, from mortality to immortality, from illusion to realization. It is, in its myriad variations, the single goal of the classic mystical quest and of all spiritual disciplines. *Regressive transformations* are those that take the opposite direction, from limited "normal" consciousness to even greater limitation or imprisonment, to deeper darkness, more extreme fragmentation and separation, into the chaotic depths of madness, depression, and the states of consciousness associated with violence, injury, and disease. Jung referred to these regressive changes as "diminutions of personality."[27]

By *digressive transformations,* I mean those changes in consciousness that are neither progressive nor regressive but simply different. Some kinds of hypnotic or trance states might be cited as "state" examples as well as possession by spirits, as reported in traditional cultures. Other instances of this kind of transformation discussed by Jung include those brought about by identification with a group, whether a mob, race, nation, or political party, and those brought about by identification with a cult hero. To these, a modern observer might add the transformations wrought by identification (plus idealization and imitation) with a popular star of the sports or entertainment world; and the changes in individuals subjected to various programs of "thought reform," brainwashing, behavior modification, aversion therapy, programming, reprogramming, or deprogramming.

The subject of this book is primarily progressive transformation, although discussions of regressive transformations are included for the sake of comparison and elucidation. The focus of attention on these progressive transformations—otherwise known as evolutionary, psychospiritual, or mystical transformations—carries with it the implicit judgment that these are better, more worthwhile, and more important to study. Indeed, I would go so far as to state that humanity is truly at an evolutionary choice point: we know in our hearts that either we are going to have to grow up very fast, change ourselves in radical ways, or we will destroy major portions of the biosphere and perhaps ourselves as well. We have a desperate need for greater awareness of our own inner dynamics and processes if we are going to survive the present global crisis.

Transformation is different from transcendence. Finally, there is a variation on the theme of transformation that is often overlooked yet very important: the distinction between *transcendence* and *transformation*.[28] To put it simply: to *transcend* is to go beyond; to *transform* is to make different. We transcend a given state of consciousness or a personality characteristic by rising above it (note the spatial metaphor) or by moving beyond it. For example, we may transcend a state of fear or anxiety by moving into an attitude of love and trust, or we may transcend a sense of separateness by meditating on the perception of oneness. The thought patterns of fear or separateness remain in our minds and may be reactivated at another time. It is as if we were stopping the music by lifting the tone arm off the recording. In psychological alchemy, transcendence is associated with the element of air, with its upward motion, and with the process of *sublimatio,* where an impulse is channeled into a "higher" expression (for example, sexual energy is channeled into creativity).

Transformation in the stronger sense (sometimes also called transmutation), however, implies that the patterns of thought or perception are actually changed. The structures and functioning of our psyche become different. Some writers speak of this as a transformation of energy: the energy of fear or anger is transmuted into a different form of expression. If, as a result of unitive experiences and spiritual practices, a person no longer has the sense of separateness, even in ordinary, everyday consciousness, then the personality structure itself has been transformed. In the soundrecording analogy, the engraved patterns on the record have literally been erased or remade. Transformation is symbolized by the element fire and is associated with the notion of purification and with *solutio,* the dissolving of problems or barriers.

Sri Aurobindo, in his writings, distinguishes between transcendence as ascent, and transformation as ascent followed by descent. This is also, I believe, the significance of the mysterious lines in the Hermetic text *The Emerald Tablet:* "It rises from the earth to the heavens, and again descends to the earth, and receives the power of things superior and inferior. By this means thou shalt have the glory of the world."[29] In the simplest terms, transcendence is ascending to heavenly realms, as in a mystical experience, whereas transformation is bringing heaven down to earth, so that it is "on earth as it is in heaven."

Even when we try to analyze and elucidate the process of transformation by means of metaphors and analogies, it remains fundamentally elusive and mysterious. I will let the old Chinese master Chuang Tsu have the last word here: "When one is changing, how does one know that a change is taking place? When one is not changing, how does one know that a change hasn't already occurred? Maybe you and I are still in a dream and have not yet awakened. Be content with what is happening and forget about change; then you can enter into the oneness of the mystery of heaven."[30]

but in fact we are asleep, dreaming that we are awake. Some people feel insulted by the suggestion that they might be asleep when they think they are awake. But those who experience an awakening, even if only momentarily, are usually delighted at the revelation.

The metaphor of awakening implies an important philosophical world view: the view that our perception of reality, our ordinary awareness of the world, is a kind of dream, illusory and transient, and that it benefits our life to try to awaken from this sleep. This notion is akin to what is usually referred to as the idealist philosophy, which holds that reality is subjective, illusory, a creation of ideas or images. As we shall see, there are some very compelling reasons for such a world view, and there is much in our experience that makes sense when looked at from this perspective.

A typical account of an awakening is the following, from a student in one of my classes on altered states of consciousness. The student, a man in his thirties, was meditating when he became aware of an immense energy field that passes through, encompasses, and unites everything.

> I had the sensation that the energy field was both palpable and impalpable, both moving and not moving I felt I had awakened to another level of consciousness. What I usually experienced as reality, phenomenal reality, seemed in the process of merging with or dissolving into this energy, which was a greater reality. When my normal consciousness returned, the veil fell. I could not "see" the energy field anymore. I must have fallen asleep again.[1]

Ordinary Awareness as Dreamlike

The idea that our ordinary consciousness, our world, our life, is dreamlike has found expression in the writings of many spiritual traditions, as well as in poetry and philosophy. According to this metaphor, both living and dying are sleeplike. Shakespeare's Prospero, in *The Tempest,* declared that "we are such stuff as dreams are made on;

and our little life is rounded with a sleep." In many folk belief systems, dying is also regarded as akin to sleeping. We speak euphemistically about putting an animal to sleep, and in Greek mythology Hypnos (sleep) and Thanatos (death) were brother gods. In a variation on this metaphor, we sleep while living and awaken when we die. We shall encounter this theme again when we discuss the metaphor of death and rebirth.

If the end of life is compared to awakening from a sleep, the beginning of life—birth—is often compared to falling into a sleep. In Wordsworth's ode *Intimations of Immortality* we read: "Our birth is but a sleep and a forgetting: / The Soul that rises with us, our life's Star, / Hath had elsewhere its setting, / And cometh from afar." This parallels Gnostic doctrines of incarnation as a fall into matter, a descent into form, and the notion propounded by many philosophers and psychologists that childhood conditioning produces a state of amnesia, a shutting down or reduction of the free and open, fluid awareness of the infant. Some Gnostics used the myth of Endymion, a Greek youth who had been put into a permanent sleep by Zeus, as an image of our condition. Thus, according to these teachings, we normally live a kind of passive, static existence in which vitality is minimized, and we are fascinated by the dreamlike images and fantasies of our inner worlds.

The old Germanic legend of Sleeping Beauty is an enchanting parable on this theme. The princess Beauty symbolizes the human psyche, and the wicked witch who curses the infant at birth represents the process of early conditioning, which brings about oblivious, unawakened consciousness. According to the story, the adolescent princess Beauty pricks her finger on a poisoned spindle, becoming subject to a sleep-inducing spell. "Spinner" is also a German colloquial expression for someone with crazy ideas. Metaphorically speaking, this represents the notion that the developmental crises of adolescence trigger confused thinking that causes the personality to seek escape and relief in deep, forgetful "sleep." The castle and its residents symbolize the body and different parts of the personality. The castle is lifeless: all the people in it, including Sleeping Beauty's parents, the servants, and the cooks, are asleep. Personality and body consciousness are steeped in narcotic oblivion and remain that way until the prince, who is the awakener, arrives, and everything comes alive. The prince is the royal self, the higher self, the one whose kiss or touch awakens us.

In the Gnostic text known as the Gospel of Truth, in a passage referred to as the nightmare parable, we find ordinary existence described as a nightmare: "And everyone has acted as though asleep at the time, when he was ignorant. And this is the way he has come to knowledge, as if he had awakened." Those who remain unawakened are described as "creatures of oblivion." Jacques Lacarrière, a modern writer on the Gnostics, states that for them, "sleep is to consciousness what weight is to the body: a state of death, inertia, a petrification of psychic forces. to awaken, to be alert, to keep vigil, these are the recurring themes in Gnostic texts."[2]

The modern Russian magus and teacher G. I. Gurdjieff, who was strongly influenced by Sufi and Gnostic ideas, constantly emphasized the mechanical, somnambulistic quality of our everyday consciousness: we do not think or do; it thinks, it does. We have no awareness of our mental processes; they simply flow along, following the automated lines of habit and conditioning. We think we are awake, but in fact we are asleep, dreaming that we are awake. According to Gurdjieff, objective consciousness, which is brought about by sustained, systematic effort at self-observation and self-remembering, is a state that compares to ordinary consciousness as the latter compares to dreaming sleep.

It becomes clear that when the ancient philosophers and seers described life or the world as dreamlike, they were uttering suggestions: their statements are prescriptive as well as descriptive. We must realize we are asleep before we can hope to wake up; even then, it is hard enough! They are saying, in effect: look at your experience *as if* it were a dream / sleep, and then perhaps you will have a chance to awaken from it. In a famous verse, the Buddhist *Diamond Sutra* says, "The phenomena of life may be likened unto a dream, a phantasm, a bubble, a shadow, the glistening dew, or lightning flash, and thus they ought to be contemplated."[3] By recommending that we regard reality as a dream, the Buddha is pushing or challenging us to awaken, even if only a little.

The second-century Buddhist philosopher Nagarjuna, in a commentary on this sutra, says:

> There is no reality in a dream, and yet, while one dreams, one believes in the reality of the things one sees in the dream. After one wakes up one recognizes the falseness of the dream and laughs at oneself. Just so, in the dream state of fettered existence a man has a belief in things which do not exist. But when he has found the Path, then, at the moment of enlightenment he understands that there is no reality in them and he laughs at himself.... Man, by the force of the dream state resulting from ignorance, believes in the existence of all sorts of things which do not exist, such as I and mine, male and female, etc.[4]

In other words, our ideas and feelings around self, around possessions, and around relationships are seen from an enlightened, transformed perspective to be dreamlike and unreal. The objects and people of the world we know, which we hold to be real, are seen by one on the path of transformation as exactly analogous to the images of dreams and fantasies.

A parallel description of the human condition is given by the fourth-century Christian theologian Gregory of Nyssa, in a passage on what he calls Angelic Vigilance:

> All who are concerned with the life of heaven must conquer sleep; they must be constantly awake in spirit, driving off, like a kind of drowsiness, the deceiver of souls and the destroyer of truth. By drowsiness and sleep here I am referring to those dream-like

> fantasies which are shaped by those submerged in the deceptions of this life: I mean public office, money, influence, external show, the seduction of pleasure, love of reputation and enjoyment, honor, and all the other things which, by some sort of illusion, are sought after vainly by those who live without reflection. For all these things will pass away with the flux of time; their existence is mere seeming; they are not what we think they are.[5]

Thus, the teachings of transformation from many cultures and religions agree in pointing out the sleeplike nature of our ordinary consciousness, and they share the popular belief that all of us are pursuing dreams—of honor, wealth, pleasure, happiness. The teachers of spiritual transformation take the analogy one step further and say it is possible and desirable—even necessary—to awaken from these dreams. For regardless of whether they are nightmares or pleasant fantasies, these dreams that we seek or avoid are essentially illusions, the transient creations of the imagination.

In the sleep state of consciousness, we each are aware only of our personal, private world; other people may appear in our dreams, but they are our subjective images of them. When we awaken we realize that we exist in a shared, seemingly more objective reality. However, Gurdjieff and other philosophers of transformation argue that ordinary waking consciousness is just as private and subjective as dreaming sleep. In the following epigram, the ancient Greek sage Herakleitos is referring to both levels of the metaphor: "Those who are asleep live each in a private world; those who are awake live in the one Great World."

Dreaming, Sleeping, and Waking in Everyday Life

Since the discovery in the 1950s that rapid eye movement (REM) usually accompanies dreaming and that different kinds of EEG brain waves, as well as respiratory and muscle-tone patterns, distinguish dreaming and nondreaming sleep, Western psychology has acknowledged three normal states: sleeping, dreaming, and waking (not considering, for now, the altered states induced by certain drugs or special procedures such as hypnosis).

The ancient Indian philosophers of the Upanishads long ago formulated a notion that there are four basic states: the three just mentioned plus a fourth state of relaxed, quiet yet alert unitive awareness (*turiya*), the state usually brought about through meditation. Thus we find Western psychology, with its external observational methods, reaching conclusions similar to those reached by the Eastern seers through internal observations.

The characteristic cyclic changes in these different states, and the accompanying brain changes, have been carefully studied and measured in sleep laboratories. Generally, when falling asleep, we start in light sleep, descend through several levels, and reach the deepest sleep around 30 to 40 minutes later. Then we ascend through the levels, returning to light sleep, where we almost wake up (sometimes do, in fact), and enter the REM dreaming stage around 90 to 110 minutes after first entering sleep. This cycle is usually repeated several more times in a night, with variations in the lengths of different stages. Thus, several times during the night's sleep we approach waking, like an underwater swimmer coming up close to the surface; we dream and then descend once again to the lower depths of dreamless oblivion. The level of arousal, or wakefulness, varies continually, in regular cycles as well as in smaller, random fluctuations.[6]

For the waking state a similar situation holds. Using remote measuring devices, sleep researchers have recorded brain waves from subjects going about their daily routine. Thus they have discovered that most people frequently and repeatedly enter into short microsleep periods lasting from thirty seconds to three minutes, which are clearly indicated by their brain waves but of which they themselves are totally unaware. These findings regarding periodic, unaware brain sleep states provide interesting neurophysiological support to the Buddhist,

they may interact with other individuals, known or unknown to them in waking reality. "Mutual dreams," in which two or more people simultaneously have the same dream, may be much more common than the rareness of report would suggest.[10]

In groups and cultures that practice conscious (lucid) dreaming, the domain of consciousness we are in when dreaming is regarded as being as real as the domain of everyday waking reality. This view, that the dream is a reality, is the mirror image of the view—discussed above— that the world, the supposed waking reality, is a dream. The teaching that emerges both from ancient meditation traditions and from the frontiers of modern scientific research is that waking and dreaming consciousness are in several important ways more alike than they are different. Their status as reality is quite similar in many respects.

I take this to be the meaning of the famous story of Chuang Tsu, the Taoist sage, who reported that on awakening from a dream one day, he could not remember whether he was a man who had dreamed he was a butterfly, or a butterfly dreaming he was an old philosopher. We might say he had equated dream consciousness and ordinary waking consciousness so well that he could not then distinguish between them.

Transformation as an Awakening

The shift in awareness from ordinary, subjective dreaming to lucid, objective dreaming seems an appropriate metaphor for transformative awakening. Just as it is possible to awaken, to become lucid, in a dream, so it is possible to attain moments or periods of heightened awareness—"wakefulness"—in waking life. Such experiences involve a radical alteration in the range and scope of awareness and thus clearly qualify as transformative experiences.

The experience of awakening to lucid awareness, in the psychospiritual sense, can occur in a variety of different ways. These varieties of awakening are parallel to the varieties of transformation experience discussed in the Introduction.

The awakening may be sudden or gradual. Triggered by a sound, a word, a touch, a flash of insight, it may feel like an abrupt and dramatic discontinuity in the flow of our normal, somnolent consciousness. Or it may instead be a progressive series of gradual and partial awakenings, of mini-satoris: periods of heightened awareness followed by periods of sinking back into inertia, into the habitual dream fantasies of conditioned consciousness.

The awakening may be momentary or lasting. Some psychedelic drug states are experienced as brief previews, as it were, of the more awakened consciousness possible for human beings. Other methods, involving consistently applied discipline and psychospiritual practice, such as meditation, would be necessary to convert the preview into a permanent aspect of the individual's awareness.

The awakening may be ecstatic or traumatic, and it may involve a reversal of the feeling state that one inhabits during the dream that precedes it. Just as the awakening from a terrifying nightmare is marked by a sense of relief, even an ecstatic feeling of liberation, so the transition from ordinary, conditioned consciousness to awakened consciousness is often exhilarating and joyous, marked by a sense of healing taking place, a peaceful resolution of inner conflicts, and an upsurge of creative inspiration. Yet just as awakening from a beautiful, happy dream can be disappointing or shocking, so we may experience a "rude awakening" when sudden pain, emotional shock, the threat of death to oneself or a loved one, traumatic illness, or disappointments bring about what is appropriately referred to as an "eye-opening" experience. When we awaken from a pleasant, though illusory, "dream," we are "dis-illusioned." This kind of disillusionment can produce growth and positive transformation if we accept it as a challenge to recognize the deeper dimensions of our life.

The awakening may be involuntary, induced perhaps by the compassionate gesture or incisive word of a wise teacher or friend or perhaps by an unexpected "accidental" coincidence of circumstances that serves to break our trance and make us "come to our senses." In systems of yoga, meditation, or other kinds of spiritual practice such as the Gurdjieffian self-remembering, however, the awakening is intentional and purposive, even planned.

The desirability of planned wakefulness is vividly illustrated in Christ's parable about the master away from home. The "master of the house" symbolizes the inner self, and the "servants" represent the various subpersonalities, or egos. "Be alert, be wakeful. You do not know when the moment comes. It is a man away from home: he has left his house and put his servants in charge, each with his own work to do, and he has ordered the doorkeeper to stay awake. Keep awake, then, for you do not know when the master of the house is coming."[11]

In the tradition of Indian yoga, we find the metaphor of awakening in the teachings concerning kundalini, which is said to be in ordinary consciousness a serpent coiled asleep in the "root center" (*muladhara*) at the base of the spine. This kundalini is a kind of energy, which, as a result of yogic practices, may begin to flow in sinuous, serpentine motions through the body, rising up toward the "crown center" (*sahasrara*) at the top of the head. While it has long been assumed that these kinds of psychophysical energy and transformations occur only in practitioners of yoga, it is now recognized that kundalini phenomena (swirling, hot currents of energy coursing through the body, accompanied by hyperalert and energized feeling states) can and do occur in anybody. I have experienced them myself, and so have numbers of my acquaintances and psychotherapy clients.[12]

Meditation can also be seen as a planned effort at awakening. Modern consciousness researchers conceive of meditation as the intentional rechanneling or refocusing of attention. One very widespread form of meditation, exemplified in the Buddhist Vipassana system, involves continuous impartial observation of one's breath, feelings, and thoughts. This activity would naturally develop an observing attitude, very similar to the attentive witness stance of lucid dreaming. While it is often believed that meditation is a passive and tranquil state, producing relaxation akin to sleep, this is not, in fact, the goal of meditation. While there is outward immobility, the meditator is inwardly moving through progressive levels of concentration with increasing degrees of awareness and insight. In Daniel Goleman's words, "Virtually every system of meditation recognizes the awakened state as the ultimate goal of meditation."[13] The name *Buddha* itself means "the Awakened One."

In Gurdjieff's system, "self-remembering" is the key process. "Only by beginning to remember himself does a man really awaken. And then all surrounding life acquires for him a different aspect and a different meaning." Gurdjieff goes to great lengths to describe the kinds of obstacles that prevent human beings from waking up—the principal obstacle being that humans do not realize they are asleep. Even if they do, however, it is necessary to plan and organize the effort of awakening, providing for oneself the equivalent of alarm clocks—external devices to help one awaken; and one has to work cooperatively with others, especially with teachers or leaders who have awakened somewhat more.[14]

In these approaches of yoga, meditation, and other spiritual disciplines, conscious, intentional transformative awakening is regarded as a kind of *initiation:* a teacher, guru, or master provides the impetus that initiates the student's acquaintance with other realms and levels of consciousness. This is often the first step on someone's spiritual journey. Evelyn Underhill, in her books on mysticism, writes that awakening is the first step on the mystical path. However, since awakenings can occur in progressive series, it is clearly possible for there to be later, additional awakenings. Indeed, some believe that the change of state that occurs at death is a kind of final awakening, a time when we last become detached from our body-bound consciousness and see our life objectively, as a dream or film that just ended.

In Greek mythology, the master initiator, the awakener and psychological teacher is the god Hermes, the Roman Mercurius: he touches people's eyes with his staff to summon them to the awakening, the heightened state of consciousness of death. He is the initiator in the Egyptian alchemical mysteries of transformation, later referred to as Hermetic. In one wellknown myth Hermes gives Odysseus a magical herb that will allow that courageous hero to withstand the bewitchment of Circe. The witch-goddess had turned Odysseus's men into swine: metaphorically, this means she induced in them an animalistic sleep state, where they were conscious only of their "swinish" nature. Hermes the god is the herald who carries messages from the gods to human-kind. In psychological alchemy, Mercurius is that part of our psyche through which insight and knowledge come from the "higher" (divine, transpersonal) realms to the human, personal realms. He is the prince who awakens Sleeping Beauty; he is the archetype of the Awakener.

The transformation of consciousness described metaphorically as an awakening can take two different forms: rising beyond or detaching from body consciousness (transcendence) or changing and sensitizing body consciousness itself (transmutation). In the former process, associated particularly with the ascetic and monastic traditions of East and West, there is a withdrawal of attention from the outer, physical world and a heightened awareness of the inner psychic and spiritual realms. Saint Teresa wrote, "In the orison of union, the soul is fully awake as regards God, but wholly asleep as regards the things of this world." And Ramakrishna, the great Indian yogi and saint, stated: "One is aware of pleasure and pain, birth and death, disease and grief, as long as one is identified with the body. All these belong to the body alone and not to the Self. Attaining self-knowledge, one looks on pleasure and pain, birth and death, as a dream."[15]

The latter process, transmutational awakening, occurs when the body itself is regarded as the temple of spirit. This implies then that the physical elements of the body become transformed: organs, tissues, cells, minerals, molecules, atoms become awakened to the presence of spirit or Self within.

The only way to describe this experience is as a feeling of being present within the body and the personality: one has sensitized awareness of both external and internal realities, the physical and the metaphysical realms. This kind of approach is associated more with the alchemical tradition, Tantric and Taoist teachings in the East, as well as Zen Buddhism in certain respects. Transmutational awakening experiences are also common with the use of psychedelics, in which people report feeling every cell of their body charged with aliveness and sensitized to an exquisite degree.[16]

The question may be raised whether the awakening experience is necessarily always benign, or whether it could be dangerous. Could not the shock of an unexpected opening of the mind or the trauma of a painful realization plunge an individual into depression or attract an injury or accident? There are times when we seem to be functioning perfectly fluidly in some difficult, even dangerous, activity and when our experience is dreamlike, and if we were to awaken from this state, we might well bring about a disastrous disturbance. Traditional wisdom suggests that the somnambulist walking on a rooftop should not be awakened lest he lose his footing on changing states of consciousness. The Sioux medicine man Black Elk reports a striking incident of this sort: in a battle with white soldiers he repeatedly charged into a barrage of gunfire without being hurt. He felt himself to be in a dream, protected by an invisible shield. At a certain moment he suddenly "woke up" and immediately felt the hot stabbing of a bullet wound in his abdomen.[17]

Moreover, the Kundalini Yoga experience has been reported to manifest in some individuals as an extremely painful, almost psychotic "kundalini syndrome." Gopi Krishna, an Indian scholar who practiced Kundalini Yoga without benefit of a teacher's guidance, has given vivid descriptions of the uncontrollable energies that flamed, seared, and roared through his body for months, threatening to literally burn him up. Such experiences underscore the need to practice kundalini techniques under the guidance of a competent teacher; otherwise, the intensity of the awakened kundalini energy can be too great for a nervous system insufficiently prepared for the much higher "voltages" coursing through the body.[18]

In a wider sense, it is certainly true that an awakening experience, especially a traumatic one, could in fact have undesirable consequences. A man suddenly confronted by the imminence of his own death *could* have the kind of transcendental experience that has been reported in the literature—leading to self-examination and renewed interest in spiritual development—*or* he could plunge into chronic fear, resignation, and depression, perhaps attempting to mask these through escapist behavior such as alcoholism.

While this kind of situation does undoubtedly occur, one could well argue that the opposite danger is much greater: most of us are asleep most of the time, and we bring about physical, emotional, and social "accidents" and injuries—through lack of awareness, blind inattention—to a far greater extent than we probably realize. To take only a few minor examples: would we spill food, cut a finger, speak a hurtful word, or bang up our car if we were really awake at the time? The mindless violence, senseless confusion, and meaningless trivialities that characterize so much of unconscious human life surely cause huge amounts of frustration, despair, and suffering. Or consider war: Gurdjieff calls it a "mass psychosis" in which millions of sleeping men fight and kill millions of other sleepers. To awaken from the permanent nightmare of ordinary existence certainly seems like a worthwhile idea, even though the awakening may cause momentary shock, confusion, insecurity, or panic. In the long run, if we trust our true, inner nature, it is bound to lead to a life of greater vitality and a deepening sense of the preciousness of existence.

When we awaken in a spiritual sense, we become aware of something, a central core being, that is always unchangingly present and fully pervasive throughout our psyche. This is Essence, the Self that is immortal and omnipresent. As the *Katha Upanishad* states: "That being who is awake in those that sleep, shaping desire after desire, that indeed is the pure. That is *Brahman*, that is called the Immortal."[19] When awake, we are more aware of our inner self and of the external world; we are more in touch with past history and future possibilities as well.

We are urged to *awaken from* the dream of our so-called reality, in which we have been subjectively enmeshed; and we are urged to *awaken to* the divine nature inherent within, the Teacher, the Friend, the Self. This notion parallels the idea of life after death as a resurrection, a kind of revivifying of the dead. In the words of Saint Paul: "I tell you a mystery. We shall not all sleep, but we shall all be changed, in the twinkling of an eye, at the last trumpet."[20] The last trumpet is the wake-up call for the final transition, to a new and higher level of consciousness.

Thus, the metaphor of awakening relates to the idea of coming alive from a deathlike sleep-consciousness to a unitive, nonjudgmental awareness of the true inner spirit. Awakening also relates to the metaphor of returning to one's source or primordial home, to the "higher" realms of consciousness from which we descended at birth and which we have forgotten.

The Zen philosopher D.T. Suzuki wrote: "What is awakened in the Zen experience is not a 'new' experience but an 'old' one, which has been dormant since our loss of 'innocence.'...The awakening is really the rediscovery or the excavation of a long-lost treasure... the finding ourselves back in our original abode where we lived even before our birth."[21]

The awakening sound of divine messengers: Jacob sleeping on the road, dreams of ascending and descending angels (Gen. 28:12). (Title page of *Mutus Liber*, "Silent Book," a collection of graphic alchemical allegories, 17th-century France)

Uncovering the Veils of Illusion

If the doors of perception were cleansed
every thing would appear to man as it is—infinite.
—WILLIAM BLAKE

It is an ancient notion that the world perceived in our everyday consciousness is a shadow play of appearances, illusory and evanescent, and that the transformation of consciousness involves transcending or dissolving this web of images. In chapter 1, on the metaphor of awakening, we saw that in Buddhism and other wisdom teachings the world of appearances is said to be like a dream. We also find this world described in terms of several other analogies: it is like stars, we are told, because faint and unreachable; and like dewdrops, bubbles, clouds, or lightning, because short-lived and constantly changing; like dreams and magic shows, because unreal and illusory; and like veils or coverings, because true perception of reality is somehow distorted by appearances.

The themes of evanescence, illusoriness and obstruction occur again in the following beautiful verse attributed to the eleventh-century Buddhist scholar-mystic Naropa:

A magic spell, a dream, a gleam before the eyes,
A reflection, lightning, an echo, a rainbow,
Moonlight upon water, cloud-lands,
Dimness before the eyes, fog and apparitions,
These are the twelve analogies of the phenomenal.[1]

Several additional related metaphoric images are mentioned here: reflections, echoes, rainbows, moonlight on water—these are also fleeting, insubstantial phenomena; visual dimness and fog, like clouds and cataracts, obscure and distort our vision of reality.

The aspect of transformation symbolized in these images is related to the idea and the experience of *discovery,* which is "un-covering"; to *disillusionment,* which is "abandoning of illusions"; to *revelation,* which is, from the Latin *revelare,* "pulling back the veil" or "unveiling"; and, of course, to awakening from a dream. It is also related to the experience of *insight,* as "inner sight," or seeing that sees beneath the surface appearance; and to *enlightenment,* as an experience of more light, produced by the removal of obscuring veils or coverings. And it is, finally, related to the transformation of the personality, because there are coverings, masks, or sheaths enveloping the central self—which, as they are removed or dissolved, provide an experience appropriately described as "self-disclosure" or "unmasking the self."

An example of a profoundly transformative conversion experience is described in the same imagery by William James in his *Varieties of Religious Experience.* He cites the account of Alphonse Ratisbonne, a Jew who had a conversion experience in a Catholic church in Rome in 1842:

> I did not know where I was: I did not know whether I was Alphonse or another. I only felt myself changed and believed myself another me. . . . In the bottom of my soul I felt an explosion of the most ardent joy. . . . All that I can say is that in an instant the bandage had fallen from my eyes; and not one bandage only, but the whole manifold of bandages with which I had been brought up. One after another they rapidly disappeared, even as the mud and ice disappear under the rays of the burning sun. I came out as from a sepulchre, from an abyss of darkness; and I was living, perfectly living I can explain the change no better than by the simile of a profound sleep or the analogy of a man born blind who should suddenly open his eyes to the day.[2]

The experience of having coverings or blinders removed is frequently reported in psychedelic states and is associated with a sensitized perception of luminosity and vibrancy in vision. Aldous Huxley's account of his mescaline experiences in *The Doors of Perception,* published in 1954, first suggested the relevance of this metaphor for these visionary states. The feeling of the self being "uncovered," analogous to the peeling of the layers of an onion, is also extremely common in the deeper transformative experiences.

Eastern teachings explain the cause of these obstructions by reference to the concept of *avidya* (Sanskrit for "not-knowledge"). This term is commonly translated "ignorance" but may more appropriately be regarded as "unconsciousness," or metaphorically, "blindness." According to both Hindu and Buddhist teachings, *avidya* is the condition of being born into this world, an inherent feature of human life. One text states: "*Avidya* overpowers beings through the lack of vision, or through false vision, just as a cataract overpowers the eyes."[3] In other words, ordinary human consciousness is obstructed, blind, unconscious, a play of illusions (*maya*). Genuine consciousness is possible, but only through yogic and meditative practices.

In some of the writings of transformational philosophers, we find the analogy of our perception and our thinking being obscured by fog or clouds. A famous fourteenth-century English text of mystical literature, *The Cloud of Unknowing,* states: "Anything that you do not know or have forgotten may be said to be 'dark' to you, for you cannot see it with the inward eye. For this reason it is called a 'cloud,' not of the sky, of course, but of 'unknowing,' a cloud of unknowing between you and your God."[4] This is the cloud of ignorance (*avidya*), of unconsciousness; the cloud that blocks the light of the inner sun, the light of spirit.

If ordinary, unawakened consciousness is clouded or obstructed, then transformed consciousness is comparable to seeing in the clear, unobscured light of the sun. William James writes: "In conversion or religious regeneration, . . . a not infrequent consequence of the change operated in the subject is a transfiguration of the face of nature in his eyes. A new heaven seems to shine upon a new earth."[5] Everything we look at in such states seems illuminated with a kind of pristine, luminous beauty, comparable to the light of a new day dawning.

In Buddhism we find the fascinating idea that not only vision but also thought is obstructed, with "thought-coverings" (*citta-avarana*). These thought coverings are the result of emotional cravings and aversions, which cause us to have mental blocks, or conceptual blind spots, in certain areas. Transformed consciousness is a state in which the individual is freed from the suffering, the emotional ups and downs, that stem from these unconscious mental blocks. In the words of the *Heart Sutra*, "A bodhisattva, through having relied on the perfection of wisdom, dwells without thought-coverings (*citta-avarana*). In the absence of thought-coverings he has not been made to tremble, he has overcome what can upset, and in the end he attains to enlightenment (*nirvana*)."[6] In this state one is no longer attached, through either craving or aversion, to the world of sense objects, of phenomenal appearances. One sees and lives in what one modern seerwriter, Stewart Edward White, called "the unobstructed universe."[7]

The symbolism of clouds points not only to the occluding and darkening of our thought and perception but also to its transitory, illusory nature. Clouds, like bubbles, dewdrops, dreams, fog, echoes, and rainbows arise and fade on the screen of our awareness and do not appear to us as solid things or objects. They are intangible, and hence they do not seem very real. Yet the sages and teachers tell us that we should look at things and sense-objects as no more real or substantial than these evanescent phenomena. When we do, we experience a kind of detachment, a bemused acceptance of the inevitability of change, a lessened desire to possess and to hold.

The individual is then aware of, awakened to, the presence of the inner self, the true Buddha nature. Just as when we recognize the dream we can awaken, so when we see the phenomenal world as the play of appearances it is, we can realize our true nature, we can attain "self-realization." In the Indian philosophy of Vedanta, this is the realization of *Atman-Brahman:* the Self (*Atman*) is realized as being one with the Absolute (*Brahman*). In the words of the ninth-century philosopher Shankara, "*Brahman* is not the universe of the senses. Everything is a manifestation of *Brahman.* The appearance of the world as other than *Brahman* is unreal, like a mirage in the desert."[8]

The World Perceived as Maya

According to the Vedanta philosophy, only *Brahman,* Absolute Beingness, is real; all else is illusion, mirage, flickering shadows, dreams. The Indian philosopher-seers used the concept of maya to refer to the illusory, evanescent quality of the phenomenal world. *Maya* is usually translated as "illusion," because of the Vedantists' insistence that only Absolute Beingness, *Brahman,* is real. Originally, however, *maya* derives from root words meaning "show" and "measure." Later, *maya* came to mean "power," particularly creative and magical power, the power that creates the magic show of phenomena. On the individual human scale, maya is the power that deludes us into taking the phenomenal world for real, the power we have to project outward the created images of our own mind. Our thoughts create our reality. Shankara tells us we "superimpose" our concepts of space, time, and material objects onto the external world, when actually there is only unchanging, infinite Beingness. He says this is as delusional as the man who mistakes a rope for a snake in the dark, who superimposes his image of a snake on what is really only a rope.[9]

An eloquent description of the realization of the world as a projected play of illusory images is found in Gopi Krishna's account of his experiences with the awakening of kundalini.

> The phenomenal world, ceaselessly in motion, characterized by creation, incessant change and dissolution, receded into the background and assumed the appearance of an extremely thin, rapidly melting layer of foam upon a substantial rolling ocean of life, a veil of exceedingly fine vapor before an infinitely large conscious Sun,

constituting a complete reversal of the relationship between the world and the limited human consciousness. It showed the previously all-dominating cosmos reduced to the subordinate position of an evanescent and illusory appendage.[10]

This is the perspective that may be attained in a transformative experience, regardless of where it occurs or in what cultural context. It is also the perspective that transformational thinkers recommend as preparing the way for such a transformative breakthrough.

Maya, then, is the magic picture show of the mind, which is projected with such power and vividness that we are deluded into taking it for something real "out there." There are fascinating parallels between this view and the emerging world view of modern physics, particularly in relation to quantum theory, with its notion of the interdependence of the observer and observed reality. As physicist Fritjof Capra states:

> As we penetrate into matter, nature does not show us any isolated building blocks, but rather appears as a complicated web of relations between the various parts of the whole. These relations always include the observer in an essential way. . . . The properties of any atomic object can only be understood in terms of the object's interaction with the observer. In atomic physics, we can never speak about nature without, at the same time, speaking about ourselves.[11]

The Buddhists take this notion of the world as created, imagined illusions one step further: To them the ultimate reality is void or emptiness (*sunyata*). And since all outwardly perceived objects are themselves illusory, only the infinite emptiness within them is real. This kind of awareness—of the world as having characteristics of "no-thing-ness"—has also been called a state of "consciousness without an object." In a famous verse from the *Heart Sutra*, we read, "Form is emptiness, and emptiness is not different from form, nor is form different from emptiness: indeed, emptiness is form."[12]

This, also, is not just a concept but may be an actual perception. A woman describing her experience in meditation reported that "my perception of everything around me and of my own body and personality was exactly balanced between awareness of 'form' as one aspect and of 'emptiness' as open space. It was like a double perspective, the inside and the outside of a sphere simultaneously, convex and concave, form as surface and space as container. I felt myself moving in awareness just exactly along the 'edge' between form and formlessness. The latter was like a kind of cliff, or abyss, of infinite depth."[13]

The paradoxical equivalence of form and emptiness formulated by Buddhist philosophers also has its parallel in modern quantum-relativistic physics. To quote Capra again:

> The field theories of modern physics force us to abandon the classical distinction between material particles and the void. Einstein's field theory of gravity and quantum field theory both show that particles cannot be separated from the space surrounding them. . . . They have to be seen as condensations of a continuous field which is present throughout space. . . . Here, then, is the closest parallel to the Void of Eastern mysticism in modern physics. Like the Eastern Void, the "physical vacuum"—as it is called in field theory—is not a state of mere nothingness, but contains the potentiality for all forms of the particle world.[14]

A well-known variant of the theme of illusion and reality is Plato's parable of the cave: we human beings, Socrates tells us, are like prisoners chained to the wall of a dark cave, in which fires cast flickering shadows on the walls—and we identify these shadows as the events and phenomena of the real world. Outside the cave, there is the lighted world illumined by the daytime sun, but when one of us prisoners manages to break free from our chains, he or she is dazzled by the great radiance and only then realizes that what has ordinarily been taken for real is a play of shadows. Here, as always, the transformation of consciousness involves a radical restructuring of our mode of perception: as we awaken, we recognize we have been asleep; as we see clearly, we realize that we have been fascinated by illusory images.[15]

According to these ideas, there are no "real" things out there that can be identified or described separately from how we as observers see them. Matter and the perception of matter are interdependently interrelated, modern physics tells us. The ultimate ground of matter is only a kind of emptiness, like space, that is filled with potentialities. Our perception, our consciousness, somehow contains veils, coverings, or screens through which or onto which we project these visions that we call phenomenal reality. William James, in describing the insights he obtained from his experiments with the psychedelic nitrous oxide, stated:

> Our normal waking consciousness, rational consciousness as we call it, is but one special type of consciousness, whilst all about it, *parted from it by the filmiest of screens* [emphasis added], there lie potential forms of consciousness entirely different.... No account of the universe in its totality can be final which leaves these other forms of consciousness quite disregarded.[16]

The Transformation of Vision

With this metaphor then, the psychospiritual transformation is described as analogous to a transformation of visual perception—from clouded to clear, from blind to seeing, from veiled to revealed. The experience is also described as an emerging out of darkness into light, becoming un-blinded, and as the removal of multiple coverings from our eyes. The "cleansing of the doors of perception" that occurs in some mystical and psychedelic states, and sometimes as a consequence of meditation, has been amply described and documented in the literature of consciousness research.

Sometimes the transformation experience can be so overwhelming that visual perception is changed literally as well as metaphorically.

A striking example from the early history of Christianity is the conversion of Saul of Tarsus to Paul, on the road to Damascus. After the flash of illumination that knocked him off his horse, Saul was blinded for three days. A healer named Ananias came to him and told him he would help him with his sight by laying on of hands. "And immediately it seemed that the scales fell from his eyes, and he regained his sight. Thereupon he was baptized" (Acts 9:1-19). In this case, the impact of the conversion vision was so strong that he was first blinded (perhaps as a kind of lesson) and *then* his eyes were opened.

If the transformation of vision occurs in the opposite direction, we have what I have called regressive transformation. For example, psychiatrists may speak of the "clouded sensorium" of the psychotic. A depressed or grief-stricken person may feel a cloud hovering over her or his head. An observer with sensitized perception (clairvoyance) can "see" the gray, brown, or dark veils and coverings that seem to surround the face and body of a person in an emotionally distraught or despondent state. William James quotes an asylum patient who said, "I see, I touch, but the things do not come near me, a thick veil alters the hue and look of everything."[17]

The closed mind is often accompanied by relatively closed narrow eyes, and we have all encountered the pinpoint gaze of people who distrust or dislike what they see. Conversely, when a person has an "eye-opening" inner breakthrough in consciousness, this can well be manifested in a more open facial expression and wider, more radiant eyes. And the notion that our pupils dilate when we take delight in what we are seeing has been part of folklore for a long time and entered the field of advertising and market-survey techniques as well.

In some writings, the transformation of vision involved in spiritual transformation has been described as a change from outer to inner focus, from the material world of the senses to the spiritual worlds revealed by inner sight. It is also a shift from the familiar world of space and time to the transcendent worlds, where "every thing appears as it is—infinite," as William Blake said; and where we can see things from the perspective of eternity. Blake, one of our greatest visionary artists and poets, said he wanted "to open the immortal eyes of Man inwards, into the Worlds of Thought, into Eternity."

Some philosophers and psychologists state that inner, spiritual vision and outer, physical vision are somehow in competition with each other, that we cannot focus both inwardly and outwardly at once. Jung seemed to believe this, since in his view, the function of intuition, which gives us inner knowing, and the function of sensation, which gives us outer knowledge through the senses, are always opposite.[18] There is an alternate view, which I personally favor, that says that transformation requires the balancing of two perspectives. This is more akin to the shamanic concept that we must learn to master both ordinary and nonordinary reality, that we must be able to see and to "see," to perceive both the obstructed and the unobstructed reality.

This inward vision, the eye of wisdom, is related to the function of *clairvoyance,* which literally means "clear seeing," seeing without obstructions, without coverings or veils. This kind of vision sees the subtle auric energy fields that surround and interpenetrate all living things; it sees into the essences of things, into what the seventeenth-century seer-mystic Jacob Boehme called their "signatures," their interior lineaments or designs. Students of psychic abilities also recognize *clairaudience,* or "clear hearing," and *clairsentience,* or "clear sensing." The implication of this kind of language is that there are aspects of reality that exist but are normally not perceived by us because of some kind of obstruction or limitation. For certain individuals and in certain states of consciousness, it is possible to perceive these other, more subtle energetic phenomena.

The transformed vision we are speaking of here can also involve greater depth and dimensionality: ordinary, unawakened perception tends to have a flat, two-dimensional field, whereas heightened, sensitized perception has a depth and almost spherical feel to it. In experiments with hypnosis, Bernard Aaronson demonstrated that an individual under the hypnotic set to "see greater depth" does in fact do so, and feels euphoric, with expanded, near-psychedelic awareness. An individual with the opposite mental set—to see less depth—feels alienated and tense, and tends to withdraw.[19] Ecstatic experiences, with or without drugs, are often accompanied by a kind of spherical expansion of visual space.

Some philosophers speak of not just two kinds of vision, but three. The symbolism of three eyes was developed by the medieval Scholastic philosophers and by Indian Raja Yoga as well, in the concept of the "third eye." The medieval theologians taught that we have (1) the eye of the flesh, which sees worldly things, (2) the eye of reason, by which we know the mind and concepts, and (3) the eye of contemplation, by which we know transcendent, spiritual realities. The way of true wisdom involved the ability to consciously function with and differentiate these three sources of knowledge.[20]

In the Indian yoga teachings, we find a different meaning given to the notion of three eyes. Here the left eye is lunar, related to night, the feminine, the receptive, whereas the right eye is solar, related to daytime, the masculine, and the dynamic-expressive. The vision of these two must balance and alternate rhythmically. The third eye, in the center of the forehead, was regarded as the eye of inner vision, intuition, and clairvoyant perception when awakened through yogic practices.

Blake began to speak in the later part of his life of the "fourfold" vision that he was given:

Now I a fourfold vision see,
And a fourfold vision is given to me;
'Tis fourfold in my supreme delight
And threefold in soft Beulah's night
And twofold always. May God us keep
From single vision and Newton's sleep.[21]

"Newton's sleep" is Blake's sarcastic term for the unawakened state of consciousness that sees only the external world, the material universe of Newtonian physics. Twofold vision is the complementarity of inner and outer, subtle and physical perception. "Soft Beulah's night" refers to the state of poetic inspiration, the poet's muse or anima. And "fourfold vision" is complete, whole, all-inclusive vision: this could refer to the four functions (thinking, feeling, sensation, intuition), to the four cosmic directions, or to any number of fourfold schemata of understanding.

The fourfold pattern is always related to the mandala, the central symbol of individuation, integration, or wholeness. One could say that a key component of the transformation of vision in psychospiritual development is the perceiving of the visual field as a kind of mandala. American Indian vision seekers have reported that they see the "circle of the Sky" touch the "circle of the Earth," forming one great hoop. This mandala, perceived in visionary states, has depth as well; in other words, it is a sphere with a six-armed cross inside. It is Buckminster Fuller's sphere of "omnidirectional awareness," moving always with us. And in Indian Tantric Yoga, the practitioners meditate with a mandala until they have succeeded in projecting and integrating their mental contents into this circular diagram. In this way the meditator comes to realize that our ordinary perception of the world is also a projected image.

Beyond threefold and even fourfold vision, there exists the symbolism of multiple eyes: in Hindu and Buddhist art one finds statues and paintings of divine or enlightened beings that have eyes all over the body, on the arms, legs, torso, palms, etc. This image symbolizes an awakened state in which awareness or light or presence has entered into every part and aspect of a being. The image of the eye signifies awareness in action, movement, gesture, expression, as well as heightened perception.

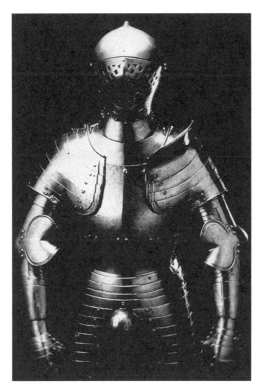

The armored individual: Wilhelm Reich's metaphor for character structure embodied in muscular tension patterns. (16th-century European military armor)

Such symbolic expressions in religious or yogic art can be, and have been, readily transferred to practical application in the growth processes of modern individuals. For instance, a student in an art-therapy class spontaneously drew a self-portrait and then drew a large eye around the figure. Doing this drawing, which one could call a metaphor for self-awareness or insight, had the effect of lifting her out of a prolonged depressive mood.

Another experience illustrates the relationship between changing vision and changing emotional state: once during a psychedelic experience, I saw the branches of a tree moving and sparkling with vivid, glistening colors. A feeling of anxiety arose in me during a conversation with my companion. I noticed that the tree branches stopped moving and the colors drained out, until the branches were blackish gray. As I observed these changes and succeeded in relaxing the anxious tension, the branches fluttered again, and the colors flowed back in. Visual appearances and emotional mood changed in synchrony.

I suggest that many people have had similar experiences in a variety of different situations. When we are afraid of or annoyed at something, the visual field tends to take on fearful or threatening hues and shadings. When we regard others with the eyes of love or attraction, they begin to look lovely and attractive. Beauty, it has often been said, is in the eye of the beholder—and so, of course, are ugliness, aggression, greed, and threat.

The transformation of vision is a metaphorical "cleansing of the doors of perception," in Blake's memorable phrase. It is a purifying of the perceptual channels, so that we are no longer limited to seeing in the darkness of the cave of our own illusions. Blake spoke of "melting apparent surfaces away, and displaying the infinite which was hid." When the surface appearances are dissolved, when we can "see through" someone or something, we become aware of how our own emotional states affect the appearances we perceive. We can then own and withdraw our projections and recognize the distortions and blinders that result from past karmic conditioning.

Unmasking the Self

Veils cover our eyes, obstructing and distorting our view of reality. Similar veils obstruct our perception of ourselves, our self-image, thus distorting and occluding awareness of our true nature or identity. Carl Jung's psychology speaks of this artificial, illusory self-concept as the persona: the mask we manufacture for the sake of appearances, a kind of cover identity that hides our actual self. The persona was actually the mask used by Roman actors to speak through as they acted their roles, and *persona* is the basis of our word *personality*. This suggests that personality, or ego, is a kind of cover, or mask, and that the "real" individual is hidden beneath the mask.

Wilhelm Reich's genius was to see and point out that this

self-image cover is actually embodied in the muscular tension patterns that he called the armor. Reich and his followers have amply demonstrated that profound changes in personality and feeling can occur as the muscular armor is directly altered or dissolved. We are normally not conscious of the armoring, but it is manifested in our behavior and thinking.[22]

We express ourselves with our armoring or through it; we are therefore limited in our expressive range by the defensive emotional tension patterns woven into the muscles and tissues of our bodies. A more organic metaphor for the mask of character was formulated by the thirteenth-century mystic-theologian Meister Eckhart: "A man has many skins in himself, covering the depths of his heart. Man knows so many things, but he does not know himself. Why, thirty or forty skins or hides, just like an ox's or bear's, so thick and hard, cover the soul."[23]

Clothes also symbolically represent the personality or character, the front with which we face the world, our habits of expression and behavior. The English word *habit* still has meanings connected to clothing, as in the term *riding habit*. And perhaps most intimately, the skin itself is symbolically perceived as equivalent to or related to the persona. Alan Watts spoke of the "skin-encapsulated ego," the typical self-image whose perceived boundary is the skin. Under the sway of this skin-ego image, I think, "I am being touched" when somebody touches my skin. If, on the other hand, I feel touched emotionally by someone's word or gesture, then my self-image is expanded well beyond the material skin to the "emotional body."

The mask, the armor, the clothes, the skin—all are symbols for personality or character. Corresponding to each of these symbols of personality are metaphors for the transformative experience. In an experience of conversion, insight, or revelation (unveiling), the individual may experience a mask being removed or a rigid character armor being dissolved or clothes being taken off, so that he or she feels naked (and then may have to deal with all the emotional charge and shame surrounding nakedness). The person may also experience the feeling of his or her skin boundary dissolving, the inside and outside becoming continuous and flowing together. Each of these metaphors has clear structural similarity to the idea of removing veils or coverings from perception.

A person who experiences the dissolving of body boundaries will interpret it differently according to his or her prior beliefs and expectations. For someone totally identified with his or her body image, the experience of its dissolution could be catastrophic. And this phenomenon would be interpreted by most psychiatrists as a symptom of weak ego boundaries, or "depersonalization." On the other hand, for someone familiar with Buddhist or other mystical literature who anticipates this kind of experience and has a sense of identity that includes the body but is not limited to it, such an experience could be a sought-after ecstatic release into an expanded state of consciousness. In the words of Shunryu Suzuki, "When you become you, Zen becomes Zen. When you are you, you see things as they are, and you become one with your surroundings."[24]

Several other related metaphors of self-transformation that appear to encompass the same theme exist in the world's literature. In older, primal cultures, many of these come from observations of the animal world. For instance, the snake's shedding of its skin was often regarded as a teaching concerning regeneration and transformation of self. The bird that breaks the shell and emerges from the "crack in the cosmic egg" is another image. People frequently feel themselves to exist within a hardened "shell," analogous to Reich's armor, which they find difficult to break out of. The insect in its larval stage, completely enfolded in its cocoon and unaware of its latent capacities, is yet another metaphor for the undeveloped, unactualized self. Adolf Portmann has pointed out that the larva "masks" the insect's mature, developed form. Similarly, the persona acquired in childhood masks the adult self.

The idea that in the process of growing up, of becoming mature or adult, there is a kind of unmasking, a more direct seeing of oneself, is also implicit in the famous passage of Saint Paul: "When I was a child, my speech, my outlook, and my thoughts were all childish. When I grew up, I finished with childish things. Now we see only puzzling reflections in a mirror [through a glass, darkly]; but then face to face. Now my knowledge [of myself] is partial; then it will be complete, even as God's knowledge of me."[25] When the personality confronts the Self, there is no hiding, no puzzling darkness, but only direct and complete self-knowledge.

A vivid account of such a radical and complete unmasking and self-confrontation is given by William James, quoting the experience of one J. A. Symonds:

> ... time, sensation, and the multitudinous factors of experience which seem to qualify what we are pleased to call our Self.... At last nothing remained but a pure, absolute, abstract Self. The universe became without form and void of content. But Self persisted, formidable in its vivid keenness, feeling the most poignant doubts about reality ... the sense that I had followed the thread of being to the verge of the abyss, and had arrived at demonstration of eternal maya or illusion. Often have I asked myself, on waking from that formless state of denuded, keenly sentient being, which is the unreality? The trance of fiery, vacant, apprehensive, skeptical Self from which I issue, or these surrounding phenomena and habits which veil that inner Self and build a sort of flesh-and-blood conventionality?[26]

A powerful mythic expression of this theme is the story from the ancient Near East of the descent of the goddess Inanna into the underworld. This is symbolically an initiation mystery tale, which describes the tests one must pass on the way to self-knowledge and inner unification. As the goddess descends into the underworld of the dead, she passes through seven thresholds, and at each one she has to remove one ornament or covering: at the first, her crown; the next, her earrings and facial jewelry; then her necklace, her breast shields, her bracelets, her jeweled belt, and finally her pelvic garment. These seven stages of descent relate to the uncovering, or opening, of seven energy centers. The "ornaments" may be taken to symbolize the conventional, conditioned self-images that obstruct and cover the natural expression of life energy through the centers.

Undefended, unadorned, and without any of the usual social disguises, with her centers opened, she has to confront her ancient sister Ereshkigal, the terrible goddess of death and the underworld. She has to endure horrible sickness and torment and be as dead for three days before she can be released back to the normal world of the living.[27]

Beyond the obvious and widespread symbolic identification of veils with the clothes, masks, and armor that express character, there is also another, deeper meaning to these symbols. The perceptual experience of piercing or removing a veil is like traversing a kind of threshold or boundary region between planes of consciousness. Ancient teachings held that each human being has many bodies, or forms, separated from one another by "veils," "curtains," or "skins." Birth, or incarnation, involves taking on bodies, clothes, or skins—the Self or Spirit becomes embodied. The phrase in the Book of Genesis about the "coats of skins" the Lord made for Adam and Eve may be a reference to this idea.

Indian yoga psychology speaks of the series of "sheaths" (*koshas*) with which the Self-Spirit-*Atman* is clothed, the outermost and densest one being the physical body. This physical body is referred to as *anna-mayakosha*, the "sheath form made of food." Higher, less densely material forms are made of "breath," of "feeling," of "mind," of "bliss."

During the incarnational descent into form, we take on one after another of these veils. In an extraordinary passage written by an Islamic Rifa'i dervish, quoted in R. A. Nicholson's *The Mystics of Islam*, we find the incarnational descent described as a passage through seventy thousand veils:

> Seventy thousand veils separate Allah, the One Reality, from the world of matter and sense. And every soul passes before his birth through these seventy thousand. The inner half of these are veils of light; the outer half veils of darkness.... Thus the child is born weeping, for the soul knows its separation from Allah, the One Reality.... the passage through the veils has brought with it forgetfulness.... He is now, as it were, in prison in his body, separated by these thick curtains from Allah.[28]

Regardless of whether we count seventy or seventy thousand, the descent into bodily form is always seen as a taking on of veils, clothes, or sheaths; or a falling into sleep, a forgetting.

On the other hand, the journey to God, or to the Self, is always experienced as an uncovering, a removal of veils. Meister Eckhart refers to this ascending, evolutionary transformation in the following passage: "In being lifted up, the soul is made naked before the idea of God, for God's begetting; the image of God is unveiled and free in the open soul."[29]

Ignorance and lack of understanding are always symbolized by blindness, deafness, or clouded or covered thinking. Insight, true perception, and spiritual awareness are experienced as unveiling, re-veiling, dis-covering, dis-illusionment.

Saint Paul writes:

> To this very day, every time the Law of Moses is read, a veil lies over the minds of the hearers. However, as Scripture says, "when one turns to the Lord, the veil is removed." Now the Lord of whom this passage speaks is the Spirit; and where the Spirit of the Lord is, there is liberty. And because there is for us no veil over the face, we all reflect as in a mirror the splendor of the Lord; thus we are transfigured into his likeness, from splendor to splendor; such is the influence of the Lord who is Spirit.[30]

Breaking through to cosmic consciousness: the seeker, thrusting his head
through the ceiling of ordinary reality, encounters a vision of celestial grandeur.
(Alchemical etching, 17th-century Germany)

Turning inward, toward the Lord, the Spirit, *Atman*, brings about
the ascent through the dimensions, the experience of transcendent
reality, with clairvoyant vision of the inner domains and subtle body
sheaths. It also brings about the unmasking of the persona, the dissolving of conditioned self-images.

As the eye is unveiled, the I is transformed.

From Captivity to Liberation

3

To know consists in opening out a way whence
the imprisoned splendor may escape.

—ROBERT BROWNING

Escape from prison has been one of the most consistent metaphors for the process of human transformation, both in the myths and texts of the ancients and in the psychological writings of modern thinkers. Liberation from the bonds of karma, escape from the ceaseless round of *samsara* (existence), freedom from the snares of illusion, deliverance from the clutches of sin—these are but some of the traditional expressions that allude to this aspect of transformation. The confined and bounded quality of ordinary human consciousness is evident to all of us: we may feel trapped in a relationship, tied down by obligations, bound by job demands, attached to possessions, fixated on someone we desire, or generally "hung up." The pattern of psychological defenses can and does become a rigid bodily armor. Psychoanalysts tell us we are the "prisoners of childhood" or write about "man in the trap."[1]

Plato's famous parable of the cave incorporates a metaphor of both illusory perception and imprisonment. Humans are compared to prisoners chained to the wall of a dark cave, watching with fascination the illusory flickering shadows cast by fires on the stone walls of the cave. This metaphor tells us that our illusory perception of the world is based on our being attached, tied to the rock wall, which is the material world. "The soul [psyche] . . . has been captured, it is in chains. It is said to be in a tomb, and in a cave; yet by turning again towards ideas, it frees itself from its bonds."[2]

Turning toward ideas means turning inward, toward self-knowledge, self-realization: *Atman*, Spirit, Self is unbounded, unconditioned, unlimited. According to the Vedanta philosopher Shankara, "A liberated being, endowed with knowledge of *Atman,* abandons attachments to the limitations of form, and becomes pure being-consciousness-joy, like *Brahman.*"[3] Spirit/soul is bound and imprisoned in matter/body. Liberation is both possible and desirable—indeed, necessary.

The myth of Prometheus powerfully expresses the archetype of imprisonment. Prometheus, whose name means "foresight," was one of the race of Titans, who were the biblical "giants on the earth," offspring of an older generation of earth deities different from both gods and humans. Prometheus was the bringer of fire, the culture hero who in the early stages of humanity's development taught the arts of civilization. Psychologically he represents the spirit in every human being that brings the fire of life down to earth. Bringing fire to earth symbolizes bringing life into body and form: it is embodiment, incarnation.

The price we pay for the Promethean project of creative incarnation, according to this metaphor, is imprisonment. Prometheus, the heroic human spirit, is as in Plato's parable, chained to the rock, trapped in material form. Every day vultures rip and tear at his liver, which every night is restored and regenerated. The liver may be regarded symbolically as the organ of living, expressing vitality and life force. The vultures are the harbingers of entropic decay and degeneration. Prometheus, then, is every one of us, as we are trapped in the limitations of material form and ravaged by the inevitable forces of old age, decay, and disease.

The imagery of the material world as a prison appears emphatically in the Gnostic texts as well as in the writings of Neoplatonist philosophers and medieval Christian mystics. For these philosophers, the world in general and the body in particular constitute a fortress, a dungeon, a tomb, a garment of chains—a condition marked by weight, cold, and immobility.[4] Mystics such as Saint John of the Cross regarded the body as a prison for the soul, which longs to be freed from it, to transcend it.[5]

Such imagery is perhaps an extension of the more common notion of the body as a sheath, shell, vehicle, or house. In dreams, explorations of a house, or damages or repairs to a house, are often metaphors for actions and experiences involving the body. If I become acutely conscious of limitations and obstructions my body presents to me, images of prisons, traps, nets, or labyrinths naturally come to mind.

In an extraordinary passage from the writings of the Buddhist sage Naropa, the world of sense objects, *samsara*, is compared to an unusual variety of metaphorical prisons and traps:

> Samsara is . . . a dungeon dark, a deep swamp of three poisons, . . . 'Tis like being bound hand to neck by Mara, or immersed in a pond of beastliness. . . . It is the net of fate . . . and living neath the floating shadows of old age and birth, entanglement in bondage. It is a flame flickering in the wind, untruth, a dream, bewilderment.[6]

I take these images to mean the emotional reactivity to sense experience, the endless grasping for and avoiding of the objects of our sensory world, which exposes us to being immersed in or ensnared by

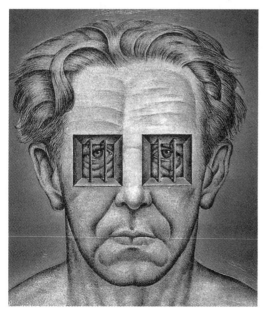

Man imprisoned by the fixed perceptions of the conditioned mind. (From an advertisement for antidepressant medication, 20th-century USA)

contradictory sensations of pleasure and pain, craving and suffering, delusion, illusion, false ideals and ideas.

Among modern philosophers and writers, the existentialists in particular have identified and described the prisonlike and angst-producing aspects of worldly existence. Søren Kierkegaard, the melancholy Dane, in his books Fear and Trembling and Sickness unto Death, wrote of the "demonic shut-upness" that results from the conflicts in our being and of the "dread" that results as we accept the "absurdity" of these oppositions. One senses that most of the existentialists never found a way to escape from the prison of existence: they only developed detailed and elaborate descriptions of its dimensions. The French philosopher Albert Camus, in his book The Myth of Sisyphus, adopted a posture of poetic rebellion, struggling forever, like his titanic hero, to roll a boulder up the mountain, or trying to find meaning in "the whirlpool's shrieking face." Jean-Paul Sartre's play No Exit, about four people locked hellishly and inescapably in one room, is another powerful statement of this theme.

A personal experience that provided me with a very different perspective on and understanding of the psychological meaning of imprisonment may be relevant here. In 1961 and 1962 I and several other graduate students at Harvard University worked with Timothy Leary on a psychedelic drug research project involving convicts in a maximum security prison. The purpose of the research was to attempt to produce insight and change through the judicious use of psilocybin (the active ingredient of the sacred mushrooms of ancient Mexico) in a supportive group environment. To minimize the prisoners' feeling of being experimental guinea pigs, we adopted a policy of research staff also partaking of the drug with the prisoners on an alternating basis.[7]

So I had the first six or so psychedelic experiences of my life behind the bars of a maximum security prison. To this day, I vividly remember the extraordinary experience of having my visual field expanded until it became a 360-degree circle or sphere, within which the prison walls, the bars on the windows, and the locks on the doors had become meaningless. Though still visible and real, they seemed ineffectual in imprisoning the human spirit, which soared unconstrained that day.

These experiences taught me that we can have inner freedom even while in an outer prison. The converse is of course also true: we can have inner bondage even while outwardly apparently free. The inner prisons, the shutters and locks of the mind, are more subtle and less obvious—yet perhaps for that reason more insidious. Since we do not ordinarily see them, we have no incentive to try to escape. As Gurdjieff says, if we do not realize we are in prison, we have no chance of escaping at all.

A widespread variation of the imprisonment theme is the idea of a treadmill, a wheel, a ceaseless round of existence. Here we find symbolic expressions of the frustrations of repetitive routine work, the futility of the daily grind. A man or woman tied to a meaningless, repetitive job might very well feel like a prisoner, with awareness contracted, perception numbed or blinded. He or she might feel condemned or punished somehow, or trapped by bad past karma. The story of Samson is relevant here: this hero of the Israelites, a liberator, a slayer of enemies, was finally caught (through the well-known ruse of the faithless Delilah) and put to work grinding corn on a treadmill in prison. Like Samson, we might sense that our life purpose has to do with liberation, but instead we find ourselves imprisoned. "Ask for this great deliverer now," wrote John Milton, "and find him eyeless in Gaza at the mill with the slaves."[8]

Other images portray life as a repetitive wheel or round. People involved in hellish psychotic experiences might find themselves identifying with the Greek myth of Ixion, who was bound to a fiery wheel and condemned to roll forever through the heavens. Obsessive workaholics might identify with Sisyphus, who was condemned to repeatedly push a huge stone up a mountain, only to have it always roll down again. The fourth century Byzantine mystic Gregory of Nyssa wrote

point of view, illness and paralysis only intensify and exacerbate an already existing, "normal" captivity.

This metaphor tells us that because of the law of karma, we are the prisoners of our own past actions. We cannot avoid or escape reaping the consequences of what we have sown before. Our thinking is bound and conditioned, fixated on fears and painful past experiences. Likewise, our behavior is limited and restricted. We are as though addicted, that is "hooked," in relation to sense stimuli and pleasures. We are *fascinated* (which means "bound") by glamour and idealisms, such as wealth, fame, power, and beauty. We are *attached* to the objects of our desires—and to our aversions. A middle-aged married woman, for instance, said in therapy that she felt "nailed down by petty concerns."

In modern times this metaphor of imprisonment has reemerged in several interesting variants, which are remarkable chiefly for their distinctive somatic, even anatomic specificity. Reich's theory of armoring, for instance, says that "the muscular armor is functionally equivalent to the character armor."

> In thus loosening the character incrustations, we set free the affects (feelings) which had previously undergone inhibition and fixation. ... Part of the work shifts from the psychological and characterological to the immediate dissolution of the muscular armor. ... I could not avoid the impression that the physical rigidity, actually, represents the most essential part of the process of repression. ... This muscular attitude is identical with what we call "bodily expression."[10]

Alexander Lowen, a psychiatrist who was a student of Reich and who further developed Reich's ideas, states that "all unresolved emotional conflicts become structured in the body in the form of chronic muscular tensions." Lowen has some interesting observations about the expression "being hung-up" and how this is manifested in somatic reality. "A person is said to be 'hung-up' when he is caught in an emotional conflict that immobilizes him and prevents any effective action to change the situation."

In an individual who has the "hung-up syndrome," according to Lowen, the upper torso may actually be held up, as if suspended by an invisible coat hanger, with the shoulders pulled up and back in fear.[11] Being "hung-up" is a form of captivity with both psychological and somatic aspects. In medieval times, this state of consciousness was expressed in symbols such as the Hanged Man of the Tarot.

Another highly relevant and innovative approach to body structure is the "structural integration" work of Ida Rolf. This involves deep, often painful, massaging of the body in order to bring it into better alignment with the axis of gravity. In Rolf 's system, the key connecting structures of the body are the fascia, the connective tissue that covers muscles and links them with bones. These fascia become rigid and distorted in the course of life, and they are actually loosened and lengthened in the structural integration work. Don Johnson, a philosopher and practitioner of Rolfing, as it is also known, describes how the fascia function as a kind of internal physical armor, as rigid walls that actually limit and constrict the free motion of our bodies.

> Fascia is the forgotten organ of the body. It starts just below the skin to form an inner covering for the entire body. . . . Fascia is the primary vehicle of change in the body—for good as well as ill. A severe leg fracture, for example, will cause the fascia in that area to become like gristle. This knot inhibits the free movement of the neighboring muscles. In other places, lack of use or poor posture will give rise to shortening of fascial planes and adhesions of these planes to bones and muscles, also limiting body movement and the flow of fluids through the flesh.[12]

Thus, from this modern research on the integrated totality of psychological and physical structures and functions, a whole new picture of the body-mind complex is emerging, which confirms in striking anatomical detail some of the ancient metaphorical and symbolic themes of the body as a constricting, binding, prisonlike structure. T. S. Eliot wrote that "the enchainment of the past and future (is) woven in the weakness of the changing body."[13] These structural formations and deformations constitute the "prison" of the body, limiting its mobility and restricting the free flow of somatic and emotional energy.

Those who have personally experienced Reichian bioenergetic therapy, Rolf 's structural integration, or the work of other such pioneers as Alexander, Feldenkrais, or Trager can testify to the strikingly liberating changes that can occur with these approaches; and they become aware of the binding limitations they have been unconsciously living under.

Other kinds of inner transformation process work, particularly those forms of meditation and yoga that emphasize close attention to bodily structures and functions, can also lead to this realization. The individual may become aware of internal images, feelings, and sensations that represent the body in terms of prison metaphors. Typical is this account, from a student of Agni Yoga:

> In working to release loads and tensions from my body, I frequently experience the obstruction as an armor plating locked on or around the muscle or organ; and as this is unlocked, sheaths of metallic-like stuff fly off and disintegrate. Sometimes these obstructions literally have the form of hasps and locks and chains. As these are unlocked and the systems freed, the experience is of greater ability to breathe, to flex, to move and to relate.[14]

Yet another kind of experiential validation of the metaphor of the body as prison comes from what are known in parapsychology as out-of-body experiences. Such experiences, which I believe are much more common than is generally assumed, have been described in detail by Robert Monroe in books entitled *Journeys Out of the Body* and *Far*

Journeys, and they have been fairly extensively studied by parapsychologists.[15] The consensus from people experiencing this phenomenon is that leaving the body is always experienced as a kind of flying or floating, a release and freedom from the usual physical limitations. Similarly, the consensus about the experience of returning to the body is that it always feels like coming into a more limited, bound, heavy, immobile state. Shirley MacLaine, in her autobiographical account of her psychic and out-of-body experiences, writes, "I melded back into my body. My body felt comfortable, familiar, but it also felt restricting and cumbersome and limiting."[16] Regardless of what kind of scientific or psychological interpretation we give to this kind of experience, the universal agreement on the subjective, experiential characteristics is quite remarkable.

If we accept the notion that experiencing the body as prison and restrictive armor is fairly common, both in illness and in certain kinds of therapy, yoga, and psychic experiences, the question still arises as to why some individuals might be more predisposed to this kind of experience than others. Clearly, some people do feel very free, agile, and expressive in their bodies and may not resonate to the prison metaphor very much. A possible answer to this question is given in the research with LSD psychotherapy conducted by Stanislav Grof. Grof found that subjects in this kind of deep exploration (and this has since been verified with other kinds of nondrug experiential therapies) can relive aspects of their birth trauma.

He observed that there is a profound connection between feelings of being trapped, bound, shut in, imprisoned, and the apparent memory of the second stage of the four-phase birth process. In this model, this is the stage (called BPM-II) in which powerful uterine contractions are impinging on the fetus but the cervix is closed, and there is as yet no passage out. Grof has proposed that each stage of the birth process functions as a kind of matrix ("basic perinatal matrix") around which later physical and psychological experiences that have the same form and feelings are organized. He describes the typical stage II experiences as follows:

> The activation of this matrix results in a rather characteristic experience of "no exit" or "hell." The subject feels encaged in a claustrophobic world and experiences incredible physical and psychological tortures. This experience is characterized by a striking darkness of the visual field and by ominous colors. Typically, the situation is absolutely unbearable, and at the same time appears to be endless and hopeless; no escape can be seen.... Agonizing feelings of separation, alienation, metaphysical loneliness, helplessness, hopelessness, inferiority, and guilt are standard components of [this phase]. The individual trapped in the "no exit" situation clearly sees that human existence is meaningless, yet feels a desperate need to find meaning in life. This struggle often coincides with what is experienced as the attempts of the fetus to escape from the closed uterine system and save its life.[17]

One could speculate that the sensory and perceptual memory of this kind of birth-related experience could be what underlies the metaphysical world view of existentialism, with its focus on anxiety, alienation, and helplessness, and its despairing and desperate search for meaning. We can also see that these kinds of perceptions, if somehow activated spontaneously instead of in a controlled, purposive psychotherapy situation, could readily precipitate an individual into a hellish psychotic state. As Aldous Huxley pointed out, such experiences under psychedelics are quite comparable to the visions and hallucinations of schizophrenia—and, he might have added, to the initiatory experiences of apprentice shamans.

Some of the more dramatic images and feelings associated with this birth stage and metaphor include being trapped in a metallic cage or huge impersonal machinery; being sucked into a gigantic whirlpool or cosmic maelstrom; being swallowed and devoured by an enormous dragon, python, or whale; being tied, bound, gagged, and immobilized; or being caught in the sticky web of some monstrous spider. And there are mythic counterparts to all these experiences— Jonah in the belly of the whale; Theseus tracking the Minotaur in the labyrinth; Inanna hanging on the peg in the underworld; Odin hanging on the world tree Yggdrasil; Prometheus chained to the rock; Christ hanging on the cross; and the sinners in Dante's *Inferno* encased in tree trunks or frozen in lakes of ice.

When, in the course of a transformation process, someone is going through this kind of hellish imprisonment experience, it can be of great value to see that the experience has been known and described for ages and that many people have had similar experiences in other eras and countries. We are not alone, and we are not the first to go through this. Such recognition contributes in no small way to the individual's ability to continue and complete the process of transformation.

Perhaps the best-known mythic "prisoner" besides Prometheus is Osiris, the green-skinned vegetation and river god of the Egyptians who becomes the lord of the underworld. His story embodies the archetypal pattern of incarnation as captivity, followed by liberation. Osiris, like Prometheus for the Greeks, Christ for the Christians, and Odin for the Nordic peoples, symbolizes the immortal spirit in the mortal human. Each of these figures is trapped, chained, hung, or fixed, a condition that represents the limited, contracted condition of human, earthly, bodily existence. Each human being is an immortal deity in mortal bodily form. As god, each one is unbounded light and splendor; as incarnated human being, each one is trapped, bound, imprisoned. The spiritual essence, or beingness, within each human being is the "imprisoned splendor" that the mystics experience and describe.[18] Odin hanging on the world tree, Christ on the cross, Prometheus bound to the rock, and Osiris trapped in the coffer are all images of the archetype of imprisoned splendor, from which each one of us is destined to be liberated.

In the story of Osiris as told by the Greek historian Plutarch, the god is tricked by his arch-rival Set into lying down in a beautiful wooden coffer that has been carved exactly to his dimensions, which is then locked and thrown into a river. Floating down the river to the sea, the coffer then lands and is incorporated into a tree trunk; the tree, with the god still inside it, becomes the wooden framework of a house. Subsequent parts of the myth relate how Osiris is liberated from his imprisonment by the divine strategems of his consort Isis.

I offer the following interpretation of this myth.[19] The four transformations the god goes through—coffer, river, tree, house—represent the four "inner bodies" on the incarnational descent into bodily form on earth. The chest or coffer, with its carved designs, represents the mental body. The river is the flowing astral dimension, also known as the emotional body. The tree symbolizes the etheric, or perceptual, dimension, associated with the treelike sensory nervous system. The house frame represents the physical body, the most material, utilitarian form. Each of the forms into which the god-man successively embodies himself represents more of a contraction or limitation.

Like Osiris, each one of us has "come down," has involved or embodied into progressively more and more limited forms, more and more constricted, denser bodies, to the maximal density of the physical. We usually are most identified with this densest material form, the "skin-encapsulated ego." In this physical house / body form, we may become aware of the most intimate details of our imprisonment: the armored muscles, rigid fascia, hardened flesh of our somatic dungeon. And like Osiris, each one of us has the potential to transform captivity into freedom, to break through, to transcend or dissolve the limitations imposed on us by personal karma and by the process of incarnation itself.

Knots, Ties, Nets, and Bonds in Relationships

Obstructions to the free flow of awareness and energy in the body that give rise to the imagery of imprisonment are frequently experienced and described as "knots." These knots may actually be tensed and contracted muscles; or they may be congealed and congested connective or vascular tissue. We all know about the knot of anxiety in the stomach and the lump of inhibited sadness in the throat. These kinds of knots may make us feel tight, tense, or tongue-tied, unable to express our feelings through words or gestures.

In the subtle body, with its energy channels (*nadis*) and energy centers (*chakras*), there may be corresponding knots and ties. In the Indian Upanishads, there are references to "knots in the heart" (*granthi*) that must surely mean obstructions in the heart center. "When all the knots that fetter the heart are cut asunder, then a mortal becomes immortal," says the *Katha Upanishad*. The heart center, like the other centers, is a gateway to the higher realms, the transpersonal dimensions. Thus when the blocks in that gateway are removed, the full splendor of the immortal being of light can be experienced and known. The *Mundaka Upanishad* states, "When the knot of the heart is unloosened, and all doubts are cut off, then man's work is finished, then is seen That which is above and below."[20]

In our personal experience, the area of human life that probably gives rise to the most complex and difficult "knots in the heart" is the area of emotional and sexual relationships. We may be *fascinated* (which originally meant "spellbound") by the charm of a loved one. There are the ties of dependency, as in being tied to a mother's apron strings. When we solemnize a relationship in marriage (a state some have referred to as "the tender trap"), we speak of "getting hitched" and "tying the knot." People often feel trapped in a marriage or relationship that has become fixed, rigid, or routine. And when a love relationship ends, there may be a painful feeling of a tie being cut, or an agonizing, constricting knot in the heart. The psychiatrist R. D. Laing wrote a whole book of poems, *Knots,* on the convoluted entanglements of both normal and disturbed relationships.

The Huichol Indians of Mexico have an interesting custom: before setting out on their annual sacred tribal pilgrimage, they make knots

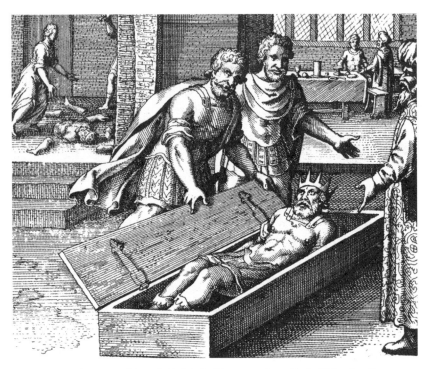

Spirit imprisoned in material form: Osiris is locked into a wooden coffer by his brother, Set. In the background, Isis gathers up his scattered members (see chapter 5). (From *Atalanta Fugiens*, an alchemical treatise by Michael Maier, first published 1617 in Prague)

in a piece of string for every intimate relationship they've had in the past year. They then burn the knotted string to symbolize the burning away of attachments. This is a metaphor for the purification of emotional knots and ties by inner fire, the alchemical *calcinatio*, as we shall see in chapter 4. In psychedelic or other kinds of deep experiential psychotherapy, a person may experience the dissolving or loosening of a knot or lump in the heart center and may experience difficult, tense, anxious, angry, or sad feelings toward a loved one releasing at the same time. As the personal and interpersonal knots are untied, then the heart and mind become more open to receiving and perceiving the light-fire of spirit, "that which is above and below."

The symbolic meaning of knots is not all bad. As Mircea Eliade points out, "Knots have opposite meaning: they can bring about illness, or cure it or drive it away; protect against bewitchment or bewitch; hinder childbirth or facilitate it; preserve newborns or make them ill; bring death or prevent it."[21] There is, for example, the "endless knot," which is one of the eight emblems of good fortune in Chinese and Tibetan Buddhism. And the horizontal figure-eight knot is, of course, our symbol for infinity. Some see the two loops of this figure as representing the intertwined connection between spirit and matter, between inner and outer worlds of life.

Another, related kind of metaphor is being caught or enmeshed in a net. We have already noted that the feeling of immobilizing netting in the body may be based on such structures as rigid fascia, hardened and congested connective tissue, or tense nerve networks. In relationships we may get the feeling of being somehow entangled or trapped in a web or net of expectations, obligations, illusions, and perhaps deceptions. If we find someone attractive, we may be captivated, bewitched, spellbound, or enthralled.

This theme was given a perceptively humorous rendering in the Greek myth of the liaison between Ares and Aphrodite. When the god of war and the goddess of love engaged in amorous dalliance, Aphrodite's husband, the lame smith Hephaistos, was informed of this by Helios, the sun god. The jealous Hephaistos then fashioned a gossamer-thin yet extraordinarily strong net of golden threads. In a surprise move, he threw it over the couple as they lay in their bed of passion. Thereupon he invited the other gods to come and view the plight of the lovers. At the sight of the undignified entanglement of the impulsive Ares and the affectionate Aphrodite, the heavens echoed with the resounding, good-natured laughter of the Olympians. Just so, we may often feel ridiculous to the point of embarrassment at the indignities to which our romantic passions expose us.

Family relationships that involve ties of dependency and love can become so entangled and confused that one or several individuals may feel "caught in a bind," suffering anguish and conflict. One important theory of schizophrenia holds that this condition is at least partly caused by "double binds," contradictory and unresolvable patterns of communication.[22] The child may get conflicting messages (for example, the voice speaks love and the eyes show hate), and this is a bind; what makes it a *double* bind is that the child cannot leave the situation. Adult patterns of communication are often equally contradictory, confused, and entangled, resisting the efforts of even the most skillful therapists or counselors to unravel.

Nets, like knots, have paradoxical meanings and values. The opposite feelings we have about them are reflected in etymology, for language contains and reveals psychological truths. For example, the words *net* and *noose* come from the Latin *nectare*, "to bind, fasten, or tie." But this is also the root word for *node, nexus,* and *connection.* Our ties bind us but also link and connect us. We may be imprisoned, in "bondage," but we desire close emotional "bonding" with family and friends as well. While we may get trapped and entangled in nets, we also use them to catch fish. And we have "networks" of relationships among people, which serve the purposes of communication and mutual support. The same Latin word *ligare*, "to tie or connect," underlies *ligaments*, which connect bones; *obligations*, which tie us to our fellow man; and *religion*, which supposedly should reconnect us with the divine.

A net, tie, or bind is experienced as limiting or immobilizing if we are caught or trapped in it involuntarily: then we are the victims. If, on the other hand, we use it consciously and intentionally, then the tie, network, or connection provides the channels through which communication and exchange of energy can flow.

In ancient civilizations there were deities who used ropes, nets, or nooses to bind and immobilize demons and to bring illness and death to human beings. These were the gods of fate, the lords of karma. They included Indra in Vedic India, Uranus in Greece, Odin in Scandinavia, and Jehovah, of whom all-suffering Job said, "He hath put his net around me." This theme of "the god who binds" is related to the similar idea, found in other cultures, of the Fates. These are often three ancient goddesses who spin out a thread for each individual: one goddess starts the thread, one continues it, and one cuts it at death.[23] Fate is that pattern of events we cannot escape from; we are trapped or bound in it, we are its victims.

The dual meanings of these symbols hint at the process of liberation. The net is not only something in which we are trapped and entangled, it is also the network for communication and energy exchange. The entire world is seen, especially in the Indian traditions of Tantra (a word related to words for weaving and texture), as a vast, interconnecting web or woven fabric. Modern scientists have similarly concluded that all phenomena are interrelated in complex networks of energy transformation. Teilhard de Chardin's concept of the noosphere, a network of thought encompassing the planet, is one such idea. The notion of networks of individuals who share a common interest and provide information and support to one another has enormous potential for furthering individual and social transformation.

The transition from the state of consciousness where we feel trapped or entangled in a net, to the state of consciousness where we are consciously and intentionally participating in a network is one aspect of the process of liberation through transformation. The question is, how does one escape from prison? How can the knots be untied or loosened? How can the limiting net be changed into a liberating network?

Strategies of Escape and Liberation

This transformative process, like the others discussed in this book, can vary in a number of ways: it can be abrupt or gradual, it can be temporary or lasting, it can be a spontaneous discovery or one aided by an outer teacher or liberator, and it can come through grace or through conscious effort. While my values favor the second possibility in each pair—a progressive, permanent, guided, and intentional approach—this does not rule out the possibility that liberating experiences can and do occur suddenly, temporarily, spontaneously, effortlessly.

I follow Gurdjieff's view that the single most important prerequisite for escaping from prison is awakening.

> You do not realize your own situation. You are in prison. All you can wish for, if you are a sensible man, is to escape. But how to escape? ... If a man is at any time to have a chance of escape, then he must first of all realize that he is in prison. So long as he fails to realize this, so long as he thinks he is free, he has no chance whatsoever.[24]

We must realize that we are in a trap or a labyrinth; that our character and body are armored and constricted; that there are knots and nets in various areas of our consciousness and our life. If I don't perceive my imprisonment, my boundedness and limitations, there is really no motivation for change.

Closely related to the need for awakening to one's situation is the factor of intention: we must want to escape, will it, desire it, long for it. In any kind of psychological work or exploration of altered states of consciousness (with drugs, hypnosis, meditation, or other methods), the importance of mental set—intention—has long been recognized. While intention by itself may not be sufficient—since the road to hell is proverbially paved with good intentions—techniques and methods practiced without clear and strong intention are probably going to be ineffective. To quote Gurdjieff again, "If liberation is possible, it is possible only as a result of great efforts, and above all, of conscious efforts toward a definite aim."

Transcendence, symbolized by flying or other upward movement, is one of the traditional ways of escape, and it applies at all levels. We can transcend the painful armoring that blocks the expression of passionate feelings by giving up, or "rising above," those passions. We can transcend the entangling knot or net of a confused relationship by giving up the desire to hold and possess. And as the traditional texts have it, we can, through transcendence, attain release from the bondage of material existence. Using techniques of consciousness alteration as advocated in shamanism, yoga, meditation, and mystical literature, we can rise up out of the "vale of tears," the dungeon of *samsara*.

Transcendence is a going beyond, an alteration of consciousness, that leaves the existing system in place. For example, an out-of-body or psychedelic experience may release us from the body's armoring temporarily, but we return to it afterward. There is a difference between escaping from the prison and actually transforming the prison—that is, dissolving the armor. The value of transcendent experiences lies in the fact that they afford us a kind of preview, a vision of the freedom that is possible, that can serve as inspiration and motivation for the intentional work of liberation.

Direct healing work on the body-mind complex can be very effective in the process of loosening the knots, thus freeing awareness. This can range from the physical alteration of fascial structures, as in Rolfing, and various ways of dissolving muscular rigidities through breathing or movement, to subtle inner techniques of psychophysical yoga.

Yogic methods involving inner "fire" (discussed in chapter 4, on purification) may also be used. The inner fire, what Krishnamurti called the "flame of attention," can burn up the knots, melt the metallic armorings, or open up the constricting walls of emotional defensiveness. The alchemical process of *solutio,* which refers to the dissolution of structures in fluidity, is also appropriate. Alchemical "water" is the realm of feeling, so *solutio* is a metaphor for the dissolving of hardened reaction patterns in the warm, nurturing flow of feeling forgiveness.

Another approach to escape-liberation is the analytical tracing back to find the origins of a defensive armored posture, emotional knot, or relationship entanglement. Theseus found his way out of the labyrinth by means of the golden thread of Ariadne. This might be seen as a metaphor for the process of depth psychological analysis:

following the thread of meaning, reversing and retracing every step that we have taken in the tortuous twists and turns of the defensive, rational ego-mind.

Several different animal figures have traditionally been associated with the theme of liberating the prisoner or escaping from the dungeon of earthly existence. Chief among them are probably birds: from the ingenious Daedalus to the Birdman of Alcatraz, we have had prisoner heroes who have passionately studied the flying of birds. *Flight* means "escape" (fleeing) and "winged motion in air" (flying) as well as, metaphorically, the ascent and traversing of higher dimensions of consciousness. To people who are undergoing transformative processes, birds often appear in dreams, visions, and other kinds of altered states—indicating that the transcendent power of the bird is operative within their psyches.

In some Asiatic as well as Native American cultures, demons, like birds, are often regarded as allies in the quest for liberation. In Tibetan and Indonesian shamanic folklore, the demons, or "wrathful deities," are representative of the dynamic forces of "breaking through": they are the guardians of internal borders and thresholds, the boundaries between states of consciousness. With their bulging eyes and ferocious mien and gesture, they provoke attention and awakening; they startle the initiate yogi or shamanic practitioner into fierce hyperalertness.

Guidance is certainly helpful if not essential for liberation: one can best escape from prison with the help of those who have escaped before. Osiris is freed from the tree / house through the wise skill of his female consort Isis; Theseus finds his way out of the labyrinth with the golden thread provided by his anima-guide Ariadne. Human beings have ever prayed to their gods and goddesses, their teachers and guides, for help in delivering them from the snares and traps of the enemies of life. And the liberation, the deliverance into peace, the release of the imprisoned splendor has been most generously aided and facilitated.

The transformation from a state of captivity to a liberated state is, I believe, reflected in the difference between our concepts of fate and destiny. Fate, which corresponds to what the Indian tradition calls karma, is unavoidable, fixed, and based on the past, either on what has been decreed (fate) or on our past actions (karma). We feel ourselves to be the passive victims of fate, caught in its web or net. Destiny, on the other hand, which corresponds more closely with the traditional Indian notion of dharma, is future oriented, free, and flexible: it is our purpose or destination, what we choose to be and do. We fulfill our destiny by exercising our free will. But until our will is, in fact, freed from the fateful, binding consequences of our past karmic actions and tendencies, we cannot really exercise that freedom. We have free will in theory, potentially, but not in practice or actuality—until we are liberated. When, through the process and practice of transformation, we no longer experience ourselves as victims of our fate, we can become masters of our destiny.

Purification by Inner Fire

Will transformation. O be inspired with flame,
Where something eludes you, resplendent with change.
—R. M. Rilke[1]

Fire is the transformative element par excellence. From the earliest times men and women have been in awe of the power of the fires of nature—the sun, lightning, volcanoes, wildfires—and have perceived or imagined great fire deities that lived in the flames. Since the sun was experienced as the power that originated and maintained life, so God, as the spiritual source and basis of our existence, was often conceived of as sun or fire. We are moved to echo the words of Herakleitos, "Everything becomes fire, and from fire everything is born."

The concept of energy plays a similarly central role in the modern scientific world view. We have learned that we live in a sea of energies and radiations, covering a vast spectrum of vibratory frequencies, only a minute portion of which is perceived by the unaided senses. The fundamental law of the conservation of energy tells us that energy is neither created nor destroyed, only transformed. And Einstein's formula $E = mc2$ tells us that mass and energy are equivalent, that things and objects are basically packets of energy bound into matter.

In the evolution of humankind and of social life, the domestication of fire was an epochal event celebrated in numerous myths of a fire bringer, such as Prometheus. Humankind's creative ingenuity exploited the transformative power of fire for human use—in cooking, smithing, metallurgy, technological invention, industrial applications, and, most of all, in warfare and weaponry—"firearms." The inviting warmth and comfort of the fireplace, where we share visions and stories, has contributed to familial and tribal bonding for hundreds of thousands of years. In his studies of primitive religion, Sir James Frazer listed many rites in which torches, bonfires, burning embers, and even ashes were considered capable of stimulating the growth and well-being of vegetation, animals, and humans.

As humans observed the qualities of fire in these processes, it was natural to draw analogies between external fires and internal processes in the body and psyche. Fire and flames became symbolically associated with ardor, sexual passion, anger, excitement, vitality, inspiration, and vision, because of the feelings of heat and energy that we experience coursing through the body during such emotional bodily states. The dramatic power of fire to bring about total destruction or transformation of matter led to its becoming associated with inner and outer processes of purification, purgation, destructuring, and the dissolving of limitations and obstructions.

However, it is clear that much religious and psychological literature speaks of fire as more than a symbol: fire and heat are spoken of as actual inner experiences. We are all familiar with the intense feelings of heat and fiery energy that occur in the body during fever. According to age-old empirical medical traditions, a fever is not so much a symptom of illness as a sign that the body is purifying itself by burning off toxins and bacteria, and thereby accelerating the healing process. There is an analogous process, a psychic fever perhaps, when a person feels that he or she is being purged or purified of something alien and harmful.

Religiously inclined individuals may regard such experiences as involving heavenly or spiritual fire energy, the mystical fire of union with the divine. Others may experience them as painful, feeling as if plunged into hellish torment. Or they may be felt to be the forces of purgatory, cleansing and purifying. Such experiences can occur unexpectedly and spontaneously, in mystical ecstasies or in chaotic psychoses. However, there are also ancient and still-active traditions of yoga, psychological alchemy, and spiritual disciplines in which methods of arousing or utilizing inner fire or heat are intentionally and consciously practiced for psychophysical transformation and purification.

Fire Deities and the Spirit of Fire

Significantly, the association of fire with divine spirit is widespread and ancient. Many people are afraid of fire and hence do not resonate to the idea of fire as a positive, transformative energy within themselves. I once shared this feeling to a degree but found that through my studies of Agni Yoga (the yoga of fire) and of alchemy, my perspective changed completely and became much more positive. I was fascinated to discover that so many ancient peoples and contemporary native cultures value fire and regard it as sacred.[2]

An energy field of purifying flame envelops the adept of the yoga of fire: Tantric deity in yab-yum embrace with yogic consort. (From the Buddhist Vajrayana tradition, 18th-century Tibet)

Fire deities abound in every ancient culture. Among the Greeks, Helios, the sun god, drew his chariots of fire across the sky each day; Hephaistos was the crippled master-smith, who, aided by subterranean fire genii, fashioned invincible weapons and shields for gods and men; and Prometheus was the hero who brought fire, hidden in a fennel stalk, to mankind. Esoterically, Prometheus symbolizes every human being, bringing the fire of Spirit down to the earth plane of matter. "Fire in the plant stalk" is metaphorically equivalent to "Spirit in matter" and "the Word become flesh" (incarnation), as has been discussed in Chapter 3.

In the Vedic religion of ancient India, Agni was the brightest and most powerful of the gods, praised and revered in numerous hymns of the *Rig Veda,* perhaps the world's oldest mythic sacred literature.[3] He was the "flame born," visualized as a red giant with flames shooting from his mouth and rays of light pouring out of his body. Through sacrificial offerings of food in the Agni ceremonies, the Vedic priests cultivated a link to the gods. Metaphorically speaking, according to Sri Aurobindo, "Agni is the force or energy aspect of consciousness."

The practices referred to as *tapas,* usually translated (by Christian scholars) as "austerity" or "penance," originally signified "heat," "fire," and "ardor." According to the *Rig Veda,* "Out of the flaming *tapas,* order and truth were born." Thus, the practices (*tapas*) associated with the fire god Agni brought about orderly and truthful transformations of consciousness. Esoterically, *tapas* refers to the yogic practices of "inner fire," akin to the Tibetan Tantric Buddhist practice known as *dumo* and the contemporary Western meditation practice known as Agni Yoga or Actualism.[4]

In the later Indian literature, the mythology of the Puranas and the yogic texts of the Tantras, the great fire god is Shiva the Transformer, who, together with his female counterpart Shakti, is the divine teacher and inspirer of Tantric practitioners. Shiva Nataraja is the image of the god dancing in a ring of fire, trampling on a demonic dwarf whose name means "forgetting." Thus, he symbolizes the power of inner fire to overcome ignorance, to awaken, to destroy the limiting obstructions that "dwarf" our true potentials. As Agni was the patron deity of Vedic priests and seers, Shiva became the protector and prototype of yogis and ascetics, practicing the austere purification disciplines of Raja and Tantra Yoga. Shiva is a dualistic, paradoxical deity: both male and female, ascetic and erotic, destroyer and transformer.[5]

In the prophetic books of the Hebrew Old Testament, there are numerous allusions to the purifying power of fire and to the fiery nature of divine reality. God speaks to Moses from a burning bush and appears to the Egyptians in a pillar of fire. The prophet Elijah is taken up to heaven in a chariot of fire (2 Kings 2:11–12). The prophet Ezekiel sees visions of a cloud glowing with fire and, within it, four gigantic beings facing the four directions (Ezek. 1:4–14). Daniel sees a vision of a man whose "body gleamed like topaz, and his face shone like lightning, his eyes flamed like torches, and his arms and feet sparkled like discs of bronze" (Dan. 10:6). Thus we get a picture, from the scriptures that form the basis of much of Western consciousness, of God and godlike beings made of pure fire or energy, existing perhaps in another dimension but visible in visionary states of consciousness.

These fiery beings or manifestations of God can, and do, interact with and have an impact on human beings in this reality. The chief impact of the fiery Spirit is purification, the burning away of tendencies and impulses to wrongdoing or falsehood. The author of the Psalms says those who hate God flee before him like smoke in the wind; "like wax melting in fire, the wicked perish in the presence of God."[6] Metaphorically, this can be seen to refer to evil tendencies in our nature that are melted away when we invoke the presence of God or Spirit.

In the Gospels there are several references to Christ's nature as a being of fire. In the Gospel of Luke, Jesus says: "I have come to set fire to the earth, and how I wish it were already kindled. I have a baptism to undergo." Here Jesus seems to be anticipating his own ordeal. In other passages, he is the bringer of the purifying fire. Matthew quotes John the Baptist as saying: "I baptize you with water, for repentance . . . but the one who comes after me...will baptize you with the Holy Spirit and with fire. . . . The wheat he will gather into his granary, but he will burn the chaff in a fire that will never go out." And in the Gnostic Gospel of Thomas, Jesus says, "Whoever is near to me is near to the fire, and whoever is far from me is far from the Kingdom."[7]

This notion of Christ as a bringer of fire for the purification and transformation of the world is a far cry from the traditional image of the meek lamb of God or the sorrowful martyr. In these passages Christ is like the fire deities of the ancients: a powerful, dynamic, warrior spirit who separates the "chaff" from the "wheat" among people. And, again taken in the interior sense, these passages say that through the fiery Christ Spirit within, the useless and trivial tendencies in our nature (the "chaff") will be consumed, and only the truthful, valuable, and authentic (the "wheat") will remain.

In many ancient mythic traditions, in alchemy and in fairy tales, we encounter the archetypal figure of the fire-breathing serpent or dragon. Often this is a dragon who lives inside a mountain, where he may guard a treasure, a "pearl of great price." The fire dragon embodies the creative spiritual forces of nature. For the European alchemists, as for Chinese Taoists and most shamanic native cultures, the world of Spirit and the world of nature are unified, not separated as they are in the Western rationalist mentality. Fire is symbolic of the energizing, vitalizing forces in ceaseless transformation. We may see and sense and feel these energies in and around us all the time, but especially clearly in certain power places in nature and in states of heightened awareness.

The alchemical texts refer to it as "liquid fire," "living fire," "elemental fire" (*ignis elementaris*), or "invisible fire." It was regarded as the force or principle of generation and regeneration in all organic life, as well as in inorganic matter, which to the alchemists was very much alive. One text refers to this energy as "the universal and scintillating fire of the light of nature, which carries the heavenly spirit within it."[8] The fire dragon was regarded as one aspect of Mercurius, who is mythologically the god Hermes-Mercurius, the initiator and teacher, and psychologically the energy of awareness or mind.

In Chinese mythology there are two kinds of fire dragons, and neither is associated with destruction, danger, or evil, as is the dragon in Western mythology. Celestial dragons represent the cosmic generative power, referred to symbolically in the first hexagram of the *I Ching,* "The Creative." The ancient Chinese believed that atmospheric electricity was a manifestation of this celestial dragon and that lightning was its procreative intercourse with the feminine earth. The terrestrial dragons were regarded (as in the West) as guardians of the hidden wealth of the earth. Their movements caused earthquakes, and their "veins" were the electromagnetic lines of force in the earth and the streaks of precious metals and minerals. For the Taoists, as for the alchemists, meditation and spiritual practice consisted to a large extent of attuning and harmonizing with these fiery beings, who were the embodiments of natural forces and energies.[9]

Hell, Purgatory, and the Fire of Purification

Although fire is symbolically associated with divine spirit and life energies, as we have seen, a very different kind of meaning of fire is equally widespread. In almost every major religious tradition, fire is an important, though not necessarily the only, element of hell, the place of damnation and punishment. In contrast to the soothing warmth, sparkling light, and blissful melting feelings of divine love typically found in descriptions of heaven, the inferno is typically a place of raging, smoking, toxic flames, of burning lakes and boiling oil, of unbearably fiery torment and unspeakably disgusting demons. It is, however, also true that the iconography of hell, both in the Judeo-Christian and Hindu-Buddhist traditions, includes extreme cold and eternal ice as well as heat; and experiences of being crushed, squeezed, torn, dismembered, prodded with sharp instruments, or forced to swallow burning and disgusting fluids.[10]

The significance of this universal imagery of heaven and hell for the experience of transformation is derived from the following psychological fact: both heaven and hell are states of mind or states of consciousness—they are within us. "Heaven" is a state of consciousness in which we experience blissful, ecstatic, paradisaical emotions, sensations, and thoughts, whereas "hell" is a state in which we experience their opposites—terror, rage, anguish, despair, torment, disgust, horror, and so on. The depictions of these "places" in religions mythology and art are clearly external representations of inner experiences.

Aldous Huxley, in his book *Heaven and Hell,* first pointed out the similarity of the classical descriptions and depictions of these places to the experiences of people under psychedelics, in visionary states, or in the grip of psychotic terrors.[11] Psychotics typically describe having all the same feelings and sensations attributed to the residents of hell in the classical theological literature of the East and West, including feelings of being on fire or intolerable burning sensations all over the body. The parallels are so striking that one is led to surmise that *hell* is the prepsychological term for psychosis or madness. To be insane is to be in a state of consciousness marked by painful torturing sensations and feelings of hopeless despair and anguish—which are, after all, the defining characteristics of hell.

While there is a close experiential analogy between madness and hell, I am not saying that only psychosis is hellish. Since hell and heaven are states of consciousness, one can "enter" them from other states—dreams, for example, or drug-induced states. The nightmare is a dream of madness and of hell. Likewise, the ability of hallucinogenic drugs to trigger hellish, psychotic-like trips is so well known that they were first referred to as psychotomimetic. A toxic delirium and illnesses marked by severe chronic pain are other conditions of psychosomatic "hell."

In giving a psychological interpretation to the terms *heaven* and *hell*, I am by no means suggesting that these are nothing but inner states, unrelated to external reality. Anyone who has had firsthand experience of war, imprisonment, torture, or other forms of individual or social violence needs no reminder that hell can be, and often is, manifested externally in ways that can indeed drive one insane.

Traditionally, one of the distinguishing features of hell is its time-lessness. Even when, as in the Buddhist traditions, hell is regarded as one of the six transitory worlds of *samsara*, the sufferer in hell feels trapped and doomed forever. It is a situation of "no exit" and no sur-cease from unbearable anguish. This no-exit feeling characteristically accompanies the psychological hell of schizophrenia. Gopi Krishna, when undergoing the hellish aspect of a kundalini awakening, also felt that the relentless, glaring, and searing heat would not end but would consume his body entirely. I myself have had an experience of "hell," under the influence of the shortacting psychedelic DMT. Subjectively, the experience was unbearably unending, although it lasted only three minutes in "real time."

The difference between hell and the state referred to as purgatory would seem to lie in exactly this factor: hell lasts forever and there is no way out, whereas purgatory is a temporary phase one goes through in order to be purged and purified. Hell is usually envisioned as a pit or an abyss, whereas purgatory is seen as a path one must walk or, as in Dante, a mountain one ascends in purposive struggle and conscious suffering. From the perspective of the psychology of transformation, the hellish state of mind, the psychotic's feeling of being forever the victim of implacably hostile powerful forces, needs to yield to the recognition that one is involved in a temporary process, a transitional stage that has a definite purpose or "end."

In LSD-triggered psychoses I have witnessed, the crucial turning point toward resolution always seemed to be the recognition of being on a journey, in a process, or in a temporarily altered state of consciousness. The purifying inner fires are then no longer experienced as torture, a shirt of flame one cannot remove, but instead are regarded as a necessary purgation, accepted—even welcomed—for their transformative power. Stanislav Grof observed that encounters with consuming fire are a frequent component of psychedelic experiences and are usually accepted as transformative. "The individual who has discovered all the ugly, disgusting, degrading, and horrifying aspects of his personality finds himself thrown into this fire or deliberately plunges into it and passes through it. The fire appears to destroy everything that is rotten or corrupt in the individual and prepares him for the renewing and rejuvenating experience of rebirth."[12]

This attitude of accepting the pain of purgation, of even welcoming it and seeking it, underlies much of the self-denial and mortification of ascetics and monastics, expressed in deliberate renunciation of pleasure, in penitence, self-inflicted pain, and deprivation. It leads to the ecstatic paradoxical utterings of Saint John of the Cross: "O burn that burns to heal, O more than pleasant wound"; or to the alchemical philosopher's "sweet wound, soothing pain" (*vulnus dulce, suave malum*). Taken to an extreme, the attitude leads to the violent self-torture of the medieval Christian flagellantes. Among the Plains Indian tribes of North America, sacrificial ordeals such as the Sun Dance, in which the initiate is hung up by hooks inserted into his flesh or has strips of flesh cut from his body, also fall into this category.[13]

For the average person undergoing a transformative experience, whether spontaneously, or purposely in the course of psychotherapy, the importance of what one could call the purgatorial attitude is this: pay attention to the pain, learn from it, remember your intention in this process, remember it has a beginning and an end. Consciously experienced purgatorial purification can teach us a posture of humility and receptiveness, as we learn to understand the messages of the body and the psyche and to regard their signals as a guide to growth. This is also the attitude of traditional Asian medicine and of modern holistic healing approaches: symptoms, pain, and illness are seen as signs that something is off balance in the totality of the body, mind, and spirit; something needs to be purified.

In the writings of the mystics, the inner fires are described as purifying by burning off the coverings or accretions, comparable to the skins and veils discussed in Chapter 2, that obscure the soul. A medieval Christian text, the *Treatise on Purgatory,* states, "Your souls are covered by a rust, that is by sin, which is gradually consumed away by the fire of purgatory."[14] Jacob Boehme wrote, "If the love of God but once kindle a fire within you, you shall then certainly feel how it consumes all that it touches; you shall feel it burning up yourself, and swiftly devouring all that you call I and me."[15] In modern psychological terms, what Boehme is saying is that false identifications and self-concepts, egotistical habits and fixations are consumed in the fires of purification.

In the Hermetic-alchemical tradition, the two metaphors most often used for interior purifying fire are the fire of cooking, which breaks down foodstuffs for easier digestion, and the fire of smelting, which burns away the dross in order to reveal the shining metal. A seventeenth-century alchemical text entitled *The Sophic Hydrolith* states: "The old nature is destroyed, dissolved, decomposed, and, in a longer or shorter period of time, transmuted into something else. Such a man is so well digested and melted in the fire of affliction that he despairs of his own strength."[16]

The following report of an alchemically oriented psychotherapy session, which was amplified with the use of the empathogenic psychoactive substance MDMA, vividly illustrates the psychological and physical transformations that can occur, given the appropriate intention and preparation.

I became aware of major energy blockages in my spine just below my belly button. I had already had powerful energy releases after spinal massage, and I requested the therapist to massage my spine at the place I felt blocked. I was studying ancient alchemy at the time, and imagery from that tradition began to take on reality. The Neoplatonic concept of matter being the densest, darkest aspect of God's light became real. Not dark, but black, hard, dense, old, putrid, rotten material began to emerge from this place on my spine and flowed throughout my body. This contamination of my body was being released. It was like the base metal of the alchemists, gross, dense, hard, and black. . . . The therapist suggested I bring the purifying "philosopher's fire" to this place on my spine and so intensely heat the material as to transform it. I was ripe for this and experienced something like fire but not fire. It was like a fire of consciousness: bright, white, hot, intense, and eternally burning—like the center of the sun. The dark, dense matter blocking my spine became white hot, the impenetrable vault was being transformed by heat; its structure was being destroyed. All the details of my past had become condensed and packed into my body, and it was now all simultaneously being broken up in a blazing bonfire created by the heat of pure consciousness. Still now, but particularly for many days afterwards, my emotional reaction to ordinary events was and will always be different. I don't compromise my feelings as much as I did previously, and I am in touch with them to an infinitely greater extent.[17]

Purifying transformative experiences of this kind are by no means limited to drug states. In a class on "Alchemy and Depth Psychology" I have taught, students who were reading and meditating on alchemical themes and symbols began to have dreams and inner visions that corresponded to many of the key processes of alchemical transformation. One of these processes, *calcinatio*, the heating of a solid to burn off liquid, is analogous to the body's purifying fevers and sweats. Another, *solutio*, the dissolving of solid to a liquid form, is a metaphor for the dissolving of rigid, fixed perspectives ("thought forms") and defensive structures.[18]

One student in the class who was studying these fire-related processes had this dream:

> I was in a large vat of oil with a woman. On the far side a fire began to burn spontaneously. I began to run out of the vat, but the woman I was with fell and needed my assistance. We were surely in danger of burning alive. The flames were approaching closer. I stopped running, went back, and pulled the fallen woman up to the ladder and safety.

The dreamer definitely knew that this dream referred to and illustrated a purification process, akin to the yogic *tapas* and the alchemical *solutio*. The interaction with the woman indicated his need to confront and dissolve the separation from his anima, his feminine psyche.

The common theme expressed in these accounts, which was confirmed in my own experiences in the practice of alchemical fire yoga, is that there is a process experienced subjectively in the body as fiery and hot. This process brings about definite changes in the psychophysical totality: a dissolving of emotional and mental fixations, a melting and releasing of hard, painful tensions in the body, a cleansing of the "doors of perception" so that inner and outer realities are seen more clearly, and a reduction of separative factors blocking inner unification. These changes are experienced as healing, both physically and psychologically, and as accelerating the individual's growth toward a more integrated, whole sense of self. The changes are universally experienced as good and valuable, though the process itself can at times be quite painful.

What exactly this fiery process is has always been a mystery. The alchemical and purgatorial "fire" is obviously not the fire that burns in the sun or in the fireplace. It is like those fires, but subtle, fluid, elemental, invisible. And it can come under our conscious control or direction. The present paradigms of physics and psychophysiology are incapable of dealing with such phenomena. However, much pioneering work has been done on verifying and measuring healing life-energies or "subtle energies," and ultimately I believe science will be able to give a coherent account of such radical transformative processes.[19]

Sri Aurobindo has given the following description of the changes brought about by the purifying inner fire:

> As the crust of the outer nature cracks, as the walls of inner separation break down, the inner light gets through, the inner fire burns in the heart, the substance of the nature and the stuff of consciousness refine to a greater subtlety and purity, and deeper psychic experiences become possible. . . . The soul begins to unveil itself and manifests itself as the central being which upholds mind and life and body.[20]

Several of our other transformation metaphors are used here: in the first stage of hell and suffering, in which our defensive walls break down, we may "crack," reducing separative tendencies. Next, the purifying fires in the heart transmute our emotions and perceptions to subtler, higher-frequency experiences. Ultimately, the fires burn off the veils, bringing us to unmask ourselves before the central soul-self.

The following image from the alchemical tradition encapsulates the paradoxical process of inner purification presented here. The alchemists' symbol for the central self, the divine spirit, is the king, the inner ruler. The image is twofold: in the foreground, the king is depicted lying on the ground as though dead; a wolf is gnawing at his side. In the background of the picture, the wolf is shown burning in a bonfire, from which the king emerges unscathed.

At first, the royal self is as though lifeless; we are dis-spirited, our will and inspiration sabotaged by predatory aggression and greed, symbolized by the wolf. Then these lower egotistic drives, the animal tendencies, are burned away and purified. The divine inner being is revealed and liberated. "The wolf devoured the king, and after the wolf had been burnt, it returned the king to life."[21]

Kundalini and the Yoga of Fire

Kundalini is both an energy or fire, and a serpent. At the cosmic level the fiery serpent or dragon symbolizes atmospheric and terrestrial electromagnetic energy currents; at the individual level, the serpent fire represents generative and regenerative energy. According to the teachings of Tantric Yoga, some of this energy is expended or expressed externally in sexual release. In order for it to be used for transformative purposes, however, it must be raised up internally, which is equivalent to a transmutation of the energy. Thus, the serpent fire of kundalini is said to rise up through the body. This is both a metaphor and an actual psychophysiological experience.

When the kundalini is awakened through conscious yogic practice, the fiery energy passes up through the body's energy centers, energizing them and burning off the "coverings" that block their expression, finally to unite with the spiritual consciousness in the crown chakra at the top of the head. Brought up through the body, this power promotes healing and longevity; raised to the throat and head, it stimulates creativity and intuition. In the Indian Tantra Yoga texts, there are said to be three channels through which the kundalini energy rises upward: the central channel (*sushumna*), also called a staff, which corresponds to the central vertical axis; and a solar (*pingala*) and lunar (*ida*) channel, which coil like twin serpents up the right side and left side respectively, and which correspond to the sympathetic and parasympathetic branches of the vegetative nervous system.

In the medical traditions of ancient Greece, the staff with the single serpent coiling around it was known as the staff of Asclepius, the god of physicians and healers, and has become an emblem for the art of pharmacy. The staff with two serpents coiling around it was the caduceus, the staff of Hermes-Mercurius, the messenger of the gods and teacher of humans. Often, the twin serpents of the caduceus have wings at the top, corresponding in locale with the upper centers of the body. Winged animals of any kind symbolize transcendence and sublimation, the "raising up" of generative energy to the higher centers. This double staff has become an emblem for the medical profession, and both kinds of serpent-staff are found throughout the literature of alchemy. Because of the similarity in the symbolism, one can regard alchemy and Tantra Yoga as the European and Indian formulations of basically the same psychophysiological transformational process and practice.

Gopi Krishna, a modern Indian scholar, has published a detailed account of his experiences with the awakening of the kundalini energy, including the painful and near-fatal effects of the energy when imbalanced or when the body has not been sufficiently purified prior to its activation. In recent years many individuals in the West—who have not had any prior exposure to or knowledge of the literature of Tantra Yoga—have reported similar experiences of fiery heat rising and surging painfully and uncontrollably through the body. The American psychiatrist Lee Sannella has assembled a number of such cases and suggested that such a "kundalini syndrome" may often be unrecognized for what it is and misdiagnosed as a psychotic episode—which it becomes only when not handled properly.[22]

Experiential accounts of contemporary individuals, whether Western or Indian, show a remarkable degree of convergence with one another and with descriptions in the traditional Indian literature. According to this literature, if the body is to tolerate the high-intensity energy of the activated kundalini, the *nadis*, which form a vast, intricate network of subtle nervelike energy channels, must be purified of obstructions and accretions. If this purification has not taken place, the energy becomes violent, a searing and corrosive flame that causes illness, fever, delirium, insanity, and eventually death from the body's literally burning up.

Gopi Krishna described his initial experiences thus:

The self (king), being devoured by greed and aggression (wolf), is then transformed and liberated by the fires of purification. (From *Atalanta Fugiens*)

I found myself staring fearfully into a vast internal glow, disquieting and threatening at times, always in rapid motion, as if the particles of an ethereal luminous stuff crossed and recrossed each other, resembling the ceaseless movement of wildly leaping lustrous clouds of spray rising from a waterfall.... Sometimes it seemed as if a jet of molten copper, mounting up through the spine, dashed against my crown and fell in a scintillating shower of vast dimensions all around me.[23]

Continuing over several months, the raging internal fires that he was unable to control in any way brought him to the brink of death. He finally realized that the energy was one-sided: the solar, right-sided aspect alone was harsh and corrosive (corresponding to the alchemical *sulphur*). When he consciously invoked the lunar, left-sided counterpart energy (the alchemists' *salt*) as a soothing, cool luminescence, his experience changed dramatically into one of pleasurable internal stimulation. This shift brought about a rapid recovery, accompanied by heightened awareness and psychic perception. Gopi Krishna's experience suggests that the balancing and harmonizing of the two polarities is as important to the transformation process as the activation and raising of the energy per se.

Variations in the patterns of energy flow are frequently found in the esoteric yogic literature as well as in the spontaneous experiences of modern individuals. The disturbed and disturbing bioelectric energy discharges found in the kundalini syndrome can appear anywhere in the body but most often move upward. In Agni Yoga, in Aurobindo's synthesis of yoga principles, as well as in the teachings of Actualism, a modern Western school of fire yoga, the light-fire energy is consciously poured from above the head downward and is directed into various parts of the body that need purification or healing.[24] In Chinese Taoist practices, both ancient and modern, the energy is circulated through and around the body, and is variously referred to as "the circulation of the light" or "the microcosmic orbit."[25] In these systems the energy is channeled from the pelvic center up the back, over the head, and down the front in a continuing circuit. From the point of view embodied in these systems, the Indian kundalini method might be regarded as only half the process.

From the different accounts of yoga techniques as well as alchemical visions, which have in common the elemental energy and symbolism of fire, it is clear that the subjective and psychological changes brought about are basically similar, even though the technical procedures may differ. Here, for example, is an account by a student of Agni Yoga that has strong alchemical imagery:

There were many experiences of sensing light energy in the centers, and radiating out, becoming flaming consuming fire, dissolving muscular tensions, emotional fixations, and crystallized image-forms. I could "see" two-dimensional images burn up like plastic sheets; sometimes I could hear soft crackling sounds and smell the odors of putrefication as toxic bodily fluids were being purified by "gentle cooking." During body work, I felt pulsing beams of fiery energy coming from the healer's hands, breaking off what felt like chunks of psychic debris, melting the icy grip of fear-based spasms or contractions. After this kind of experience I felt lighter in weight, almost floating, as well as cleansed inside and outside.[26]

We see, then, that such experiences of modern individuals are described in the same patterns of imagery, the same symbols and metaphors, that the ancient technologies of human transformation have used and elaborated. The imagery of alchemical purification through fire and of the serpentine healing fire seems to correspond to something inherent and natural in the human being. In any given time and place, perhaps only a few people have worked consciously with these processes. Many more may have experienced some aspect of the process without realizing that it is a transformation and can be deliberately developed and supported. The fact that the process and the method have their dangers (pain, illness, insanity) is true of any human endeavor, particularly those that aim at radical self-transformation.

The Mystical Fire of Union

What remains after the fires have done their work of purification? What is the nature and value of unitive experience brought about by and based on inner fire? Since God, in religious literature and sacred myths, is often identified as a being of fire or light who purifies and transforms us, the answer becomes startlingly simple and obvious: the fire of divine spirit is both the agent of transformation and its goal or end.

The following passage from an alchemical tract called, appropriately enough, *The Glory of the World* appears to be making this point. It refers to the adept's experience of God as fire, to the vitalizing and animating qualities of inner fire and the value in cultivating it, and to its purifying effect on the mind (symbolized by Mercury).

> Take fire, . . . wherein God himself burns by divine love. It is the most precious fire that God has created in the earth, and has a thousand virtues. . . . It has the purifying virtue of Purgatory, and everything is rendered better by it. . . . The fire should be able to fix and clarify Mercury, and to cleanse it from all grossness and impurity. The Sages call it the living fire, because God has endowed it with his own divine and vitalizing power. . . . This fire unites three things, namely body, spirit and soul.[27]

It is the mystics and alchemists who really personalize this theme of God as living fire: God is no longer an immense powerful being up there in some transcendent realm. Rather, divinity is the fire of life within every being. Our innermost essence is fire and light. Saint John of the Cross, the sixteenth-century Spanish mystic, expressed it as follows:

> O living flame of love!
> How tenderly you force
> To my soul's inmost core your fiery probe.
>
> O lamps of fiery blaze
> To whose refulgent fuel
> The deepest caverns of my soul grow bright.[28]

This inner flame is both a purifying, consuming fire and the fire of the soul's love for God. As the *Treatise on Purgatory*, attributed to Saint Catherine of Genoa, says, "As she, plunged in the divine furnace of purifying love, was united with the object of her love, so she understood it to be with the souls in purgatory."[29] The human psyche is purified, transformed, and loved by the fire of God, with which it becomes increasingly unified.

Like the purifying, purgatorial fires that generally come earlier in the process of transformation, the fire of divine inner union is an actual, psychophysiological experience, not merely a metaphor. This is emphasized again and again in the literature of mysticism. The fourteenth-century English mystic Richard Rolle, in his tract *The Fire of Love*, gives this account:

> I cannot tell you how surprised I was the first time I felt my heart begin to warm. It was real warmth, too, not imaginary, and it felt as if it were actually on fire. I was astonished at the way the heat surged up and how this new sensation brought great and unexpected comfort. I had to keep feeling my breast to make sure there was no physical reason for it. . . . Before the infusion of this comfort I had never thought that we exiles could possibly have known such warmth. It set my soul aglow as if a real fire were burning there.[30]

This account is typical of the experience of many individuals to this day, who either spontaneously or in the course of psychospiritual practice or psychotherapy feel what is often called an opening, or awakening, of the heart, accompanied by spontaneous "infusions" of spiritual fire.

The sequence in transformation by fire characteristically follows the stages presented in Dante: first the inferno, then purgatory, then heaven. In the first state we feel like victims of overwhelmingly powerful, hostile, oppressive forces, the fires of madness and hell; then, in the purgatory phase, we recognize that we are on the path of purification, that we have a purpose and that our fiery suffering is intentional. Finally, the painful purgatorial fires change to the soothing, nourishing fire of divine love and union. We are then, in T. S. Eliot's phrase, "redeemed from fire by fire."

> The dove descending breaks the air
> With flames of incandescent terror,
> Of which the tongues declare
> The one discharge from sin and error.

The only hope, or else despair
　Lies in the choice of pyre or pyre—
　To be redeemed from fire by fire.[31]

An extraordinary unitive vision of the world as animated by divine spirit-fire, is found in the works of Jacob Boehme, the great seventeenth-century German mystic, an uneducated shoemaker whose transcendental visions had a profound influence on subsequent European philosophy and theology. Boehme's mystical insight was that all of life, all creation, all matter, all opposites, come from and are based in a kind of primal ground, which he himself likened to the Hermetic ideas of primordial chaos, the *prima materia*. It is a conception similar in some respects to the Chinese Tao, the Buddhist Void, and the Hindu *Brahman*. The unique aspect of Boehme's formulation is in the fact that he called this primal ground a *fire*:

> This Burning Fire is a manifestation of Life and Divine Love, through which Divine Love, as unifying principle, over-enflames and sharpens itself as the fiery aspect of the power of God. This ground is called the Great Mystery or Chaos, from which originates evil and good, light and darkness, life and death, joy and suffering, salvation and damnation, . . . for it is ground of souls and angels and all eternal creatures, the good and the evil, ground of heaven and hell and the visible world, including everything existing—since all come from that one source-ground.[32]

We have here a vision of ultimate reality, of God and the universe, that in contrast to most other formulations is much more dynamic: a unified field of all-encompassing fire energy that provides the ground-matrix of the known and unknown universe. In Jacob Boehme's vision, this primal fire ground precedes all the divisions into the dualities of spirit and nature, physical and metaphysical, good and evil, light and darkness—and in it all these dualities and separations will, in the end, be resolved.

From Fragmentation to Wholeness

5

When the ten thousand things are viewed in their
oneness, we return to the origin and remain where
we have always been.

—ZEN MASTER SENGSTAN

One of the major themes in the literature on the transformation of
consciousness is the notion that the disjointed, separated, fragmented
parts of the psyche can be and need to be synthesized into a harmonious, integrated whole. An initial condition of confusion, disorder,
and chaos gradually gives way to a state where we are functioning
from a clear center within ourselves. In this state, the different parts
or aspects of our psychological and physical totality are functionally
coordinated and unified. William James spoke of "the divided self
and the process of its unification," and Jung wrote of the process of
individuation, becoming in-divisible or whole. The experience of feeling scattered, fragmented, and confused is surely familiar to all of us
at times, and this is the psychological and experiential basis for the
metaphor of integration.

Because people often feel themselves, their psyche, and their whole
lives to be scattered or splintered, a significant aspect of the experience
of healing and growth is the synthesizing, the gathering together of
these fragments. As an example, here is the account by a twenty-five-
year-old college student of his experience during a deep altered-state
psychotherapy session:

> I put together all the bits and pieces of my past knowledge of my
> father, my mother, and brother, . . . and in an instant of realization
> I saw my fragmented emotional interior become a whole gestalt.
> I "saw" my childhood history with an adult mind and unified the

fragmented pieces of my emotions.... I have waited many years for such deep understanding.[1]

The English words *whole, wholesome,* and *wholeness* (as well as the more recent variants *holism* and *holistic*) are derived from the Old English *hal,* which means "sound," "complete," and "healthy." The same root word is also ancestral to the German *heil,* "safe," to our *hale,* and to *hail,* as a greeting. So wholeness, in the sense of integration, overlaps considerably with the concept of health. We might say that health *is* whole, complete functioning. Furthermore, the English *holy* and the German *heilig* also derive from the same root. Thus, health, wholeness, and holiness are all associated with the fundamental underlying concept of integration and togetherness, which is contrasted with its polar opposite of dispersion, scattering, and fragmentation.

There are links between this metaphor and some of the other themes we have already discussed. Fragmentation and dividedness are often seen as identical to captivity and defense: the knots and nets that trap our awareness are the same defensive mechanisms that also separate and divide our personality. The process of inner purification burns or strips away the blocks and barriers that produce the state of dividedness. This metaphor is also related to the notion of opposites and their reconciliation. From the many to the one, from duality to unity—the direction of growth and evolution is toward integration, toward oneness. Transformation toward more fragmentation, greater internal dividedness, is seen as regressive or pathological—with one important exception.

In many shamanic traditions, there exist practices of intentional fragmentation in which practitioners purposefully allow themselves to be divided and dismembered—psychically. This kind of conscious, guided dismantling of ego structures is regarded as part of the work of learning to function in different realities. We are dealing, then, not with psychotic disintegration but with intentional shamanic practice.

A further crucial point here is that separation or dissociation in the psyche is regarded as an inevitable and necessary consequence of incarnation, just as imprisonment is. A human being's nature is originally one, single, whole, and unified with God. Through entry into the world of form, however—through embodiment—we become involved with multiplicity. We live enmeshed in the thousand petty details of ordinary existence. Meister Eckhart wrote: "This treasure of the Kingdom of God has been hidden by time and multiplicity . . . and by creaturely nature. But in the measure that the soul can separate itself from this multiplicity, to that extent it reveals within itself the Kingdom of God."[2] In the core of our being we are singular and unified; at the surface of our interactions with the world, we are multiple and dispersed. In transformation we seek to recover that original unity.

Psychic Fragmentation in Ordinary Awareness and in Madness

Numerous expressions in our language attest to the implicit belief that our personality, our psyche, our mind is something that is brittle, that it can be broken or fragmented in some way. We may be "shattered" by an experience or think we are "falling apart," "coming apart at the seams," or "falling to pieces," to the point where we have a "nervous breakdown." We may "break" under cross-examination, "break up" with laughter, or "break off" a relationship, which may also make us feel "brokenhearted." I may be "shaken" by some bad news, feel "torn" between conflicting demands, be "crushed" by a rejection, or "crumble" under stress until my mind "snaps." I can get "smashed" on liquor and the next morning have a "splitting" headache. Recognizing how "scattered" our thinking and our energies often are, we tell ourselves we need to "get our act together."

We tend to deplore states of mind in which our thinking is scattered. We feel confused when we have a multiplicity of choices or have mixed motives for something. On the other hand, we tend to admire those who are "single-minded" in their pursuit of some ideal or in their practice of a devotion. We search, with varying degrees of awareness, for a unifying vision or purpose in our life. William James spoke of several "selves" that constitute a personality:

> Now in all of us, however constituted, . . . does the normal evolution of character chiefly consist in the straightening out and unifying of the inner self. The higher and the lower feelings, the useful and the erring impulses, begin by being a comparative chaos within us—they must end by forming a stable system of functions in right subordination.[3]

Many psychological theories contain ideas similar to this. Starting with the common observation that human personality and behavior are constituted of many parts and functions, psychologists have developed lists of "traits" or "needs" to account for the multiplicity and diversity of human activities. In the psychoanalytic theory of personality and its later derivatives, a person's adult personality structure represents an accumulation of numerous identifications with various role models, who were imitated at various stages of development—starting with our parents. In adult life we then find ourselves with a multiplicity of roles. It is not necessary to go into the details of these theories of human nature to appreciate the common theme of multiplicity.

Roberto Assagioli, who developed his theory of psychosynthesis based partly on the esoteric teachings of Alice Bailey, spoke of the existence in the psyche of a number of differing, and at times conflicting, subpersonalities. In his view, we are at first unconsciously identified with these subpersonalities; in time, as we become aware of them, we see them as roles we consciously play out. Some have suggested the apt metaphor of the self as a kind of orchestra with many different parts playing together. The task of transformation, then, is to attune and harmonize the different musicians and instruments of the personality.[4]

Another metaphor for ordinary psychic multiplicity is the theater. In Jung's psychology, for example, the drama of the psyche has four main characters—the ego, the persona, the shadow, and the anima or animus—while the Self would be analogous to the author, producer, and director combined. The many varieties of consciousness and identity are accounted for in his model by the multifarious images and symbols in the collective unconscious. Each of us has access to an enormous number of archetypes, myths, and symbols that live in our psyche. These archetypes and symbols serve as signposts, or centers, around which are crystallized our wishes, hopes, fears, ideals, and impulses. They are as numerous and varied as the facets of our personality.

Older typologies of human temperament were often based on the assumption that people are identified with parts or subsystems of the body. In the humoral theory, which goes back to medieval times, we had sanguine ("blood-related") or phlegmatic ("lymph-related") dispositions, as well as choleric and melancholic temperaments. In the nineteenth and early twentieth century, variants of the humoral theory distinguished temperaments on the basis of presumed hormonal preponderance: we had adrenal, thymus, and thyroid characters.[5]

It is a common observation that we identify ourselves and others with different parts or organs of the body. If I say, "I hurt" rather than "my foot hurts," I am identifying with my foot at that moment. Each part of the body has "ego," a sense of identity. We can, by self-observation, come to an awareness of where in the body our identity is centered at any given time. This kind of awareness is very helpful in charting our course through the process of transformation. In psychotherapy, for example, it is valuable to ask someone who reports feeling fear, where in the body the fear is located. The use of genital and anal organ names as terms of abuse also implies identification of the whole self with a part of the body—those particular parts being judged inferior or repulsive in some way.

I am inclined toward the view that each structural unit of the body, each organ, each cell, has a sense of identity. Each organ and cell has its ego, which is the subjective center of its aliveness. Because there are so many of these egos, it is easy to see how a sense of being scattered, disjointed, or fragmented can arise. This idea, which I adopted from the Actualism teachings of Russell Paul Schofield, is also found in the writings of Georg Groddeck, the German physician from whom Freud derived his theory of the id (originally *das Es*). Groddeck wrote, "I go so far as to believe that every single cell has this consciousness of individuality, that every tissue, every organic system, every kidney cell and every nail cell has its 'I' consciousness."[6]

Probably the most forceful statement of the fragmented nature of ordinary human personality is found in the Russian mystic Gurdjieff's teaching:

> Man has no permanent and unchangeable I. Every thought, every mood, every desire, every sensation, says "I.". . . There are hundreds and thousands of small I's, very often entirely unknown to one another, mutually exclusive and incompatible. Each moment, each minute, man is thinking of saying "I." And each time the "I" is different. Just now it was a thought, now it is a desire, now a sensation, now another thought, and so on, endlessly. Man is a plurality. Man's name is legion. . . . There is nothing in man able to control this change of I's, chiefly because he does not notice, or know of it; he lives always in the last I. . . . This explains why people so often make decisions, and so seldom carry them out.[7]

Gurdjieff goes on to argue that the arising and functioning of these different egos is controlled by such temporary factors as weather and other external accidental circumstances, as well as by the longer-lasting influences of education, imitation, religion, caste, tradition, and so forth. In this view of the variegated multiplicity of human personality, our everyday consciousness is seen as scattered and fragmented.

The physicist David Bohm, in discussing the prevalence of fragmentation on the level of the individual, of the group, and of society, points to the "rather interesting sort of irony [that] fragmentation seems to be the one thing in our way of life which is universal, which works through the whole without boundary or limit." Bohm goes on to make the important point that in considering the transformation of fragmentation, we are not talking about wholeness as some sort of remote ideal. Rather, wholeness is the original fact, which we want to reestablish. "Wholeness is what is real, and fragmentation is the response of this whole to man's action, guided by illusory perception, shaped by fragmentary thought."[8]

We need to become aware of our fragmented consciousness, to pay attention to our fragmented way of thinking and understanding reality. We need to learn to "view the ten thousand things in their oneness."

The notion that normal, everyday consciousness is characterized by scattering and fragmentation is difficult for many people to accept, and it is not a comforting realization when we observe it in ourselves. In the area of mental illness or psychological disorders, however, we can readily see that multiplicity and dividedness are a key feature. Here too, the metaphors implicit in colloquialisms are highly suggestive. We can have a "breakdown," or we may "crack up." The word *crack* is based on Middle English *crasen*, "to break," which is the ancestor of our words *craze* and *crazy*. Equally suggestive of the fragmentation metaphor is the etymology of mad, based on the Indo-European root word *mait*, "to hew," which we find related to the words *maim, mayhem,* and *mangle*. This is particularly interesting in view of the connection, discussed later, between psychic fragmentation and the metaphor of bodily dismemberment.

In psychotic states of consciousness, in addition to separation or disconnection between different parts of the psyche (to a much higher degree than in normal awareness), there may also be conflict and opposition between the different psychic fragments. Psychiatric researchers have referred to the "shattered language" of schizophrenia in describing the loose associations, the incoherence, the attentional gaps and intrusions, the nonlogical, non-reality-oriented speech of these individuals. *Schizophrenia* literally means "split mind." Indeed, the "psychotic break" is regarded by some as simply a more intense and radical version of the normal, neurotic "nervous breakdown."

In multiple personality disorder (MPD) and other dissociative disorders, the individual appears to have two or more personality fragments manifesting at different times; these personalities are separated from one another by an "amnestic barrier." In other words, the different characters in the interior drama don't know one another. In response to repeated unavoidable traumatization, two or more fragments of identity, sometimes called "ego-states" or "alters," are created that maintain a continuity of their own, often with different names and different personality characteristics. Dissociative conditions, including multiple personalities, may be much more common than psychoanalytically oriented psychiatry believes.[9]

Since we all have several roles and identities that we play out in everyday life, one could say we are all multiple personalities to a certain extent. The psychoses and dissociative disorders are merely more extreme forms of psychic fragmentation and multiplicity. The shattered psyche of a psychotic requires a healing transformation that is essentially similar to the spiritual transformation of normal, scattered consciousness to integrated, unified consciousness. In both cases, we go from fragmentation to greater wholeness.

Shamanic Dismemberment: Osiris and Dionysus

The experience of psychological and psychosomatic fragmentation is symbolized in a very direct, concrete manner in the ancient images and rites of shamanism. Following the lead of historians of religion such as Mircea Eliade and anthropologists such as Michael Harner, we can regard shamanism as a set of practices in which altered states of consciousness are induced by various means, including chanting, drumming, dancing, and use of hallucinogenic plants. Such an altered state is experienced by the shamanic initiate as an inner journey in which she or he enters another world for the purpose of connecting with a source of power, obtaining a vision, or bringing about a healing. The metaphor of the shamanic journey as a transformative altered-state experience will be discussed in more detail in Chapter 11. Here we are concerned with the shamanic initiation experience of being symbolically cut up or dismembered, and with the related concepts of initiatory sickness and the "wounded healer."

Eliade has amply documented the occurrence of dismemberment initiations in shamanic cultures of North and South America, Africa, Australia, Central Asia, and Indonesia. In these cultures, it is an accepted and expected part of shamanic apprenticeship to suffer an illness or a wound, or to have an inner experience of being dismembered and reconstituted. The illness of the shamanic seeker can be very real, and by going through it and overcoming it, the would-be healer is in a way following the ancient adage "physician, heal thyself." Through such experiences, the would-be shaman's healing power is tested and demonstrated for the members of the community. In some cases, the illness may be more psychological. The parallels between some shamanic vision accounts and psychotic experiences have often been remarked upon. The differences, however, are equally important: the shamanic experience is intentionally incurred, as part of a training sanctioned and approved by the culture, while the psychotic experience is involuntary and unwanted, and has no social support—in fact, it entails social stigma.[10]

Shamans in training may have initiatory visions in which they see and feel themselves being (metaphorically) dismembered, or cut open, or flayed, or reduced to a skeleton. In some of the Australian aboriginal tribes, the would-be medicine man is "cut open" with stones; the abdominal organs are "removed" and replaced by crystals, which give him curing and clairvoyant power after he is put back together. In Siberia and among the Eskimos, the initiate is divested of flesh and contemplates his skeleton before being reassembled. In other cultures there may be a "stripping" of the skin, followed by its being washed or replaced by a new one. It is important to realize that such apparently gruesome inner experiences are sought out by the shaman in training, for they are followed by the feeling experience of the body being renewed and by the acquisition of magical or healing powers.

To the practitioner who is a member of that shamanic culture, such visions have the nature of a religious experience. The initiate feels he or she is being delivered from the limitations of the ordinary world and empowered to perform visionary, healing, and protective work for himself or herself and the members of the community. Michael Harner has for years conducted training workshops in shamanic practices for modern Westerners and has reported that altered-state journeys and dismemberment visions can readily occur in a contemporary context and are usually experienced as being both healing and renewing. According to the shamanic teachings, when the person's body is reconstituted, it is given new organs that are healthier, stronger, and free from disease. The healing reconstruction of the (inner) body may be performed by the spirit of an ancestor or a power animal. I recall one very moving experience in a shamanic journey triggered by drumming, in which after being "killed" and left lying lifeless on the ground, I was revived by my spirit-horse passing its huge, warm, soft nostrils over every part of my body, breathing new life into me.

Healing experiences of being dismembered and then reassembled in a healthier, stronger form are also commonly reported in the accounts of those who ingest hallucinogenic or entheogenic plants as part of a shamanic practice. Particularly the Amazonian plant brew known as *ayahuasca* or *yagé*, which has a powerful purgative effect, can induce literally gut-wrenching experiences of being devoured, dismembered, or disembowelled. With this, as with the Mexican magic mushroom *teonanácatl*, the work of disassembly and reconstitution may be carried out by the diminutive elflike beings that are felt to be the spirits of those plants. Here is an extract from an account of an *ayahuasca* experience, by a psychologist in his fifties:

> The ayahuasca jungle elves, the little green guys, are carrying away what look like armor plates and metallic pieces. I get the sense they are taking apart pieces of a structure, to wash and polish them and tune them up for better functioning. Suddenly I realize the structure they are dismantling is my self. I yell after them (inwardly), "Hey, wait, that's *me* you're carrying away there." Without missing a beat, they reply cheerfully, "Not to worry, we'll put you back together, you'll be fine." All the time they are singing in the rhythmic chants of the *icaros* we are hearing. I had experienced, and heard of, shamanic dismemberment experiences before, where you are pounded and pulverized, or sliced and cut up, as a prelude to eventual reconstitution. But this was the first time I experienced this kind of civilized, courteous, efficient dismantling. The green elves were taking apart my character armor, and giving me back an improved, more flexible, more comfortable body-mind persona.[11]

Perhaps the most dramatically powerful of such rituals that has been documented is the *chod*, or "cutting-off" rite, of the Tibetan Lamaist tradition, which represents a fusion of the original Bön shamanism with Vajrayana Buddhist teachings from India. In this rite, the initiate retires alone to a deserted cemetery or charnel ground, invokes various demons and "wrathful deities," and invites them to cut up and devour his body. Here are the instructions for one such rite:

> Then imagine this body, which is the result of thine own karmic propensities, to be a fat, luscious-looking corpse, huge enough to embrace the universe. Then visualize the Radiant Intellect, which is within thee, as being the Wrathful Goddess and as standing apart from

the body, having one face and two hands and holding a knife and a skull. Think that she severs the head from the corpse, cuts the corpse to pieces and flings them into the skull as offerings to the deities. Then think that by the power of mantras, the offerings are wholly transmuted into *amrita* [divine essence or nectar], sparkling and radiant.[12]

This text makes clear that the dismembered body is transmuted to a higher, "lighter" form, just as the substitution of crystals for internal organs among the Australian medicine men symbolizes their becoming filled with light and power. In these examples, such ritual visualizations of personal destruction are regarded as an inherent and inevitable feature of the transformative initiation. Dismemberment is always followed by healing and renewal, intensified fragmentation by wholesome integration.

In the Tibetan and several other shamanic traditions, the dismemberment of the (inner) body is often visualized as being accomplished by demons or monsters; the healing and reconstituting may be done by the practitioner's teacher or guru or by a spirit ally or power animal. From another point of view, the destructive demons or "wrathful deities" are in essence also allies: they assist in the labor of transformation and liberation. They are personifications of the fiercely energetic forces of "breakthrough"—even though to the ego experiencing their violent power, they appear to be causing breakup and breakdown. The shaman-yogi must learn to tame these demons, which reside, of course, within the psyche, and he or she must learn to redirect their energies toward enlightenment and transformation.

The relevance of these ancient shamanic rituals and practices to the modern individual lies in their emphasis on transformation and awareness. Such is the power of these vivid and dramatic inner visions that they can give a new center and a new direction to the psyche of the practitioner. A similar role is played by myths of dying and dismembered gods and by the mystery cults based on these myths.[13] The myth of a god or hero functions as a prototype, or exemplar, for the individual, telling us to follow the example of the god who can let himself be dismembered and then reconstituted.

We have already discussed (in chapter 3) the myth of Osiris, who was trapped inside a coffer, a tree, and a house, as a metaphor for the human experience of captive embodiment. In another part of the myth of Osiris, the symbolism of dismemberment and reintegration is elaborated. The story goes that Osiris, the green god of vegetation and the flowing river, was captured again by his enemy-brother Set, the fierce god of desert heat and aridity. This time Osiris was cut up into pieces that were scattered all over the world. His consort Isis again saved him, by finding and reassembling the fragments—except that his generative member could not be found. So Isis fashioned a new one and impregnated herself by it. Osiris went on to become the Lord of the Underworld. Their son Horus continued the struggle against Set in the natural world.

Such a myth has many levels of meaning: on the ecological and geo-graphical level, it represents the interactions at the boundary between two ecosystems—the hot, arid desert and the fertile river valley. On the level of psychospiritual transformation, the story of the dismember-ment of Osiris is a metaphor for the fragmentation of personal identity in the world of ordinary existence. We have psychic pieces of ourselves all over the place. Isis, in putting Osiris back together, represents the feminine spiritual counterpart, the female soul or anima, capable of synthesizing and integrating our scattered selves. The myth applies equally to men and women: the dynamic, expressive aspect (Osiris) gets scattered and lost in the toils and splinters of material existence; the nurturing, receptive aspect (Isis) heals and "makes whole." The cure for dismemberment is re-membering: remembering who we actually are. This is the process of self-remembering and recollection that plays such an important role in Gnostic and Sufi teachings.[14]

In the Greek myth of Dionysus, the connection between the experience of bodily fragmentation and the psychic dissociation of insanity is clearly revealed. Dionysus is also a vegetation god, specifically associated with the cultivation of wine and other inebriants. He comes from an older, preOlympian layer of religious culture, in which earth goddesses and gods were still preponderant. He is the god, the spirit, the archetype, of divine intoxication, ecstasy, *enthusiasmos*. He drives mad those who do not acknowledge his divinity, hence he is also the god of madness, mania, dismemberment, dissolution, and death.[15]

Dionysus, like Osiris, has several births and several deaths. The variant of his story most relevant to the present theme is that of Dionysus-Zagreus, whose name means Great Hunter. At the instigation of Hera, who was jealous because he was the offspring of Zeus and a human woman, he was captured by Titans as a youth. Before being caught, he changed himself rapidly from one animal form into another, ending in the body of a bull. In this form he was caught, cut to pieces, cooked in a cauldron, and devoured by the Titans. However, his father, Zeus, managed to save his heart and remake him from this one organ. In a variant, the pieces were reassembled by his grandmother Rhea. The story of Dionysus' fragmentation, like that of Osiris, can be seen as an expression of the archetype of conscious, intentional self-dismemberment. The shape-shifting theme clearly shows that this myth contains residues of older shamanic traditions.

We can see the devouring Titans as the teachers and guides who lead the youthful Dionysus through the kinds of experience his followers would later incorporate in the rituals of the mystery cults. Dionysus, like every human being, is part god, part human. In childhood he is dismembered, just as we all become fragmented and dissociated as a result of the conditioning processes of ordinary existence. And through the intervention of the divine principle, in the form of either the divine father (Zeus) or the divine mother (Rhea), the human life is saved and healed. Like Osiris, Dionysus becomes ruler of the underworld, equated with Hades. He is the one who crosses and recrosses the boundaries between worlds, who shatters our carefully constructed conventional realities, driving us into madness or liberating transformation—depending on our level of preparedness and the quality of our intention.

Following Nietzsche, classical scholars have said that Apollo and Dionysus represent two central mythic strands in ancient Greek religion: the Apollonian, which is lyrical, poetic, harmonious, musical, and aesthetic, and the Dionysian, which is intoxicated, abandoned, chaotic, wild, and irrational. The myth tells us that if we do not acknowledge or recognize our own instinctual, violent, and ecstatic impulses, they can drive us mad. If we do recognize and acknowledge them, those violent and paradoxical impulses within us can be transformed and integrated. In modern literature the character of Zorba the Greek is a prime example of the Dionysian temperament: we may recall his statement that you have to be a little bit crazy to really cut loose and be free.

Individuals in the midst of a transformation process that includes fragmentation or dismemberment experiences would do well to study the mythic imagery of Osiris, Dionysus, and the related stories of the Indian Kali. In these myths we can see how such a madness-inducing experience can be transformed and how it can eventually lead to integration.

Alchemical *Separatio* in Meditation and Psychotherapy

In the Hermetic tradition of consciousness transformation, the process of *separatio* most nearly corresponds to the metaphor of dismemberment. Through *separatio,* the elements of our nature, which are initially in a state of undifferentiated chaos, are carefully distinguished, separated, discriminated. In Buddhist meditation practice this is the function of "discriminative wisdom." It is a kind of sorting out of the separate parts of our totality, seen as a prerequisite to subsequent integration. Jung used the German word *auseinanderset-zen,* literally "setting apart," a kind of conscious analytic confronta-tion, to describe the recommended attitude toward the contents of the unconscious. Or, to put it another way, the destructuring of the old personality, both physical and psychic, must precede the restructuring of transformation.[16]

As used in alchemy, the "elements" have both physical and psycho-logical meanings. Physically, they represent component states of the material body: earth the solid, water the fluid, air the gaseous, and fire the bioelectrical. Identifying and then integrating these aspects through meditation, imagery, and discriminative awareness is the first phase of the alchemical integrative process. Psychologically, the four elements correspond to the levels of personality consciousness and Jung's functions: *earth* the physical body and the sensing function, *water* the emotional body and feeling function, *air* the mental body and thinking, and *fire* the perceptual body and the intuitive func-tion. Thus, the alchemical meditative process of *separatio* consists in a kind of conscious discriminative sorting out of our confused, chaotic thoughts, feelings, perceptions, and body sensations.[17]

Separatio, as conscious, intentional discrimination, is akin to the process of *solutio,* as conscious, intentional dissolution: both result in a release of the spiritual energies that have been trapped or bound in the old structures. Jung wrote: "The *anima mundi,* imprisoned in matter, . . . was set free by 'cooking,' by the sword dividing the 'egg,' or by the *separatio,* or by dissolution into the four 'roots' or elements. The *separatio* was often represented as dismemberment of a human body." He also points out the connection between *separatio* and the modern concept of psychic dissociation, "which, as we know, lies at the root of the psychogenic psychoses and neuroses."[18]

An example of a dismemberment-*separatio* image occurred to a psychotherapy client who, after an emotional encounter with a psychotic, dreamed of seeing himself with his torso opened and his

Transformation through destruction: the goddess Kali dances among the severed limbs and heads of humans, her tongue shooting flame. (From the Hindu Tantric tradition, 18th-century India)

intestines pouring out. Subsequently he imagined his depression as a pit of darkness, out of which light was beginning to emerge. Other experiences in the same vein, which have been observed in psychedelic states, in psychotherapy, and in dreams of persons undergoing radical transformation, include seeing parts of one's body, especially the arms and hands, becoming elongated and flying off into space; seeing another's or one's own body as a skeleton; feeling one's skin being turned inside out and washed; or feeling as if penetrated and transfixed by hundreds of needles or swords or arrow points simultaneously (as in the legend of Saint Sebastian).

In the model of personality transformation developed by Stanislav Grof, dismemberment and *separatio* imagery stems from the third phase of the birth process, in which the fetus is being actively and vigorously, though often with enormous pain and struggle, propelled through the birth canal.[19] Experiences derived from the memory of this stage are characterized by feelings of "titanic struggle," "cosmic suffering," "volcanic ecstasy," explosions, orgies, bloody warfare, battles, dangerous adventures, dying and being reborn, and religious sacrifice as in the Aztec, early Christian, and Dionysian traditions. Clearly these are all characteristic dismemberment and fragmentation images; in psychotherapeutic transformations, they typically occur just prior to the experience of rebirth into a new and better kind of life.

An example of healing, liberating *separatio* imagery is found in this account, by a twenty-six-year-old college student, of part of a psychedelic therapy session:

> I felt shattered, broken up. . . . It was as if a sledgehammer had been slammed down on the crystallized, granitelike structures of my deepest and earliest emotional pain and trauma—something that was previously rocklike and unchangeable, like cement that had solidified in my being.[20]

In other words, healing takes place as some psychic complex is disintegrated through a cutting and breaking down process, applied to the area of hardened defenses and resistance.

Almost all these images can be found in alchemical texts and illustrations—another factor that supports the notion that the alchemists were in fact practitioners of consciousness transformation. For example, in a sixteenth-century tract entitled *Splendor Solis* ("Splendor of the Sun"), we are told of a vision of an alchemical practitioner, Rosinos, in which he sees a man lying on the ground, his limbs and head cut off. Next to the dead man stands the killer, holding a blood-stained sword. In the killer's other hand is a paper on which is written, "I have killed thee, that thou mayst receive superabundant life. And the body I will bury, that it may putrefy, and grow and bear innumerable fruit."[21] Another alchemical text advises us to "destroy the bodies until they are changed." This is conscious, deliberate destruction of psychic structures, leading to intentional reconstruction.

Alchemical separatio: cutting the cosmic egg with the fiery sword of analytical discrimination. (From *Atalanta Fugiens*)

Jung pointed out the parallels between this symbolism and that of Job's sufferings and Christ's passion—and, he might have added, the sufferings of the early Christian martyrs. The martyrs' devout, even ecstatic, acceptance of torture and death might in part have been stimulated by a perception of the similarity of Christ's martyrdom with the slain and dismembered divinities of the mystery religions of Osiris and Dionysus.

Approaches to Wholeness

There are three major keys to what could be called the strategy of transformative reintegration. These keys are also central in the other varieties of transformative experience discussed in this book. The first *point* is that we must recognize the fact of scattering and dissociation in ordinary consciousness and everyday life, just as we must recognize our dreamlike unconsciousness, our illusory images of self, and our condition of imprisonment.

The *second* major aspect of an integrative strategy is that we need to focus intention toward transformative integration, just as we need to focus intention toward awakening, toward realization, toward liberation, and toward purification. It is this aware intention of transformation that makes painful experiences of psychic disintegration, or of being trapped, confused, bound, or poisoned, bearable. With this metaphor of fragmentation to wholeness, we also see, in the shamanic, alchemical, and yogic traditions, the practice of intentional self-dismemberment and discriminative wisdom as a prelude to deeper healing integration. We shall encounter this paradoxical strategy again in discussing the metaphor of death and rebirth, where we find practices of intentional "dying," the alchemical *mortificatio.*

A *third* major aspect of strategy, common to all the transformation processes discussed in this book, is the necessity of an inward orientation.

We get scattered into multiplicity because our attention is directed toward outer things and events in an imbalanced manner; whereas by turning within, we find the single source of wholeness. As exemplified in the myth of Osiris and Isis, it is usually the outgoing masculine principle (in men or women) that gets dissipated, scattered, or dissociated from the source-self, whereas the feminine principle (in women and men) functions to contain, to heal, to nurture, and to synthesize. Osiris was worshiped as the one who has made himself whole: "I have knit myself together ... I have renewed my youth. ... I am Osiris, Lord of Eternity."[22] As we recognize that the fragmentation to which we are subject is due to a disconnection from the source of our life, the immortal self, it follows that our path to wholeness must involve a "re-membering" of that Self.

Transformation through dismemberment: "I have killed thee, that thou may-est obtain superabundant life." (From the alchemical treatise *Splendor Solis,* by the legendary Salomon Trismosin, 16th-century Switzerland)

All the various technical procedures of yoga, alchemy, and sha-manism are utilized in the process of reintegration and healing. This includes methods of visualization, of vocalization (*mantra*), and of breath control (*pranayama*). It is often said that the power of breath, as the animating wind or spiritus of divine presence, is the medium through which the healing actually takes place. For example, an apprentice shaman may feel that his or her power animal reconstitutes the body by breathing into it, just as the Creator breathed life into Adam, the man of earth. A yogi may use various breath control tech-niques to bring about a new balance of inner energies and perceptions. Breathing into deadened or disconnected parts of our body image is perhaps the surest way to awaken and reanimate them.

Transcendence and the imagery of ascension is also a major aspect of integration and unification. We "rise into" oneness. Meister Eckhart wrote: "The whole scattered world of lower things is gathered up to oneness when the soul climbs up to that life in which there are no opposites."[23] As mentioned earlier, in the ancient wisdom teachings, the highest, source level of consciousness is an undivided unity. As differences and multiplicity arise inevitably in the course of the descent of spirit into material forms, evolutionary transformation then involves a return to the original state of undivided wholeness, a theme to which we shall return in chapter 12.

Finally, singleness itself is regarded as a quality of consciousness that can be cultivated. Ancient Greek authors used the term *monachos*, "single" (which entered into English as *monk* and *monastic*), to describe the practitioner of Gnosis. Origen, one of the early Christian Fathers, said, "Where there are sins, there is multitude . . . but where virtue is, there is singleness, there is union." The Gnostic *Gospel of Thomas* speaks of a person who "when he finds himself single, then he will be full of light; but when he finds himself divided, he will be full of darkness."[24]

This singleness, perhaps single-mindedness—the undividedness of the individuated person who has a unifying vision that integrates all of life's experiences—was beautifully expressed by the American mystic and transcendentalist Walt Whitman:

> There is, apart from mere intellect, in the make-up of every superior human identity, a wondrous something that realizes without argument. . . . an intuition of the absolute balance, in time and space, of the whole of this multifariousness, this revel of fools, and incredible make-believe and general unsettledness, we call the world; a soul-sight of that divine clue and unseen thread which holds the whole congeries of things, all history and time, and all events, however trivial, however momentous, like a leashed dog in the hands of the hunter.[25]

Whitman calls this single-mindedness a "root-center for the mind" and "soul-sight." It is indeed, as we have seen, a vision that seems to come from the soul or spirit, and one that fosters a feeling of being rooted in the very ground and core of our beingness.

Reconciling with the Inner Enemy

Nil humanum me alienum.
(Nothing human is alien to me.)

—TERENTIUS

The shadow, the id, the beast, the devil, the monster, the adversary—
these are some of the many names assigned to a psychological complex
that is present, more or less, in all human beings. We can regard it as
a kind of psychic image or entity that functions as an inner opponent,
our opposite, with whom we struggle and argue as we live our lives.
To reconcile this opposition is regarded as a central transformational
challenge on the path to individuation or wholeness. We are dealing
here with what C. G. Jung referred to as *coincidentia oppositorum,*
the "coming together of opposites," the acceptance and reconciliation
of antagonistic aspects of our nature.[1]

The evaluative judgment of good vs. evil or good vs. bad is often
superimposed on or confounded with other dualities. The result of
such confounding of one duality with another is that our perceptions
of the external world then contain these built-in evaluative prejudg-
ments. When the evaluative judgment is superimposed on the duality
of male and female, we get sexist attitudes of male or female superiority and inferiority. When superimposed on the duality of human and
animal, we get images of monsters and destructive beasts, as well as
fear of our own animal impulses and passions. When the evaluative
judgment is superimposed on religious, racial, class, or national differences, we get bigotry, racism, chauvinism, and the other prejudices
that separate in-groups from outgroups.[2]

The good/evil evaluative duality has also been superimposed on
the duality of spirit and matter, or spirit and body. The spiritual realm,

the spiritual aspect of the human being is then regarded as good, light, and higher, in contrast to the material world and the physical body, which are then seen as bad, dark, lower, or sinful. Sometimes, paradoxically, the polarity is reversed: the spirit is rejected, feared, or hated, and only the physical body and the human self is regarded as real and reliable. This can occur particularly with individuals who have an image of the deity as punitive and judgmental.

The task of transformation in relation to these opposing dualities is integration: bringing about a coming together, a co-existence, of the opposites. The self and its shadow must come to terms. We must make friends with the inner enemy. Or, if not friends, then at least and at first, we must get to know the inner adversary. We must get to the point in our own self-understanding where we can truthfully say with the Roman poet Terentius, in a line much quoted by both Goethe and Jung, "Nothing that is human is alien to me."

Throughout history, human beings have experienced the complex of evil, bad, or wrong in many different ways. A common thread is a recognition, a sense, that something has gone wrong: there is a mistake, or something horrible or uncanny has occurred, something that is a threat to ordinary settled reality. This wrong, or deviation, must be corrected or dealt with in some way. Demons, monsters, devils, and malevolent spirits are the traditional mythic and religious personifications of this experience. The Freudian id and the Jungian shadow are contemporary psychological metaphors that point to the hidden, dark, negative side of our nature. We shall be exploring several aspects or variations of this theme in this chapter.

In the Judeo-Christian tradition, one of the most often repeated statements about Satan concerned his multiplicity: "Thy name is legion." There are innumerable forms that Satan, the devil, the manifestation of evil, can take—not only because, like the Trickster in shamanic cultures, he can assume different forms, but also because, as a group projection of individual minds, he has as many forms as individual minds can imagine. The multiple aspects and qualities of the evil principle that we shall discuss in this chapter give some sense of the many features and names of this figure. It is this same figure that may, if we recognize and make peace with it, turn out to be the source of a great deal of knowledge—as that of which we are unconscious, which we have kept hidden in the shadows, becomes conscious. The sense of wrongness, of a deviation or mistake having been made, that I mentioned above, depends essentially on our capacity for judgment. It was said that the result of eating the fruit of the tree of the knowledge of good and evil was precisely that Adam and Eve acquired this power of judgment. Our capacity to make swift, almost instantaneous judgments (of threat or danger) has essential survival value. So the faculty of judgment per se is not something to be eliminated or suspended. On the other hand, spiritual traditions have consistently pointed out that this judging tendency is also one of the chief obstacles to psychological development of clear understanding. Judgment, especially prejudgment, contracts and distorts our perception, as is expressed in Christ's parable about the beam in our eye, to which we are oblivious while judging the mote in someone else's eye.

According to the Jewish Kabbalah teachings, evil occurs when the function of discrimination or judgment (*Gevurah*) is separated from its natural complement—loving-kindness or mercy (*Hesed*). The implication is that discriminative judgment must be integrated with kindness or compassion for this opposition to be transformed. A similar moral attitude is implied by the Buddhist teachings that advocate a balanced integration of discriminative wisdom and compassion.

I assume that there is a difference between the good/bad and the good/evil judgment, although they have in common that they are both judgments imposed on experience. The difference is this: *bad* suggests that something is useless, worthless, inferior—to be ignored, eliminated, or possibly changed and made "better." We are not necessarily afraid of or horrified by something we think of as bad. *Evil,* on the other hand, is much more dynamic: it is a force or tendency that actively opposes the "good," that tries to destroy, negate, tear down, kill. It frightens and horrifies us. Traditionally it was said that the devil, the embodiment of evil, opposes everything one does toward enlightenment or tries to block one's approach to the realm of Spirit or God.[3]

On Integrating the Shadow

The shadow, in Jung's psychology, is described as the *dark*, meaning "unconscious," aspects of the personality. It has a quality of emotional intensity and presents a significant moral challenge to the ego-personality. Integrating the shadow is regarded as an essential step in the process of individuation. We must be able to recognize and acknowledge the existence in ourselves of destructive tendencies.

A much more difficult task confronts us when, as is often the case, the dark aspects within are not recognized, and the intense, threatening feelings are projected out, onto other people in our environment. They, the others, then are the ones who are perceived as bad, evil, or dangerous. This permits us to maintain unconsciousness of those impulses within ourselves. As Jung wrote, "Projections change the world into the replica of one's own unknown face."[4] The projections need to be withdrawn: we need to own our shadow so that its destructive impact can be neutralized within our own psyche. This is undoubtedly one of the most difficult and elusive problems a person can encounter in her or his own self-examination, in psychotherapy and in the process of self-transformation.

A principal reason for working on integrating the shadow aspect in ourselves is that we cannot recognize it for what it is when it is bound up in projections. This was Jung's analysis of the phenomenon of Hitler and the Germans: because most Germans denied the existence of shadow aspects within themselves, they did not recognize the incarnation of the collective shadow represented by Hitler.[5] Many thousands of Germans, and Jews, simply could not believe what they heard about concentration camps. And yet clearly, for a person to be susceptible to influence by the collective shadow, as the Germans were influenced by the shadow side embodied by Hitler, there has to be some correspondence in the individual's psychic constitution. We must have within us some of that same tendency. It is this personal correspondence that makes us vulnerable to infection by the collective shadow as expressed by psychopathic demagogues or propagandists. And this is the primary reason that it is necessary to own and integrate the shadow within ourselves: to make ourselves immune to the propaganda of evil.

The projection mechanism of the collective shadow can also be seen in such phenomena as the *scapegoat,* in which one member of the society or a subgroup is blamed and has projected onto her or him the various shadow tendencies of the members of the society. Another example, in families, is the so-called black sheep, the one who (unconsciously) takes on and acts out the psychopathology and moral deviance that the others deny in themselves.

In family psychotherapy, the technical term for this is *the identified patient:* this is the one who, according to the family, has "something wrong" with him or her. In the process of family systems therapy the other members of the family each have to learn what they contribute to the problem.

For Jung, integrating the shadow was accomplished primarily through making conscious something that is unconscious. This is why the symbolism of *shadow* is so apt. When we shine direct light on a shadow, it ceases to be a shadow; and when we bring the clear light of awareness into our dark side, it ceases to be unconscious and is therefore no longer something that follows us and haunts us, unnoticed, wherever we go. The transformation process that Jung advocates brings the shadow into the light of awareness.

The psychic opposition between conscious ego and unconscious shadow is often symbolized in dreams and altered state experiences as a conflict between a white and a black person, where the black or dark-skinned person symbolizes the feared shadow side. Naturally, this tends to be true primarily for white-skinned people; "black" or "dark" is unlikely to be the chosen symbol of the inner adversary for blacks or dark-skinned people. Indeed, anthropologists have reported that some South American Indian tribes have mythic images of white-skinned demons descending out of the sky in planes.

With this caveat, the following series of dreams of a young white man illustrates in a vivid way the transformational symbolism of integrating the shadow. The dreams were recorded over a period of a year and a half, and are presented here in selective extracts from longer dream reports. The dreams were accompanied, as they so often are, by corresponding changes in the man's state of mind and his relationships with others.

> In the first dream, the dreamer sees a powerful black man snatching a purse from a woman; he follows the thief and tries to subdue and arrest him.
>
> In the second dream, the dreamer is involved in a treasure hunt and is given an important clue by a young black man.
>
> In the third dream, he witnesses a confrontation between a white red-neck policeman and a black companion policeman. The black policeman is outraged at the white policeman's corruption, and the dreamer joins him in condemning the white.[6]

In the first dream there is recognition of the shadow, the opponent; the fight is joined. The second dream reveals hidden values, treasures, in the shadow side. The third dream, almost an object lesson in symbol and reality, demonstrates the difference between the appearance of shadow and the real dark side.

After this time, for this dreamer, the symbolic inner image for the shadow is interchangeably white or black. The next mask the dangerous side of his personality assumes is that of a beast. A first integration takes place.

In the next dream, there is a white vampire wearing a hat and cape, preying on old people; the dreamer destroys this white vampire. He then meets a black figure with the head of a beast, changing into the head of a man. They embrace, and the black beast-man tells the dreamer that he need not be afraid, that he is human. There is a deep emotional release as they greet, merge, and thank each other.

In the final dream, the dreamer is getting married. Just before the wedding his bride-to-be turns into the black man, whom he recognizes as his shadow side. He is "deeply relieved and happy that it is him that I will be joining with."

The most immediate conclusion of practical value for transformational practice that one can draw from this metaphor is that each of us needs to learn or discover how we in particular symbolize to ourselves the entity or aspect of our personality referred to as the shadow. In some, it might be a black person, in others a white person, in yet others a beast or animal. What distinguishes these images, how we recognize them, is that they frighten, attack, or oppose us at every turn. Each of us needs to learn to decode our private symbolic language.

Accepting the Unacceptable

While for most of us the shadow is a kind of aggregate of destructive, violent, or aggressive impulses, this need not always be the case. For example, a professional killer or psychopathic sadist who consciously and intentionally indulges in destructive or murderous actions is not necessarily expressing his or her shadow side. Such an individual has no difficulty accepting and expressing feelings of murderous hatred, and these feelings and behaviors are not the opposites of any conscious purpose or conscience in their psyche.

For such persons, there is a kind of reversal of values, where the shadow is such that the individual is inhibited in expressing feelings of tenderness, compassion, or kindness. This phenomenon, which is perhaps rare, has led some Jungians to speak of the "white shadow."

What is in the shadow here, in the darkness of unconsciousness, are the "good" feelings and impulses. For transformation to take place, the individual must integrate these "good" feelings.

People clearly differ in what traits and qualities of their nature they regard as unacceptable. For some it may be their sexuality, for others their aggressiveness, for yet others laziness or inertia. One person's shadow may be quite innocuous and acceptable to another. What makes some part of our nature the shadow is not its destructiveness or violence; it is the fact that we are unconscious of this aspect. What is unacceptable to us consciously and yet lives somehow in the unconscious layers of the psyche is what causes "shadow problems."

Thus, in some ways, the notion of something unacceptable, and therefore hidden, is perhaps more appropriate than the symbol of the shadow (something dark). A person may have a feeling of rejection or exclusion toward some part of their psyche—some thought, feeling, or impulse. This part is excluded from their awareness and from their conscious sense of self, or identity. This non-self then, this alien element, this monstrous or bestial impulse, is excluded, split off, separated from awareness, not acknowledged. In the process of individuation then, it must be acknowledged and assimilated. For wholeness, we need to accept the unacceptable. A paradoxical challenge indeed!

The psychiatrist R. D. Laing, in his book *The Divided Self,* has clearly described the process of splitting off parts of oneself, or one's self-image, in psychosis. Such splitting may take the form of a "false self" versus a "true self"; or a "good self" versus a "bad self." Laing cites examples of psychotic patients who experience themselves as machines or robots, as automata or objects, as animals or monsters— that is, something nonhuman or antihuman.

I would like to suggest the term *schizon* as an alternative for *shadow* in those instances where we are dealing with an experience of rejecting or excluding an aspect of our nature. The splitting-off of the schizon can be seen as a defensive reaction, similar in intent to projection of the shadow onto another person. We separate that part of ourselves because we find it unacceptable to ego, to our conscious self-image. That part of our identity is sent into internal exile. The schizon or shadow is perceived as a threat to the ego: it is feared, avoided, hated, or denied and ignored.[7]

To put this another way, besides projecting our shadow side onto others, another common way of dealing with it is to take the unacceptable part and keep it hidden in the unconscious recesses of the psyche, isolating it from awareness. Freud, who discovered this mechanism, called it repression—in German *Verdrängung*, literally "a pushing away." In the Basque language, the word for this unacknowledged, pushed away part of our nature that causes us to behave in violent and destructive ways is in fact oshua, which means "the hidden."[8] The well-known myth of King Minos, who had an elaborate labyrinth built in order to hide the monstrous, devouring Minotaur, gives expression to this theme. The folktale of Bluebeard, who murdered several wives and kept their skeletons hidden in a closet to which he forbade entry, is another metaphor for this process: this is the prototype of the well-known skeleton-in-the-closet motif.

We hide this unacceptable part, this schizon, from ourselves, but we are rarely able to hide it completely from others. This is because others do not have the same difficulty we have in recognizing this aspect of our character. If, for example, I have a self-image that does not allow for my expressing rage, then I will defensively hide it every time it comes up. I will be unconscious of feeling rage and of any nonverbal expression of it (through tone of voice and the like). Other people, however, are not invested in the same way in my image of myself as being without rage.

This situation is symbolized in the Old Testament story of Cain and Abel. Cain complains, after the murder of Abel, that he now has to hide from the world. But he wears the mark of the murderer. Hiding draws attention to itself. The Jewish *midrashim* commentaries tell us that after the murder of Abel, the eye of God, or in some versions, the voice of God, followed Cain all over the world. This is the eye or voice of conscience—from which we cannot hide, because it is the eye of the Self within. From the point of view of the little self, the ego-personality, this is the guilty conscience, the vengeful or punitive superego.

The eye of God, of Self, sees everything that we are and do. But in relationship to others we want to hide the *schizon*, the bad side, the antihuman behavior. We can't face it, and we don't want others to see it. Traditionally, in religious mythology, the "face" of evil is unimaginable and is not to be perceived. This may well be the motivation underlying the use of masks or disguises by practitioners of evil, such as Inquisitors, torturers, or the KKK.

The *Star Wars* film epics, with mythic insight, show Darth Vader, the personification of the dark side, wearing a metallic, inhuman mask. The mask turns the perpetrators of evil into faceless nonpersons. They are not recognized, hidden in the shadows of darkness and concealment.

For the process of transformation, the symbolism of shadow and mask underscores the importance of awareness and recognition. That which is hidden in the shadows, or behind the mask, in the depths of our own psyche, must be seen and identified. I cannot integrate some aspect of myself unless and until I can recognize it for what it is. The fairy tale of Rumpelstiltskin, the malicious dwarf, illustrates the importance of recognizing and identifying—that is, naming—that which is evil. The dwarf symbolizes the malignant lower impulses that "dwarf" our true potential. In the story, the dwarf has the princess in bondage, and she cannot become free from his hold over her until she learns his name—that is, his identity. As the tale goes, when she does find out his name and calls it out, he flies into such a rage that he literally tears himself to pieces—he "splits" apart.

By recognizing and identifying evil, we neutralize its power, which is based on concealment and masking. This is as true of collective

Dungeon and seduction scene with Mephistopheles, *Faust,* and Gretchen. (Lithograph by Eugene Delacroix for Goethe's *Faust,* Paris, 1828; reproduced from *Picture Book of Devils, Demons and Witchcraft,* ed. Ernst and Johanna Lehner, Dover Publications, 1971)

manifestations of evil as it is of the individual's intrapsychic process. If there had been more Germans able and willing to call attention to the genocidal death camps of the Nazis, that particular holocaust might not have gone as far as it did. The one thing that can stop state-endorsed torture and murder is to expose it to the eyes of the world: to document and call attention to it, as the work of the Amnesty International organization has repeatedly demonstrated.

From Denial to Affirmation

The dangerous, threatening parts of the mind, what we have called shadow or *schizon,* remain unconscious and unknown because we deny that we have them. This points up the important role of denial and negation in the splitting off of psychic fragments. It was Freud himself who first pointed out that repression, the pushing of something into the unconscious, involves a process that is an exact analogy to the linguistic function of *negation.* Denial and repression say no to an impulse, or thought, or wish.[9]

If we see someone behaving in a way that we consciously regard as bad or evil, we are likely to think (and perhaps say) "I could never do that." In other words, the thought or impulse is denied. This then creates a kind of split-off area of consciousness, referred to as the unconscious, to maintain that negation and denial. Through these kinds of repressions and denials, repeated countless times in the process of growing up and living, we create a system of inhibitions and prohibitions, defensive walls that end up being a kind of prison chamber of the mind.

The power to negate and deny has traditionally been attributed to the devil. In Goethe's *Faust* drama, Mephistopheles introduces himself as "the spirit who always says no" (*Ich bin der Geist der stets verneint*). Mephistopheles wants to seduce Faust into saying "stop" to life. He wants him to say, "Hold this moment, it is so beautiful." Psychologically, this is saying that when we attempt to impose our own ego-will on the ever-changing life process, we are in danger of falling into the denial and unconsciousness of the devil.

To recapitulate: there is a process that is experienced mentally as negation, emotionally as rejection and exclusion, and perceptually as a hiding and concealing. In the body this process is a stoppage, a blocking of the flow of life energy. The sum total of these blocks and holding patterns that hinder the flow of life energy was symbolized by Wilhelm Reich as the *armor*—the character armor, which is also a muscular armor. According to Reich, the function of the muscular character armor is to defend the ego against unacceptable impulses—that is, to block or negate the experience and the expression of these impulses.

In chapter 3, on the metaphor of imprisonment and liberation, we saw how the armor functions as a kind of prison, from which we try to break out. Reich was impressed by the extent to which the armoring process led to reactions of rage and violence, as the armored individual unconsciously tries to break through the defensive armoring. In this attempt there is an immense concentration of destructive rage, precisely the kinds of behavior that we would traditionally attribute to the devil and regard as opposed to the life force. It is for this reason that Reich concluded that the armor is the source of man's devilish violence. "I seriously believe that in the rigid, chronic armoring of the human animal, we have found the answer to the question of his enormous destructive hatred . . . we have discovered the realm of the devil."[10]

Another perspective on the role of denial and negation in the conflict of good and evil tendencies can be obtained by considering the nature of lying. In European Christian theology and folklore, one of the devil's common modes of operating was to sow seeds of doubt, to question, to suggest that perhaps something was not so. In this way, the devil was the slanderer, undermining people's faith and belief in divine reality. Denying the existence and sovereignty of God and the saving efficacy of the Holy Ghost was regarded as the most serious, unpardonable sin, inspired of course by the devil, the "one who always denies."[11]

We may experience the conflict between good and evil tendencies in our nature as a kind of struggle between yes and no, between yea-saying and nay-saying. A part of us affirms life, and another part of us denies it, opposes it. Freud identified this struggle between yes and no tendencies as the struggle between the animalistic id and the rational human ego. He argued it was a necessary and inevitable consequence of civilized existence. The experience of doubt is another yes versus no situation: when we are in a state of doubt, we are "of two minds" about something. One part of us believes it, says yes to it; another part denies it, says no.

We can see that denial per se is not necessarily evil or destructive. In fact, if an impulse is "bad" or destructive, for example, then denying it and inhibiting it may well be the path of the "good." In the most basic terms, the word *no* sets a limit; it defines a situation. Any form or pattern has a limit or boundary. That boundary says *no* to a further expansion of the process within that form. So the *no* is necessary for setting a limit to the *yes*. In the struggle between the two, we experience the chronic split in our nature. But we also generate the necessary energy for the process of transformation, as Gurdjieff would say.[12]

Purification and Elimination

A variation on the theme of something in us being dark like a shadow, or being split off like a *schizon,* is the very common image that something in our nature is covered with dirt, or polluted, or tainted, and needs to be purified. People who have had a strong puritanical upbringing are particularly susceptible to this kind of imagery. In dreams, meditations, or psychedelic experiences they may find themselves dealing with issues of defilement, pollution, and the corruptibility of the flesh.[13]

There are many examples of this particular metaphor in the New Testament. Evil spirits inhabiting an individual are referred to as "unclean spirits." Jesus drives unclean spirits out of a man and into a herd of pigs. Our sins are compared to stains on the radiant, pure soul. The soul must be "washed in the blood of the lamb" in order to remove the stain of original sin. This metaphor for evil or sin is linked to ancient purification taboos and practices, and to baptismal rites.

There seem to be two basic postures that we adopt in relationship to something that we find in ourselves that we regard as polluted or impure: we want either to purify and cleanse it, or to excrete and eliminate it. I propose that the biological excretion of fecal waste may be the organic and experiential basis for the first judgment of "bad" in the child. What is excreted is bad for the body, and young children, through instinct and learning, come to regard excrement as bad, worthless, to be eliminated. This may also explain why children and adults, in moments of sudden anger, refer to "bad" things or events as shit.

The judgment that something is bad and therefore to be eliminated becomes, in certain circumstances, a judgment that it is evil and therefore to be feared and condemned. There exists a fairly widespread association of evil and the devil with the functions and structures of excretion.[14] Martin Luther, for example, usually referred to the devil as something black and filthy, and used homely German anal terminology to describe the recommended behavior toward the devil (*wir sollen ihn bescheissen*, etc.).

In some Christian paintings of hell or the Last Judgment, the devil, chief of the demons, is shown excreting sinners through his anus. In some branches of Hindu mythology, evil is explained as emanating from certain parts of the body of the Creator, Brahma, whether it be the penis, or most often, the anus. In one mythic cycle, human beings are seen as the excretions of Brahma. This reminds us that some children believe that babies come from defecation.

According to this metaphor, then, something that is evil or bad is like a blemish, or pollution, or feces. It should be cleansed, purged, or eliminated before it corrupts the organism or psyche in which it is found. This is essentially the peculiar rationale that underlay the Nazis' bizarre theories of racial purity and how the Jews were supposedly corrupting the Aryan bloodlines. This grotesque, genocidal perversion should not blind us to the valid principle that waste matter or toxins in any organic system, if retained, become pathological and should therefore be eliminated for the preservation of health and normal functioning of that system.

In the alchemical tradition, this theme is related to the metaphor of *putrefactio,* the putrefaction of the inner fluids, which corresponds physiologically to conditions of disease, infection, or toxicity in the organism and psychologically to conditions of despair, depression, and revulsion at oneself. It is a state of consciousness in which one feels filled with something that is rotten and foul-smelling. Interestingly, doctors and nurses who work with schizophrenics have often reported a distinctive, repulsive odor emanating from their bodies. The alchemists acknowledged the pain and distress of the *putrefactio* state or condition but valued it because they saw it as the precursor to transmutation. Just as conscious dying, called *mortificatio,* was followed by rebirth, so conscious putrefaction was followed by regeneration.[15]

As indicated above, the alternative to elimination of something putrid and rotten is purification. The purification of that which was corrupt and toxic in the alchemist's *vessel* (= body) was accomplished through the use of inner "fire," which we discussed in chapter 4. So purification and elimination can be regarded as two principal means for dealing with corrupt, "bad," or "evil" elements in the psyche. As such, they are aspects of the general process of integrating the shadow and reconciling the antagonistic opposites.

From Inner Warfare to Inner Peace

In some of our experience the duality and opposition between good and evil is felt as a defensive stand-off, a separation, a gulf, a rejection: we are unconscious of the shadow aspects, blind to our faults, and want to separate from that in us which we feel is rotten. In other phases of our experience there is a more active struggle or conflict going on. We may love and hate simultaneously, or feel both attraction and aversion toward the same object or person. We may be in turmoil as our fears and inhibitions struggle with impulses of lust or aggression. In meditative states or dreams or psychedelic visions, we may witness what seems like a clash of opposing tendencies in our psyche, like armies battling in the night.

The task of personal transformation is to turn this inner warfare to inner peace. We need to come to terms with the "enemies," both inner and outer. The clashing opposites must be reconciled. Forces, tendencies, and impulses that are locked in seemingly endless conflict must learn to co-exist. I personally used to believe one had to make friends with the inner enemy, the shadow self. I now feel that making friends is perhaps not necessary, that this other side of our nature may always stay in opposition to our true nature, or "right side." We may want to keep this figure as what Castaneda's Don Juan calls a worthy opponent, for warrior training. But we need to understand this opponent. Making friends with the inner enemy may be possible; getting to know him or her is essential.

All spiritual traditions agree that the violent, destructive forces are within us. In the New Testament we read, "From whence come wars and fighting among you? Is it not from the lusts that war in your members?"[16] A text by one of the fathers of the Eastern Church, in the *Philokalia*, states, "There is a warfare where evil spirits secretly battle with the soul by means of thoughts. Since the soul is invisible, these malicious powers attack and fight it invisibly."[17]

The good Christian, in order to be saved, is exhorted to "battle" temptations and to repel demonic invaders and harmful external influences. A poem by the Persian Sufi philosopher-mystic Rumi states: "We have slain the outward enemy, but there remains within us a worse enemy than he. This *nafs* (animal self or lower self) is hell, and hell is a dragon."[18] The following line from the *Bhagavad Gita* describes the transformation: "He whose self is unconquered, his self acts as his own enemy, like an external foe. But he who has conquered himself, is the friend of his self."[19]

If we inquire into the possible experiential origin for the pattern of this particular metaphor, we are asking, how does the feeling of being

Confrontation with the shadow in the form of masked alien beings: Asaro mudmen.
(Photo by David Holdsworth, Eastern Highlands, Papua New Guinea)

in a state of conflict arise in us in the first place? I will suggest partial answers to this question from three different levels or perspectives: the personal developmental, the historical and evolutionary, and the theological/mythical.

The *personal developmental* basis for the experience of conflict and power struggle may very well be (in part) the phenomenon of sibling rivalry in early childhood. Competition between brothers and sisters for the attention and approval of the parents, and other adults, is of course extremely common. The competitive attitude may be maintained into adulthood and carried over into personal and work relationships with peers. Alternatively, it may be internalized, so that one feels there is an inferior and a superior self-image competing and struggling with each other. Fritz Perls, the founder of Gestalt therapy, called this the conflict between "top dog" and "underdog."

There are numerous myths about bitter and protracted competition between rival brothers, such as Cain and Abel or Osiris and

Set, and stories about hostile sisters, such as *Cinderella* or *King Lear,* that illustrate this theme of sibling competition. From the perspective of transformational psychology, we interpret these as referring to an internal process: both the good sibling and the bad or evil sibling are aspects of our own nature. In the words of the English Boehme disciple, William Law,

> You are under the power of no other enemy, are held in no other captivity, and want no other deliverance but from the power of your own earthly self. This is the murderer of the divine life within you. It is your own Cain that murders your own Abel.[20]

The theme of inner conflict also has probable *historical* and *evolutionary* antecedents in the age-old, long-continuing struggles between tribes and societies for territory and economic survival. Here are ancient animal and hominid memory imprints of the laws of the jungle: the principle of "eat or be eaten," "kill or be killed." The cutthroat competition of the haves and the have-nots is a deeply ingrained factor in the consciousness of the human race. Whether humanity, as a species, can transform this territorial and economic competition into peaceful and cooperative co-existence is perhaps our most fundamental challenge.

Going further back into mammalian evolution, one could speculate about the possible residues in human genetic memory of the millions of years of competitive interaction between predators and prey. The ecologist Paul Shepard has argued that the predator carnivores developed a different sort of consciousness, a different kind of attention, from the prey herbivores, related to their different lives of chasing or escaping.[21] Predator intelligence is searching, aggressive, tuned to stalking and hunting. Prey intelligence is cautious, expectant, tranquil but ready for instant flight. Is it possible that these different styles of awareness, these opposing modes of relating, form a kind of evolutionary template for the human behavior of aggressors (predators) and victims (prey)? Don't we still hunt, prey on, and victimize our fellow humans for survival? Don't we still, in the paranoid mode, vigilantly watch for threats, prepared to flee or defend?

A third level of explanation for the experience of conflict is the *theological/mythical*. Many of the ancient mythologies offer a cosmic story of the world inherently split by discord and strife. Herakleitos said, "War is the father and king of all." In the Zoroastrian religion of ancient Persia, the competition between the forces of light and of darkness was given a most dramatic expression: here we find the myth of the long-drawn struggle and alternating rulership of the world between Ahura-Mazda, the Light Creator, and Ahriman, the Prince of Darkness. This Zoroastrian conception of a fundamental cosmic dualism undoubtedly had a profound influence on both Judaism and Christianity. Zoroastrian dualism shows up in the teachings of the Manichaeans and the Gnostics, with their strong emphasis on the fundamental duality of the Creator, and the parallel duality of the created cosmos.[22]

In this complex of conflict and warfare, made up of personal, evolutionary, and mythic elements, we find the story of man's inhumanity to man: destructiveness, violence, cruelty, sadism, intentional injury and violation of another's physical or psychological integrity. Recalling the reader's attention to the earlier discussion of judgment, I offer the following perspective on these manifestations of human evil: they represent a mixture of judgmentalism and violent rage. The judgment is expressed, acted upon, in a destructive and aggressive way. That which is judged to be bad is attacked and destroyed.

To put it another way, the judgment that is rendered serves as a rationalization for the naked expression of violence or rage. The rationalization may be literary or aesthetic, as with the Marquis de Sade; or it may be spuriously racial or genetic, as in Hitler's genocidal holocaust; or it may be religious, as with the torturers of the Inquisition. The conflict of the judge-persecutor with the judged-victim is perhaps the most vicious of all the warring opposites we know. This variant too is played out within the psyche: we are ourselves the punitive judge (in Freudian terms the superego) and the punished victim of persecution (psychologically, the guilt-ridden ego).

For transformation to take place, we need to learn to become wise, impartial judges of ourselves, not punitive, vindictive judges. And again we start by realizing that the opposing enemies are all within us: we are both judge and accused, both jailor and prisoner, both executioner and condemned.

On Facing One's Demons

In traditional and contemporary folk religious belief, demons are the relatives of the devil—they are personifications of evil forces, of alien and destructive influences and impulses. They are definitely regarded as something outside of us, something not-self. In primitive or native cultures, living in a state of *participation mystique* with nature, demons, like giants, often represent the destructive, violent energies of hurricanes, storms, lightning, wild fires, avalanches, floods, earthquakes, volcanic eruptions, and the like. Inventing or imagining living beings, whether spirits or demons, guiding these forces somehow makes their terrifying character more tolerable.

Conversely, our own inner states may at times feel to us to be out of control, like the forces of nature. We then find it natural to describe these inner states as analogous to these forceful aspects of nature, as when we speak of someone as a "tempestuous character," or of being in a "stormy mood" or "flooded with grief," or having a "volcanic explosion" of temper. Our inner life, then, like nature around us, seems at times to be dominated by violent, clashing energies that seem alien and overwhelmingly powerful to us. This is one aspect of the experience of the demonic.

In the East, both Hindu and Buddhist mythology offer a somewhat different perspective on demons or *asuras,* also known as angry gods or titans. The *asuras,* in many myths, play the role of counterpart to the "good" gods, or *devas* ("shining ones"). They are the permanent opponents of the gods, analogous to a kind of cosmic mafia, with values opposite those of normal humans and gods. Usually, they oppose and challenge the gods, but sometimes they cooperate with them. For example, in one famous myth, gods and demons combined forces to produce *amritsar,* the nectar of immortality, that they both craved.

In the Buddhist Wheel of Life, which symbolically portrays six different types of personalities, or lives, one can be born into, the world of the *asuras* is one of the six worlds, one possibility for existence. Buddhists say these demons are dominated by feelings of pride, jealousy, and anger, and are engaged in perpetual competitive struggle and conflict. Thus, from a psychological point of view, we are in this

The medieval Christian image of the devil: the horns and goat legs were adopted from the Greek Pan, god of wild animal nature. (From the *Rider Tarot Deck,* created by Arthur Edward Waite, 20th century England)

world of *asuras,* in this type of existence, when we are dominated by feelings of pride, jealousy, anger, and competitive struggle. The mythic picture of the *asuras,* then, is shown to us as a kind of reminder of how our feelings, our thoughts, and our intentions create the kind of reality in which we live. The chaotic, murderous existence of the demons, and of humans dominated by demons, is an external consequence, or out-picturing, of their inner state.[23]

Yet another aspect of the demonic is shown in the Tibetan lamaist imagery of the "wrathful deities" or *herukas.* These grotesque figures with their violent, superhuman, terrifying appearance are esoterically regarded as personifications of high spiritual principles. They are the guardians of the thresholds that lead into new and higher worlds of consciousness. They are also the protectors of the *dharma,* of the true teaching. And they are the supporters and prototypes of the process of breaking through—of shattering the limitations and illusions of conditioned awareness. Tibetan Buddhist monks undergoing their initiatory training meditate on these horrendous demon images, which will subsequently aid them in their struggle with their own shadow.[24]

In Western culture, the concept of the demon has an interesting history. Our word *demon* actually comes from the Greek *daimon,* which was originally not an evil spirit at all. It was a protective spirit, a divine guardian, something like what later European folklore called the guardian angel. Plato reported that Socrates would say he conversed with his *daimon* to obtain spiritual guidance. The Romans referred to this higher spirit as the *genius,* and saw it as the source of inspiration and creativity. Every person had his or her genius. Houses, towns, and sacred places could also have this kind of power or presence, called the *genius loci,* "the spirit of the place."

It was only under the later influence of Christian dogmatism that the word *demon* came to have maleficent connotations. As is well known, Christianity, in its proselytizing zeal, turned the pagan gods of the Old Religion—such as Pan, Dionysus, and Odin—into devils or demons. Early Christian writers still made a distinction between *agathos daimon,* a "good spirit," and *kakos daimon,* an "evil spirit" or demon.[25]

Generally speaking, there appears to be a much greater tendency in the Western Judeo-Christian tradition to polarize good and evil as absolute opposites. Only the three monotheistic religions have a concept of an evil deity, the devil or Satan, who opposes God and blocks the spiritual aspirations of human beings. In the Asian religious traditions, as well as in the polytheistic religions of the ancient world, we more often find a pluralistic view that accepts a multitude of different perspectives and beings of diverse origins and values. And although there may be numerous harmful and malevolent spirits and demons, there is not one personification of supreme evil. Most deities are mixed, ambiguous characters, just like humans.

We see then that the figure of Satan, or the devil, at least in Western culture, has all the traits and qualities previously discussed as belonging to individuals dealing with their bad or unacceptable side. He is the liar, the slanderer, the destroyer, the deceiver, the tempter, the one who brings guilt and shame, the adversary, the unclean and dark one who denies and negates everything that enlarges and enhances life, who opposes everything that we value and hold most sacred.[26]

In Jungian terms, the devil represents or embodies the collective shadow of the entire Western Judeo-Christian civilization. He is, as it were, an amalgamated projection of the imagery of evil of all the thousands and millions of individuals who have believed in him throughout the centuries. As with other projections, by attributing dark impulses and feelings to the devil, someone not-self, one is relieved of responsibility for them—as expressed in that most classic of all excuses, "The devil made me do it." Satan exists and is real in the same sense that the ancient gods and goddesses are real and exist: they live in the psyches of those humans who identify with them, to whatever degree, whether consciously or unconsciously.

The legion of names that the devil can take, the many variations on these themes of clashing opposites and treacherous antagonists, are a tribute to the creative imagination of human beings.

This is the multifarious figure whose features can be detected somewhere behind the persona of every man and woman. It is the beast that haunts every beauty, the monster that awaits every hero on his quest. This being may, if we but recognize and come to terms with it, turn out to be the source of a great deal of knowledge, as that which has been kept hidden, unconscious, in the shadows, gets looked at in the light of awareness.

When we recognize the devil as an aspect of ourselves, then this deity can function as teacher and initiator: he shows us our own unknown face, providing us with the greatest gift of all—self-understanding. The conflict of opposites is resolved into a *coincidentia oppositorum,* the creative play of energies and boundaries.

On Dying and Being Reborn

7

So long as you do not have this dying and becoming,
you're only a gloomy guest on this darkening Earth.

—J. W. GOETHE

To die and be reborn is a metaphor for the most radical and total transformation that consciousness and identity can undergo. When our self-image or self-concept, the sense of identity with which (and as which) we have lived, comes to an end, then we feel as though the ego or self is dying. The pattern of this transformation metaphor is as follows: whatever I call "me" is finished and dying; then, after a period of turmoil and uncertainty, there is the "rebirth" of a new identity, a new sense of who "I" am. The transformation involves all aspects of the psyche, because it involves the central organizing principle of selfhood. The new self that is born is naturally of a childlike nature, filled with the wonder, joy, and spontaneity of childhood. Whereas in some Christian fundamentalist circles it is customary for people who have made a commitment to Christ to refer to themselves as "twice born," the original meaning of that concept goes much deeper than simply a profession of renewed faith, however sincere. It refers, actually, to the second part of a death-rebirth transformation process. The rebirth experience, to be authentic, must of necessity be preceded by an experience of metaphorically dying. This first, dying phase is inevitably anxiety provoking and problematical for most people. As William Bridges has pointed out, any kind of ending, whether that of a career, a relationship, or a project, is a kind of dying. As a culture, we do not handle deathlike endings very well.[1]

In the mystery religions of ancient times and in many traditional cultures, "death-rebirth" was and is the name of an initiatory experience. Associated with it are ritual practices such as entombment, profound isolation, or painful ordeals through which the initiate must pass. Afterward, the initiate customarily adopts a new name, perhaps a new garment, and sometimes a new role in society, all of which express the newly reborn being. Although we no longer perform the ancient rituals of death and rebirth, many people, in changing their name, lifestyle, or work, are publicly signaling that a transformation has occurred.

In the mystical literature of Eastern and Western cultures, we find many descriptions of death-rebirth experiences. Furthermore, they are seen as something to cultivate and practice. A saying of Zen master Bunan goes, "While living, be a dead man, thoroughly dead; whatever you do then, as you will, is always good."[2] Death-rebirth experiences, though painful, are highly valued because they lead to increased understanding, health and long life, peace, and inner freedom from fear. In modern literary and autobiographical accounts of transformative experiences, whether occurring spontaneously or induced by psychedelic substances, individuals have reported that they actually felt and sensed themselves to be dying, and then reborn, renewed, or rejuvenated.

As an example, here is the experience of a twenty-year-old college student on his first LSD trip. The setting was the backseat of his friend's car, driving down the freeway (not exactly the recommended set and setting).

> I had an extraordinarily powerful sense of expansion and ascent and at one point realized that I was faced with a choice of holding onto my limited identity as J. P., or going far beyond it into a space from which I might never return. In that moment my life unfolded with untold clarity. I was neither my name, nor the sum of my experiences accumulated during the past twenty years. I was not my parents' son, I had not grown up in San Jose and I was not a student at U.C. Santa Cruz. Each identification fell by the side. An irresistible force was impelling me beyond this illusion. I was to die to everything I

thought was me—all I had to do was to say yes and there would be no turning back. I saw, too, in that moment, that to try to hold on against such a force could create madness. So I assented and ascended. I lost track of space and time and at some point found myself watching what seemed to be the center of creation—a massive luminous sphere that was radiating out concentric circles of light. It seemed that creation was being recreated in every moment, and I was part of that creation. . . . I felt profoundly happy and at peace in a way I never had before. I was established in truth, light, and the unshakable knowledge of my own identity. . . . I have never stood so consciously upon the threshold of death and stepped across it. I felt as though I was leaving behind my familiar personality like an old suit. The sense of exhilaration was quite powerful.[3]

This experience has all the hallmarks of radical self-transformation, what William James would have called a conversion experience. There were long-term, positive personality changes. The old familiar self-images came to an end, and the true identity, the Self, was recognized. The feeling of crossing a threshold and the sense of participating in the process of the creation of the world are both frequently reported in the literature on mysticism and spiritual transformation. The idea that resisting the intense process could lead to madness is one we shall return to later.

Conscious Death and Intentional "Dying"

For the majority of people, the idea of death—death in general and their own in particular—is surrounded by fear and denial. In the teachings of the great spiritual and religious traditions, however, we consistently find a positive and affirmative attitude toward dying. The following epitaph was found at Eleusis, the center of the greatest mystery religion in ancient Greece: "Truly the blessed gods have proclaimed a most beautiful secret: death comes not as a curse but as a blessing to men."[4] Spiritual teachers have always insisted that the commonly held negative view and fear of death are based on ignorance and must be changed for genuine spiritual transformation to occur.

Mystics and teachers even go beyond the acceptance of death as an inevitable fact of existence to assertions of the necessity and desirability of dying with awareness, of the value of awareness of dying, and of growing through death. In a famous saying where he anticipates his own death and resurrection ("The hour has come that the Son of Man should be glorified"), Jesus uses the analogy of a seed kernel that disappears into the ground before sprouting: "A grain of wheat remains a solitary grain unless it falls into the ground and dies; but if it dies, it brings a rich harvest."[5] Saint Paul uses the same analogy in response to questions about the raising of the dead: "The seed you sow does not come to life unless it has first died."[6] Such statements express a deep awareness that new life, the birth and fruitfulness of a new identity, arise out of the death of what has preceded it.

The apparent dying, the disappearance of a seed into the dark ground prior to its emergence as a fruit-bearing grain, is being used as a metaphor for the disappearance or dying of the old ego. The transformed personality can live and thrive only if the previous personality has died. This is also the meaning of Meister Eckhart's saying that the Kingdom of God (which symbolizes the transformed, enlightened state of consciousness) is "for none but those who are thoroughly dead."[7] Both physical and psychological dying are valued because they lead to a better state, a transformed and more enlightened state. Similarly, there is an ancient tradition that the practice of dying leads to liberation and wisdom. Thus we hear Socrates say that "true philosophers make dying their profession, and to them of all men death is least alarming."[8]

A positive, less fearful attitude toward death is the necessary preparation for a transformed state of heightened aliveness. Furthermore, a reduction of the fear of death is a consequence of undergoing metaphoric, or psychological, dying. Thus it is not surprising that in folklore and mythology all over the world, the moral of many stories is that death must be treated with respect and honor.[9] Most societies prohibit verbal insult or physical assault of dying or dead individuals (except in the case of conquered enemies, who may be dishonored). Ancient funeral practices, such as the three-day wake, bespeak the respect and even awe with which those who undertake the final passage are regarded.

Many a mythic hero or heroine, including Gilgamesh, Inanna, Odysseus, the Grail knights, and the Mayan twins, undertake dangerous journeys into the underworld land of the dead in order to fathom the secrets of death and life. Such journeys pay homage to the power and mystery of death. In the Indian wisdom literature, the best-known journey of this kind is that of the youth Naciketas, told in the *Katha Upanishad*. The story is that Naciketas, as a result of a quarrel with his father, waits for three days and nights in the land of Yama, Lord of Death, and thereby earns the right to ask three favors of this mighty god. Perhaps the three-day journey to death is a metaphor for a mortal illness, which takes individuals out of their usual state into a "near-death" experience from which they return with greater knowledge.

In any event, according to the legend, Naciketas asks first to be able to restore his broken relationship with his father. His second favor is to learn how to practice the fire ritual (which takes place "in the secret place of the heart"), so that he can, through this ritual, establish his awareness of and relationship with the higher realms. The third favor he asks—which the god Yama is most reluctant to grant—is to know the mystery of life and death and the true nature of being. "Tell us about that which they doubt, O Death, what there is in the great passing-on. This boon which penetrates the mystery, no other than that does Naciketas choose." Yama then proceeds to instruct Naciketas in a long philosophical and yogic discourse, ending with, "The Inner Self [*Atman*] abides always in the heart. One should draw [him] out, as one may the wind from the reed. Him one should know as the pure, the immortal."[10]

The young man on the LSD-induced death-rebirth experience quoted earlier was, in a way, reexperiencing the ancient legend of Naciketas, when he obtained "unshakable knowledge of [his] own identity" after consciously stepping across the "threshold of death." The *Katha Upanishad* ends with the words: "Then Naciketas, having gained this knowledge declared by Death and the whole rule of Yoga, attained *Brahman* and became freed from passion and from death. And so may any other who knows this in regard to the Self."[11] Self-knowledge is the ultimate favor and reward given to those who confront their own death. In such an experience, the self that I thought I was dies, and my true Self is revealed and recognized. Such an experience may be devastating, but it is certainly humbling, and potentially ecstatic and liberating.

Many of the descriptions of the ultimate state of consciousness to be attained on the disciplined path of self-transcendence and transformation are indicative of a kind of ego annihilation, a total dying of the self and all its normal identifications. The end state of Buddhist meditation, *nirvana,* means "extinction," a "passing away" of the flames of desire and attachment. The Islamic Sufi's ultimate state of *fana* is likewise a "dissolution," a merging of individual identity into union with universal beingness. In a magnificent poem by Rumi, the great thirteenth-century Persian poet-sage, our dying is seen as a repeated phase in a cosmic evolutionary process:

> I died a mineral, and became a plant.
> I died a plant, and rose an animal.
> I died an animal and I was a man.
> Why should I fear? When was I less by dying?
> Yet once more I shall die as man.[12]

The poem tells us that we have died many deaths, as humans and in those life forms that preceded the human. Death, therefore, is not to be feared as involving a loss, since it has always led to something higher. The poem concludes with the lines, "O let me not exist—for non-existence proclaims in organ tones, 'To Him we shall return.'" Death signals the return to the divine inner source.

The Taoist philosopher Chuang Tsu has given us a wonderful portrait of the sage who has attained to this level of wisdom and freedom, through practicing the Tao.

> The true man of old knew nothing of loving life and hating death. When he was born, he felt no elation. When he entered death, there was no sorrow. Carefree he went. Carefree he came. That was all. He did not forget his beginning and did not seek his end. He accepted what he was given with delight, and when it was gone, he gave it no more thought.[13]

Every time something ends in us, it dies: thus we experience thousands of little deaths each day, each hour. Thoughts arise, die, arise again; images form, dissolve, form again; feelings well up from within, crest and recede, to emerge again later. Insofar as we are identified with these thoughts, images, and feelings, we die, are reborn, die again, are reborn, continuously. Rumi said that "every instant you are dying and returning." The German theologian and mystic Johannes Tauler spoke of the great value of such daily dying: "A man might die a thousand deaths in one day and find a joyful life corresponding to each of them."[14] Anyone who has ever had the experience of letting go of some craving or attachment and has felt the sudden lift, the ecstatic freedom that comes from this, will know the truth of these statements.

Tauler goes on to speak of the special value of consciously dying "to a scornful word, . . . to some inclination, acting or not acting against [one's] own will, in love or grief, in word or act, in going or staying." In other words, inclinations, impulses, desires, wishes, judgments—all these are born and die within the psyche. Gurdjieff 's statement on the importance of consciously dying, intentionally letting go of false identifications, is characteristically forceful and vivid:

> A man must die, that is, he must free himself from a thousand petty attachments and identifications. . . . He is attached to everything in his life, attached to his imaginations, attached to his stupidity, attached even to his sufferings, possibly to his sufferings more than to anything else. . . . Attachments to things, identifications with things, keep alive a thousand useless I's in a man. These I's must die in order that the big I may be born. But how can they be made to die? They do not want to die. It is at this point that the possibility of awakening comes to the rescue. To awaken means to realize one's nothingness.[15]

In shamanic cultures, the preparatory training of the shaman-healer typically involved either an "illness" or a "wounding," both primarily internal and symbolic but frequently accompanied by psychosomatic and physical manifestations. During this shamanic experience the shaman would let go of all his or her old attachments: a more or less total dying to the old way of living was called for. Sometimes the older shaman, while instructing the apprentice, would symbolically "kill" the apprentice. This was followed by a restoration, or reconstitution, often aided by an animal ally or spirit, into a new, more power-filled form, endowed with healing and magical abilities.[16]

In alchemy, the process of *mortificatio,* which literally means "killing" or "dead-making," was the process of consciously and intentionally "working on" the reduction of ego attachments and impulses. This was done through symbolic meditations and visualizations that emphasized, in Edinger's words, "darkness, defeat, torture, mutilation, death and rotting." These images in turn are followed by those related to growth, regeneration, fruiting, ripening, and rebirth.[17] We shall return to the theme of *mortificatio* again later.

Nearness to Death as Transformative Experience

The metaphor of death as a teacher and liberator, as the beginning of a new way of being, and as the stimulus to knowledge of divine reality, is found in all the great spiritual traditions of humankind, in Eastern and Western mysticism, yoga, shamanism, and alchemy. Confirmation of this view has come from three different groups of people: those who have almost died but returned; those who have experienced the death of a close relative; and those who are approaching death slowly in terminal illness. All three situations can be triggers for far-reaching and profound changes in consciousness and personality. Nearness to death is what they have in common, whether it is one's own death or that of another.

1. One who has been touched by the awesome hand of death inevitably has afterward a far different understanding of the meaning of life. In the past two decades, psychological research on the experiences of people who have come close to dying but have returned has been pursued and reported by Russell Noyes, Karlis Osis, Raymond Moody, Kenneth Ring, and others. Due to this work, the notion of near-death as a profoundly altered state of consciousness has gained some degree of acceptance. What is particularly striking is the unanimity of the reports and the profound changes in world view and spiritual values that occur with these "near-death experiences" (NDEs).[18]

The experiences typically include sensations of being outside the body, sometimes looking down or back upon the physical body, and feelings of a definite transition, sometimes experienced as crossing a boundary or threshold, or sometimes as passing through a dark, enclosed space, such as a tunnel or cave. After this transition, people usually report feelings of peace, unity, serenity, ecstasy, timelessness—feelings comparable to those of mystical visions and shamanic journeys. Frequently, people report seeing dead relatives beckoning to them from a region of light, or they see spirit beings made of pure light. The return to everyday reality is often accompanied by a profound sense of loss and regret and by the insistence that the experience is incommunicable. Individuals feel they have been granted a preview of what death is actually like, and that this preview is a potent catalyst for changing one's life.

In some accounts people report perceptual changes comparable to those found in psychedelic or spontaneous illuminative experiences. One such incident was told to me by the woman to whom it happened. As a college student she was out sailing with a friend. Both were inexperienced sailors and got caught in a storm. After initial panic, the woman thought that this was the end; she already saw the obituary notices. Suddenly a profoundly peaceful mood descended over her, and the spray from the waves crashing over the boat sparkled with rainbow-colored jewelled droplets. A state of timeless serenity filled her until she and her companion were at length rescued.

Another feature of the typical NDE, which also has its mythic analogy, is what has been called the life review. For some, though not all, near-death survivors, in bare seconds of real time, a movielike panorama of their lives unfolds before their eyes. A striking example was reported to me secondhand: a man had taken a high dose of LSD with a group of friends and was on a city rooftop at night. When he stepped off a three-foot-high boxlike structure on the roof, he thought in the dark that he had stepped off the edge of the roof and would surely now die. In the split second before his foot landed on the roof three feet below, he experienced the whole classic life review played out before his astonished eyes.

Such life-review visions may be the experiential basis for the metaphor of the judgment scene found in many after-death myths, where the good and bad deeds of one's life are assessed and weighed. Esoteric philosophy teaches that after death there is a review of lessons learned and mistakes made in this life. Variations on this theme abound in every culture. In Egyptian myth the heart of the deceased is weighed in a scale against the Truth Feather of the goddess Maat. In Tibetan Buddhism, it is taught that the death god Yama holds a mirror up to the just deceased in which they can see all their deeds and intentions, which will determine where they go next.

If a life-review experience, or even only a detached mood of objective reflection on one's life, is common in NDEs, it may explain why people who have had these kinds of experiences often choose to practice some kind of meditative or spiritual discipline afterwards. *Almost dying* is clearly a very powerful awakener, a turning point or conversion.

2. Equally powerful as a catalyst to realization and transformation can be the encounter with death through the death of a relative, loved one, friend, or child. My personal estimate is that experiencing the death of a loved relative is probably the most prevalent trigger for profound spiritual transformation. When someone we love dies, it is as if a part us dies as well. Even the death of an individual we do not know personally but whom we idealized or regarded highly can be the trigger for a profoundly altered state—as those who still remember vividly the stunning impact of John Kennedy's assassination can attest. The encounter with a transcendent archetype of this kind—the death of the leader—leaves images in the mind like etchings in burnished copper. Many people remember every sensory detail of that day with unforgettable clarity.

In our culture the approach to death is marked by anxiety, embarrassment, and denial. In recent years, a number of individuals and organizations have devoted themselves to exploring more humane and enlightened ways of relating to dying people. Elizabeth Kübler-Ross, Ram Dass, Stephen Levine, and others have made contributions to our knowledge of how to "work with the dying," or rather how to just be, and perhaps meditate, with the dying. Levine writes: "You relate to one who is ill the way you relate to any being. With openness. With an honoring of the truth we all share. Work to dissolve the separateness that keeps one lost in duality. Become one with the other. No help, just being. See the conditioned illusion. Break that ancient clinging. Allow both of you to die."[19]

In the work of these individuals, and in organized efforts such as the hospice movement and the Shanti project, we see a renewal of ancient ways of helping people come to terms with death, both those dying and the survivors. The surviving relatives often have greater psychological difficulties in coming to terms with death than does the dying person.

3. In situations involving terminal illness, a person approaches the final transition gradually (as opposed to the sudden and unexpected confrontation that occurs in a near-death experience) and has the opportunity to resolve old conflicts, complete unfinished business, and release fears and attachments to images of self and others. This is the vast potential of dying slowly; but unless there is support for such an intention from family, friend, or guide, it is hard for a dying person to maintain this conscious attitude. Someone needs to be there to help the person through the shoals of resistance, anger, fear, and other sharp-edged emotions. Often the guide need do no more than be there with an attitude of open, truthful, and aware support.

This modern work on the humane preparation for dying has involved the reexamination of ancient religious texts. The practices and rites of the ancient Egyptians, as collected in their Book of the Dead, have become the objects of renewed interest. Their beliefs concerning the after-death state and reincarnation are now being presented in serious, if fictionalized, accounts by such writers as Joan Grant, Elizabeth Haich, and Isha Schwaller de Lubicz.[20] In medieval Europe there were tracts known under the general title of *ars moriendi* ("the craft of dying"), written as manuals for those who attended the dying.

Tibetan Buddhists encoded their visions and records of after-death consciousness in a profound document known as the *Bardo Thödol*, subtitled *The Book of Liberation Through Hearing on the After-Death Planes,* which contains the most central doctrines of Vajrayana

Buddhism. In this text, the person attending the dying is instructed to speak the words of guidance into the ear of the departing traveler. Over and over again, the text emphasizes the importance of practicing the meditations, the yogic disciplines, before one dies, in order to be better prepared for this most difficult passage.

This *Bardo Thödol,* also known as the Tibetan Book of the Dead, was adapted by Timothy Leary, Richard Alpert (later Ram Dass), and myself as a manual for people taking high-dose LSD trips.[21] We had observed that the essential features of this map of after-death visions could easily be identified in psychedelic experiences. Instead of physical death, these trips had ego death; instead of peaceful and wrathful deities, they had heavenly and hellish visions corresponding to the person's own religious background; and instead of rebirth, they had reentry, or return to the world of ordinary, familiar identity in a transformed and renewed condition, if the experience was successful.

LSD psychotherapy has also been found to be extremely valuable for people with terminal cancer, in work done by Walter Pahnke, Stanislav Grof, and others.[22] The experience with LSD enabled cancer patients to transcend their pain-wracked bodies and become attuned to a level of consciousness that included the physical, but in the context of a more comprehensive, more unitive, pain-dissolving awareness.

In experiences with LSD or without, it is possible for people who are dying to attain this kind of transcendence of the physical in a way that alleviates much of the usual pain and fear accompanying death. One might well wonder whether this is not the natural, true way of dying designed for us by God and/or nature. This is exactly the question posed by the biologist-philosopher Lewis Thomas:

> Could it be that the sensations associated with dying are the manifestation of a physiological mechanism? Is there, in fact, such a thing as the "process" of dying? It does not seem unreasonable to me, considering the meticulously designed, orderly mechanisms at work in all other important events of living. It is not unlikely that there is

171

a pivotal moment at some stage in the body's reaction to injury or disease, maybe in aging as well, when the organism concedes it is finished and the time for dying is at hand, and at this moment the events that lead to death are launched, as a coordinated mechanism. Functions are then shut off, in sequence, irreversibly, and while this is going on, a neural mechanism, held ready for this occasion, is switched on.[23]

Thomas proposes that such a mechanism, possibly involving endorphins, the body's own pain-reducing chemicals, could be responsible for the often calm, detached, painless, even illuminative experiences of individuals who are dying. If this is true, a healing transformation is "built in" to the very process of coming nearer and nearer to death.

Death comes even to the mighty: allegorical image from the *memento mori* ("remember your dying") tradition. (Frontispiece from a book published in London, 1639; reproduced from *Picture Book of Devils, Demons and Witchcraft*)

Dying, in this very organic view, is not just the ending of life or the cessation of vital processes. It is, rather, an active process, almost a kind of physiological unwinding, a progressive withdrawing from the world of external sense objects.

Thanatos and Psychic Death

In the introduction, I suggested that there are regressive and progressive transformations. We can sink into deeper sleep and unconsciousness, as well as become more awake and aware. We can find ourselves in states where we are more bound, more trapped, as well as states that bring us toward liberation. In states of pathological psychic disorganization, the parts of the psyche are more fragmented and disjointed than is usual. At this other end of the spectrum of states of consciousness, we encounter, in terms of the present metaphor, states of greater "deadness" than are a normal aspect of conditioned existence. Such emotional deadness is the opposite of aliveness and vitality; in its clinical forms it is known as depression, rigid defensiveness, or catatonia.[24]

In madness and certain forms of psychic disorder we may experience deadness as a lowered, contracted awareness, a numbing of one's sense of being alive. This is a cold and joyless death-in-life, very different from the life-enhancing, high-spirited attitude of the Taoist sage or Zen master, who is also a "dead man in life." Some psychotics sense themselves to be dead or in the process of being killed or destroyed, as the work of R. D. Laing, John Perry, and others has demonstrated. Robert Lifton describes the concept of the "dead self" as analogous to Laing's "false self." And Laing has written of the schizophrenic's "desire to be dead, desire for non-being"; he attributes this state of "death-in-life" to the "primary guilt of having no right to life in the first place, and hence being entitled only to a dead life."[25] Schizophrenics' eyes are often said to look dead.

Lifton, who has done research with survivors of Hiroshima, compares the schizophrenic's deadness with the kind of "psychic

173

numbing" found in survivors of nuclear catastrophe or concentration camps. Just as the motionless postures of the catatonic may represent the ultimate defense against overwhelming impulses toward annihilation of self and world, so the robotlike deadness of catastrophe survivors may be their sole remaining response to the threat of total destruction. It must be emphasized that such "death-in-life" states, unlike those of the mystic, the yogi, or the shamanic initiate, are not intentional and therefore are unlikely to be followed by a feeling of renewal. There are, however, exceptional circumstances when the schizophrenic might be able somehow to complete the transformation process with the support of his community.

Following earlier theories of Otto Rank and Ernest Becker, Lifton proposed that death anxiety, or fear of death, is a central, unacknowledged motive of human life. Fear of death, for these authors, is the hidden undercurrent of human beings' ubiquitous quests for immortality.[26] In his works *Denial of Death* and *Escape from Evil*, Becker extended the work of Rank, Wilhelm Reich, and Norman O. Brown to argue that the repressed fear of death is at the root of much of man's evil behavior: we destroy another in order to symbolically stave off our own fear of destruction. On the collective scale, the exploitation of this fear of death underlies the most dreadful phenomena of tyranny, oppression of the masses, war, totalitarianism, and genocide.

To overcome the destructive, numbing effects of the denial and fear of death, we must, as always in conscious transformation, first recognize and acknowledge death and turn it into our friend and ally, into a happily anticipated final journey. Such an acceptance and affirmation of dying is not a morbid "death wish" but rather a deeply and joyously felt awareness of the transcendent continuity of life. I had the good fortune to see this kind of awareness when I had a meeting with an old Mongolian Buddhist lama, who chuckled and smiled happily whenever the topic of his impending death came up in the conversation—and he was the one who kept bringing it up.

When Sigmund Freud was sixty-three, two years before he discovered the first signs of cancer in his body, he put forward, in his book *Beyond the Pleasure Principle,* the most startling and controversial of his many innovative theories: the coexistence in all life of a death drive (thanatos) as well as a life drive (eros). It has been suggested that there is a connection between Freud's formulation of the theory and the cancerous processes going on in his body at the time.[27] His own experience, his own awareness of the death process, may have provided the experiential basis for his discoveries and interpretations.

Freud's theory of thanatos has often been criticized and is not generally accepted by his followers.[28] As a result, the insights that led Freud to postulate a death urge and the old master's vision, with its mythic and mystic overtones, has been largely ignored. Freud wanted to explain the enormous destructiveness of human behavior, which he had vividly experienced in the First World War, as well as the manifestations of sadism and masochism he saw in his patients. He felt that the life drive and the death drive, eros and thanatos, are primordial biological principles, the first tending toward unification and organization, the second toward separation and disorganization.

On the ego level the personal manifestations of these two drives are sexual libido for eros and violent aggression for thanatos. We experience them in our dreams and fantasies as well as in our outward behavior; we embody them in our own personal symbols and myths. At the physiological level, as Freud pointed out, we experience them in the complementary coexistence of anabolic ("building up") and catabolic ("breaking down") processes occurring in our bodies. The aim of thanatos, Freud said, is to reduce tension, to break down, to return to the quiescence of the inorganic world. "Everything living dies from causes within itself, and returns to the inorganic. The inanimate was there before the animate."[29]

The value of such analogies and formulations, which Freud himself admitted were highly speculative, lies in their insight into life as a

complementary duality composed of creative and destructive principles, an idea that is found in virtually every major spiritual and religious tradition, in the writings of the mystics, and in the death-rebirth
mythologies of cultures all over the world. This unitary vision of life
as a creative interweaving of two complementary strands or processes
that vary in relative potency at different stages of our life—and are
subject to influences that may distort and deviate their natural expression—has the potential for transforming consciousness in a most
radical fashion.

As we focus awareness on death, we may find, as Freud did, that
there is a perfectly natural dying (thanatos) going on in us all the
time that complements and balances the life-affirming energy of eros.
Conscious focusing on the processes of dying, and the associated
symbolic imagery of death, for the purpose of transformation is, I
believe, one of the psychological meanings of the alchemical operation
of *mortificatio*.

Alchemical *Mortificatio*

If we allow that cells have consciousness and identity, and that it is
possible for human beings to increase their awareness of the body
wisdom residing at the cellular level, then our somatic awareness of
cellular birthing and dying may well be another experiential basis for
subconscious feelings of an ever-changing balance of life forces and
death forces. We know that from two to three million of our cells die
each second, while equal numbers are being born. At this level, then,
there is no possibility of attachment to the individual life form. Cells
live out their life span in periods ranging from several days to several
months, and within seven years or so, all the cells in our body have
died and been replaced. Yet we have retained our life, and the awareness of our identity, beyond all of these countless lives and deaths.

In Greek myth, Thanatos, the god of death, was seen in some literature as a black-robed, sword-wielding figure, comparable to the Grim

Reaper of European folklore. In this guise he is the personification of death as fearful and evil. However, an equally widespread image of Thanatos was as a winged spirit who lived with his twin brother Hypnos, the god of sleep. As such, he is a very different figure, an angel of death who aids the dying on their final journey. Merciful and benign, he guides us in the great river crossing. He is familiar to us from our nightly meetings with his twin, sleep. How effortlessly we drift off and release our hold on the physical form each night! Can we be similarly calm and composed when we make the final transition? And can we be equally calm when we have to "die" to some object of our affection and attachment?

Although I do not claim to have completely transcended or transformed my fear of death, I have had sufficient experiences in altered states of consciousness to have convinced me of the validity of this benign interpretation of death. I have come to understand that the alchemical operation of *mortificatio* is actually the conscious and intentional contemplation of death-related symbols and images. One could also say it is a meditation on natural processes that are analogous to dying.

The following shift in awareness occurred to me during a session involving the process known as rebirthing, in which one is guided, through special methods of breathing, to recall and release early traumatic memories. A memory of physical pain would surface, as it were, from lower depths of unconsciousness, be reexperienced, and then be released into the stream of present awareness. At that moment, the whole complex of thoughts, feelings, and sensations associated with that memory would die. To the extent that I was still identified with that memory complex (saying, "That painful thing happened to *me*"), that part, that little ego, died. As it died, in a micromoment "I" went through the fear, pain, anger, grief, and finally release that we go through when we die. This, then, was practice in dying—practice in letting go and releasing attachments.

Mortification in the ordinary sense is not a pleasant experience. We feel mortified when our pride or vanity has been wounded, and we try as soon as possible to recover from the perceived humiliation and shame. In the alchemists' conscious, intentional practice of *mortificatio,* on the other hand, such death blows to the ego are not avoided and may even be cultivated, because they bring about liberation from attachments. Edward Edinger has pointed out how often alchemical *mortificatio* is associated with symbols of the conscious ego, such as the king, the sun, or the lion. It is the kingly ego that undergoes "darkness, defeat, torture, mutilation, death, and rotting."[30] It also involves *putrefactio,* which is decomposition, decay, and disease. Out of the decaying matter comes new life; out of darkness comes light; out of death comes rebirth; out of defeat comes triumph. "Where is death's sting, where grave thy victory?"

There are distinct parallels to *mortificatio* practices in other traditions of spiritual transformation. Buddhist monks are taught to overcome desire by contemplating the body of a young woman as a worm-filled corpse or a skeleton. Hindu renunciates wander homeless, foodless, naked, and with ashes on their head to express their detachment from all sensory-physical concerns. Christian ascetics meditate on the passion of Christ and the suffering of the martyrs, expressing their union with Christ through this identification (referred to as "the imitation of Christ"). The eleventh-century Persian Sufi Khurquani said, "Thou must die daily a thousand deaths and come to life again, that thou mayest win the life immortal."[31]

Although many partial "little deaths" are possible and valuable, when the whole ego-personality "dies," everything changes. The old self-image, the one we acquired from our parents and from society, which is symbolized by the old king in alchemy, by the dragon, or by the rotting blackness—all these have to be "killed," that is, rendered completely lifeless within us, so that they have no more power, no more of our life energy invested in them. The new personality, the new sense of identity that results from the transformational work, is symbolized by the reborn child.

One could say that through these images the alchemists showed that they regarded the processes of physical, organic death as an appropriate analogy for the ending of old self-images, beliefs, and emotional patterns. Similarly, they felt that new birth, or rebirth, was the appropriate metaphor for the new, completely changed persona, the newly developed way of perceiving the world.

The New Birth and the Eternal Child

The new being that arises and grows after the death of the old self is called by the alchemists "the philosopher's son (or daughter)," the *filius philosophorum*. In Chinese Taoist alchemy, the term used was "fetus of immortality."[32] As Jung writes, "The alchemists assert that death is at once the conception of the *filius philosophorum*."[33] The "philosopher's child" is called this because it is the offspring, or result, of philosophical work, the alchemical *opus*. This work of the philosophers (who are, in the literal sense, the "lovers of wisdom") is the practice of dying daily, as Socrates had said. From the intentional, conscious "dying," involving the release of past identifications, a new and wiser being arises and grows in us.

This rebirth phase of the transformation may be experienced in several different ways. First, there is *resurrection,* a restoring to life of a personality that has died. Alternatively, rebirth as self-realization is the replacement of the small self by the greater Self or Spirit. Third, there is rebirth as renewal, where the one who has died, metaphorically, lives thereafter in a world renewed, a heightened state of consciousness. The fourth variant is rebirth experienced as *the birth of the "radiant child"*: this is the archetype of the divine or eternal child, which, as Jung points out, symbolizes "the potential future."[34]

Resurrection. The restoration to life of an adult body that has died is described in many mythic and shamanic tales: Osiris is put together

179

again by Isis; the twins Hunter and Jaguar of the Mayan *Popul Vuh* reassemble themselves after being dismembered; shamans who have "died" may be reconstituted by their power animal or ally. Many modern practitioners of shamanic work recount how they were "cut up," "pulverized," "burned," "eviscerated," or otherwise "killed," then reconstructed by their animal helper.[35] While from a skeptical point of view, one could dismiss these as fantasies, we would still have to account for the fact that shamanic practitioners consistently report an enhanced sense of well-being after such experiences.

In the New Testament, the story of Lazarus, as well as that of Jesus himself, exemplifies this kind of physical resurrection. To a certain extent, the modern accounts of near-death experiences (NDEs) coincide with this kind of pattern. In the case of Jesus, the resurrection was into a nonphysical, "spiritual" body that yet resembled the physical in all significant respects, even to having the wounds that the physical body had suffered. The closest most of us come to this kind of experience is in suffering a near-fatal illness and then recovering—the body appears to be fully restored to health. A common feature in all these accounts is that the new body is stronger, healthier, and lighter than the old.

Self-realization. In this kind of rebirth, the little self is overshadowed or replaced by the great Self, the personal body-ego by the transpersonal Spirit, the mortal by the Immortal. Meister Eckhart says that in this experience "the soul . . . is dead to self and alive to God." A Sufi saint wrote, "Thy being dies away, and His person covers thy person." Or, in the words of the Gospel of John, "No one can enter the Kingdom of God without being born from water and Spirit. That which is born of the flesh is flesh, that which is born of the Spirit is spirit."[36] People in such states feel their own ego concerns fade into insignificance in the face of the awesome power and light of the great Self, the God within, the "diamond essence," the *Atman*.

The encounter with the Self can be an overwhelming and annihilating self-confrontation, as was pointed out by C. G. Jung. In his essay "Concerning Rebirth," Jung wrote:

> He who is truly and hopelessly little will always drag the revelation of the greater down to the level of his littleness, and will never understand that the day of judgment for his littleness has dawned. But the man who is inwardly great will know that the long-expected friend of his soul, the immortal one, has now really come, "to lead captivity captive"; that is, to seize hold of him by whom this immortal had always been confined and held prisoner, and to make his life flow into that greater life—a moment of deadliest peril! [37]

As this statement makes clear, the deadly danger exists for those identified with the small self, the personal ego. Not all encounters with Self, however, need be traumatic or even painful. There is, after all, the vast literature of mysticism that sings in rapturous tones of ecstatic union with the divine, of dyings that are peaceful and blissful, of unitive experiences that have the character of a nuptial or are likened to dissolving in an oceanic feeling of blissful oneness.

Renewal. Some accounts of death-rebirth experiences emphasize the new quality of awareness and perception that comes into existence afterward. It is as if we have entered a new world, and a kind of pristine, shining radiance suffuses everything we perceive. The emotional response to what is perceived is also new; there is a quality of joy and freshness, an outpouring of affection and enthusiasm. In a second-century Gnostic text, *Treatise on Resurrection,* we read, "It (the resurrection) is the revelation of what is, and the transformation of things, and a transition into newness. For imperishability descends upon the perishable; the light flows down upon the darkness, swallowing it up."[38] Here we find the metaphor of the newly born converging with the metaphor of vision unveiled, the doors of perception cleansed ("everything appears as it is—infinite"). The mystics say that after the death-rebirth revelation, because we see everything then with love

Resurrection from death to a heightened state of consciousness; the banners declare: "provided with eyes thou departest." (Final plate from *Mutus Liber*)

and wisdom, we are seeing it from the perspective of the infinite and eternal (*sub specie aeternitatis*).

The birth of the radiant child. The biblical admonition that "except ye become as children, ye cannot enter the Kingdom of Heaven" follows naturally from the teaching that one needs to die before entering the blessed, enlightened state. Here the death-rebirth metaphor leads us to the archetype of the divine child, the *puer aeternus.* Most discussions by Jungians of the *puer* or *puella* focus on the shadow side of this archetype and on its clinical manifestations in flighty, immature "playboys" or "little girls."

But the "philosophers' child" that is born as a consequence of the inner *coniunctio* of male and female, or the divine or radiant child is connected with numerous myths of the birth of a god in human form. The Indian legends of the boy Krishna (*Gopal*) and the Christian legends of the Christ child are only the best-known examples.

Jung described the child archetype as an anticipation of the synthesis of conscious and unconscious, and as a symbol of wholeness or the Self. The mythic child-god or child-hero always has an unusual, miraculous birth or a virgin conception—which symbolizes the psychic genesis of the new being. The child image represents a link to the past, to childhood, as well as to the future, as it anticipates a "nascent state of consciousness." The "golden child" or "eternal youth" is androgynous, because he/she represents the perfect union of opposites. Only the old self, the ordinary ego, identifies itself as male or female—and this self has now died. The "child" is both beginning and end, "an initial and a terminal creature," because the wholeness that it symbolizes is "older and younger than consciousness, enfolding it in time and space."[39]

The divine child is invincible. He or she overcomes dangerous enemies in infancy: one of the images of the boy Krishna shows him trampling a giant serpent underfoot in a dance—a metaphor perhaps for the overcoming of reptilian instinctual aggressiveness. An example from Greek mythology is the story of the baby Heracles, who strangled a serpent that attacked him in his crib. The radiant child has all the power of a god, since it is a god: it is the Immortal One that replaces the mortal personality that has "died."

In the Russian Orthodox liturgy, the triumph over death is expressed in the following words: "Christ is risen from the dead, trampling down death by death, and upon those in the tomb bestowing life." I suggest that this imagery refers to the change that occurs in the psyche as the healing, transformative power of the intentional dying is experienced. The unconscious death tendencies (thanatos) that function to oppose the body's life-preserving tendencies (eros) through disease and degeneration are gradually reduced, or rather, brought into complementary balance.

One of my teachers referred to "pockets of death" within our nature that are opened up and dissolved by enlightened awareness, thus bringing about the death of death. As we consciously accept dying and "dying," the process provides spiritual nourishment. Shakespeare expresses this idea in one of the sonnets:

> So shalt thou feed on death, that feeds on men,
> And death once dead, there's no more dying then.[40]

In the nontheistic Chinese Taoist tradition, the archetype of the eternal child is also known and treasured. The newborn child is still connected to the Tao, to the source of its life and its arising, and this is why we should emulate it. Lao Tsu says in the *Tao Te Ching:*

> He who is filled with virtue is like a newborn child.
> Wasps and bees will not sting him;
> Wild beasts will not fall upon him;
> He will not be attacked by birds of prey.
> His bones are soft, his muscles weak,
> But his grip is firm. . . .

He screams all day without becoming hoarse.
This is perfect harmony.[41]

Characteristically, the Taoists emphasize the practical value, in terms of health and well-being, of attunement to the awareness of the infant.

For the individual in a process of transformation, the imagery and mythology of the eternal child fosters a positive and life-affirming attitude: we are encouraged to confront and transform our fear of death, to embrace the process of "dying" as liberating and as bringing wisdom. We thus come to know that out of the turmoil and darkness of dying comes the sparkling vitality of the newborn self. This new self is connected to the eternal source of all life, that source from which we all derive, the divine essence within. It is hence aptly named "the eternal child."

From Darkness to Light

8

> The one thing that frightens Satan
> is to see a light in your heart.
>
> —SUFI PROVERB

Enlightenment—the process of bringing light in—is implicitly a key aspect of all the transformation metaphors we have been discussing. When we awaken, we open our eyes and perceive (with) more light. To become "lucid" (from *lux*, "light") while dreaming is to bring a quality of transparent awareness to our experience. Similarly, when the cataracts that blind us, the veils or coverings, are removed, there is more light. When the clouds of ignorance are dispelled, the light of the spiritual sun shines in brightness. Imprisoned in a dungeon or a cave, we are trapped in darkness; when liberated, we are dazzled by daylight. The alchemical purification by fire burns away the dross of conditioned, earth-bound consciousness to reveal the radiant "gold" of illumined consciousness.

For most people "enlightenment" is a process of imparting or acquiring knowledge about something. "That was an enlightening presentation you gave today." Historians of culture speak of the Enlightenment: the period in eighteenth-century Europe when a group of philosophers and scientists promoted a rational, nontheological approach to the problems of philosophy and society. This is not, however, the meaning of enlightenment for the mystics and visionaries of Eastern and Western spiritual traditions. For them, light is not an abstract symbol but an experience that is lived and felt in the mind, the heart, the body, and the inner recesses of the psyche.

Enlightenment, then, is not merely a metaphor but rather an experience of one's own inner essence, the Self, as a Being of Light.

187

Enlightenment, when defined as the rational acquisition of knowledge, deals with only one limited aspect of human consciousness—the mental. I follow the teachings of the ancients in proposing that the notion of enlightenment is meant to be taken much more literally. The process involves seeing more clearly, both internally and externally, so that there is more lucid awareness, a feeling of the light and warmth of love in the heart—ultimately a complete immersion in the ocean of light called God, Being, or Spirit. This aspect of consciousness transformation is actually a process of moving from darkness to more and more pervasive light and clarity.

The reader might object that these ideas of Spirit, or God, or Self as a Being of Light are mystical and arcane—that they involve assumptions that are impossible to prove and that modern people cannot apply to themselves. I myself once held such a skeptical view, when I was still under the influence of the rationalistic-mechanistic world view with which I had been conditioned. Only through repeated personal experiences and the parallel accounts of friends, colleagues, students, and clients was I eventually led to adopt a more open-minded attitude. I realized also that contrary to my prior beliefs, mystics were not armchair philosophers, indulging in fantastic speculations. Rather, they were, without exception, speaking from their own experiences: they were describing interior perceptions. In many cases, they were not learned intellectuals but simple, humble men and women who led active and productive lives. The unanimity of the mystics' testimony and of the images of light in myths and sacred texts is far too pronounced to be written off to chance.

It is an unmistakable fact that in the sacred literature and art of most religious and spiritual traditions, the symbolic imagery of enlightenment is central. The accounts of the mystics and seers of East and West are replete with experiences of and visions of light. The creation of the world, in the Judeo-Christian tradition, begins with God's invocation, "Let there be light," and the emergence of light out of primal darkness. Modern science, in a rather parallel fashion, sees the universe beginning with an energy explosion of inconceivable force and radiance. The Creator works with light—*is* light. The Christ is called "the light of the world." The vision of Krishna in the *Bhagavad Gita* is of a cosmic being of overwhelming radiance, "brighter than a thousand suns." Solar deities of light and fire, such as the Indian Agni, the Iranian Mazda, the Egyptian Ra, and the Greek Apollo, play key roles in all the ancient sacred mythologies. Jung called light "the central mystery of philosophical alchemy."

In some traditions the duality of light and darkness is emphasized. In Taoism light is *yang* like the day and darkness *yin* like the night. "That which lets now the light, now the dark appear, is Tao." It is a natural process of cyclic change: the Earth turns its face toward and away from the Sun. Some of the dualistic religious teachings see an ongoing cosmic struggle between the "forces of light" and the "forces of darkness." This is true of the Zoroastrians; of the Essenes, who compiled the Dead Sea Scrolls; of the Egyptians, in their stories of Osiris/Horus and Set; and of the ancient Meso-American cultures, in their myths of the conflict between Quetzalcoatl, the Lord of the Dawn, and Tezcatlipoca, the Lord of the Smoking Mirror.

Medieval philosophers made a distinction between three kinds of light and three kinds of eyes. These philosophers held that we have eyes of flesh, which see with exterior light the physical world of sense objects and matter. Next, we have an eye of reason, which sees with interior light the truths of reason, mind, and knowledge. Last, we have an eye of contemplation, which sees with higher or spiritual light the ultimate reality of oneness, the ground of being.[1]

Enlightenment of the Physical Body

"A man's wisdom makes his face to shine," says Ecclesiastes (8:1). It is a common observation that uplifting, affirmative emotions, such as joy and love, cause people's bodies and faces—their eyes especially—to light up, to radiate or shine. Conversely, moods of depression or despair cast darkening hues on a person's countenance, draining the visage of color and making the eyes appear to lack luster. We could, of course, say that such expressions are merely metaphorical and do not represent veridical perceptions. On the other hand, there is the cogent testimony of those who report luminous energy phenomena—that is, light emissions from the body—of which present-day science is as yet unable to render an account. There are age-old traditions of subtle energy fields, or auras, surrounding living organisms, and some of these phenomena have in recent years proved amenable to measurement and recording, through such means as Kirlian photography and other methods.[2]

Whatever the nature and origin of this "light" may be, it is apparent that it can, on occasion, suffuse the body with such intensity that it becomes visible to others, even those who are not normally clairvoyant. The light may become visible in certain altered states: in psychedelic states, as well as after prolonged periods of meditation, many people, myself included, have seen patterns of light and flame around the heads and faces of individuals. Thus, it appears that either the sensitized vision of the perceiver or the intensity of the phenomenon in the subject can make the inner light outwardly visible.

There is a universal tendency to depict saints and enlightened beings with haloes and auras of flame and light, and mystical literature is filled with accounts of yogis and prophets who were seen to be filled and overflowing with light. The nineteenth-century Indian saint Ramakrishna was frequently observed by his students to glow visibly. Some of these occurrences have been recorded in photographs, in which the body can be seen to have a distinct luminosity. In this century, a German traveler who visited Ramana Maharshi, another famous Indian yogi-saint, recorded his observations of the saint's transfiguration:

> While my eyes were immersed in the golden depths of the Maharshi's eyes . . . the dark complexion of his body transformed itself slowly into white. This white body became more and more luminous, as if lit up from within, and began to radiate. . . . With the same eyes which a moment ago were able to read some notes in my diary, I saw him sitting on a tiger-skin as a luminous form.[3]

An elderly lady of my acquaintance has told me of an experience where she saw the upper torso of her teacher of Agni Yoga, who was sitting in front of her, literally become transparent and dissolve into shimmering fibers of light.

The prototype of this kind of occurrence in the Christian tradition is the event known as the Transfiguration, in which Jesus took the disciples Peter, James, and John up to a high mountain, where they saw him transfigured: "his face shone like the sun, and his clothes became white as light," and he was seen conversing with Moses and Elijah.[4] In trying to understand such perceptions, the explanation of Meister Eckhart makes simple and elegant sense: "The light in the soul's core overflows into the body, which becomes radiant with it."[5]

The individuals who are experiencing the light-in-the-body phenomenon usually agree that it is both like and unlike the physical light we see around us. Often, the light is felt more than seen, which makes the experience parallel to those of fire and warmth in the body described in chapter 4. This light-fire energy is often perceived as being healing, as well as spiritually illuminating. Here, for example, is an account by a contemporary student of light-fire yoga of a breakthrough experience that came after many days of inner self-healing work:

> My body had gone into a state of near collapse . . . and I felt sick and frustrated, working with healing energy in my abdominal area. Nothing but darkness, pain, and obstruction was being experienced, for what seemed like an endless period of time. . . . All at once something broke loose and I entered into what could only be described as

a region of light. It was a vast curving plain, cool and full of delicious sensations and feelings, and it was filled with light, above, below and all around. My biggest shock came when I realized it was inside of me. "The Kingdom of Heaven is within you," it has been said . . . and with a churning mixture of shock and exhilaration I knew what that meant, and I knew that it was true.

Shock, elation, gratitude, joy—these are the common accompaniments of this kind of unexpected illumination. An informant quoted in the anthology by Cohen and Phipps describes walking home one evening on a freezing night, when suddenly,

it was a bit like a long electric shock, . . . but it wasn't mechanical, it was a person. . . . There was a feeling of heat and light rushing through my bloodstream, seeping over me and paralyzing me almost, as if some person were blowing something in me to white heat, and I was sobbing with tears of love and gratitude. There were no visions or voices, but the person communicated . . . ideas or certainties, with a sort of close intimacy, much more closely than into my ear or imagination.[6]

The light or energy is felt as suffusing the interior of the body, bringing deep feelings of love and tremendous well-being. It is perceived as intelligent and aware, bringing about a state of self-understanding both intimate and all-inclusive.

Arthur Young has pointed out the simple but profound truth that we do not actually see light. Instead, we see *by light* and *with light*.[7] We usually think of light as coming into the eyes, the eyes of flesh, with which we see the world. However, in states of illumination, light seems to also pour through the body and flow outward—at times with such intensity that it is visible to others. The eyes radiate, the face shines, and the heart "sees." Ancient sacred texts refer to the intelligence of the heart, the eye of the heart. This is the heart center, where we see with the feeling light of love. Experiences of the heart center opening are accompanied by sensations of warmth, openness, and lightness.

Corresponding to this kind of experience are many expressions in the world's sacred literature that speak of the Self, or Spirit, as a light in the heart. In one of the Upanishads we read that Atman is "the person here who is the knower among the senses, the light within the heart (*antarjyotih*)." The notion of the light in the heart is expounded also by the Vedantist philosopher Shankara: "*Atma* rises in the heart like the sun of knowledge, destroying darkness, all-pervading, all-sustaining."[8]

Islamic mysticism also refers to the light in the heart. The fourteenth-century Sufi Mahmudi Kashani writes of the light of truth that is ordinarily veiled by our humanness: as long as it shines only through this veil, we call it faith. "If this same light attains directly to the heart and the veil of humanness does not intervene, then it is the light of certainty.... The black cloud of human attributes rises up constantly and covers the face of the sun of truth. When it is

Subtle energy currents surrounding the head.

193

uncovered, . . . then the heart directly experiences the effulgences of that light."[9]

Shamanism, which can be regarded as the oldest spiritual and healing tradition on this planet, describes the initiatory experiences of shamans in training, or in healing trances, as involving light. The explorer Rasmussen quotes an Eskimo shaman as saying, "Every real shaman has to feel *quamaneq,* a light within the body, inside his head or brain, something that gleams like fire, that enables him to see in the dark, and with closed eyes see into things which are hidden, and also into the future."[10]

Healing, intuitive knowing, clairvoyance, and precognition have all been associated with this kind of inner light, especially when focused through the heart center or the midbrain "third eye" center. Light in the body is natural: it is perceived also in animals and plants, if we are to believe shamanic seers and the research reported in *The Secret Life of Plants* by Peter Tompkins and Christopher Bird.

European alchemists, particularly Paracelsus, spoke of the "light of nature" (*lumen naturae*). Paracelsus claimed that psychic perception and clairvoyant dreams in man and the instinctive prescience ("the auguries") of animals were brought about by this light of nature. "Nothing can be in man unless it has been given to him by the light of nature." Elsewhere, Paracelsus distinguishes the light of nature from another light, "outside the *lumen naturae,* by which [man] can search out supernatural things." He says these lights appear in our experience as *scintillae,* "fiery sparks." They come from the world soul and are "seeds of a world to come," sprinkled throughout the great cosmos. In man, the little cosmos, the sparks come from what Paracelsus calls the *astrum,* the "star in man."[11]

In all the great religious traditions, light has been the primary symbol, as well as original manifestation, of God, Divine Being, Spirit, the Immortal and Eternal. In some traditions, notably the Hindu and Buddhist Tantras, as well as Chinese Taoism and European alchemy, divine light "descends" to nature and into the body. Yaqui Indian shamanism, as described in the books by Carlos Castaneda, involves painstaking and disciplined practices aimed at heightening the apprentice's ability to see the human form as a being made up of "luminous fibers." Alchemy, as described in chapter 4, involved the purification of the dense matter of the body (symbolized by the alchemical furnace); as the *purificatio* is brought to completion, sparks of light (*scintillae*) begin to appear, leading to visions and insights.

In the yoga systems of the Hindu Tantras, the practitioner visualizes geometric configurations of light (triangles, stars, diamonds, circles, spheres) in the various centers and in the energy channels (*nadis*) that link these centers. Agni Yoga (yoga of fire) methods involve the channeling and focusing of light-fire energy of different color-frequencies in the centers, as well as directly in the physiological organ systems of the body. In Tibetan Buddhism, in the *Vajrayana* ("diamond-lightning way") teachings (the strand of esoteric practices designed to bring about enlightenment in one lifetime), there is also an emphasis on channeling and focusing light-energy patterns and figures. Likewise, Taoism, especially the alchemical and yogic strands of that tradition, has a practice called the "circulation of light" (or fire, or energy) through the body in certain distinctive patterns.[12] The experience of light-throughout-the-body is something that can and does happen to people spontaneously, as an integral part of a transformation process, regardless of religious or cultural belief systems. When this experience does occur, it is always felt to be something immensely positive, healing, and inspiring. It is, in fact, such a common experience that it has been incorporated into the language of all the great spiritual traditions. It is also the central preoccupation of practitioners of transformation—the shamans, alchemists, and yogis of ancient and modern times, who can justly be regarded as, in Mircea Eliade's words, "technicians of the sacred."

The Illumination of the Mind

In very broad terms we might say that enlightenment of the body is associated with healing and physical transformation, whereas illumination of the mind is associated with wisdom and greater self-knowledge. It is important to emphasize again that those who have experienced this kind of enlightenment insist that the experience is literally and actually en-lightening, that the expression is not just metaphorical. As strange as this may sound to one who has not experienced it, the contents of the mind itself, its thoughts and images, can become filled and suffused with light, just as body structures and tissues can. Thus, the notion of the "mind's eye," which perceives with inner light, makes perfect sense experientially.

The distinction made between exterior light (of the body, the flesh) and interior light (of the mind, the consciousness) parallels the distinction between the light of nature and the light of spirit developed by Paracelsus and other philosopher-mystics. In the eighteenth century, these ideas were given cogent expression in the writings of that great clairvoyant scientist of consciousness, Emanuel Swedenborg, who wrote:

> It has often been granted me to perceive and also to see that there is a true light that enlightens the mind, wholly distinct from the light that is called natural light. I have been raised up interiorly into that light by degrees; and as I was raised up my understanding became so enlightened as to enable me to perceive what I did not perceive before, and finally such things as I could not even comprehend by thought from natural light.[13]

The Indian Vedanta philosophers also equate the "light in the heart" (enlightened body) with the "sun of knowledge" (illumined mind), as was shown in the passage quoted from Shankara. This inner knowledge-light is said to be "all-pervading, all-sustaining, radiating throughout the world"—very much like the networks of thought energy, the collective tapestry of consciousness that links all humans and all forms of life. These are paradoxical utterings, because the reality is difficult to convey. The enlightening of the body and the illumination of the mind are different experiences, but the light involved in both is the same. The mental and the sensory-physical are two distinct bands in the spectrum of awareness. Either one can be dark and obscure, or illumined with radiance.

Buddhist texts, although they deny the independent existence of any substantive self, are remarkably congruent in their descriptions

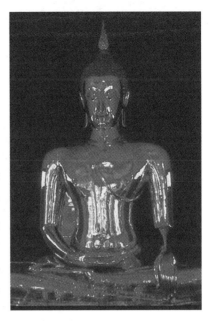

Complete bodily transformation by illumination. (Golden Buddha, 15 feet high, 18th century Thailand)

of interior light. The Tibetan Book of the Dead describes the radiant light that appears to a person at the moment of dying: "This mind of yours is inseparable luminosity and emptiness in the form of a great mass of light, without birth or death."[14] Another text states that when in meditation, Buddha had a "ray named the ornament of the light of knowledge rising from the cranial suture, shining above the head."[15] Again, the integration of mental and physical experiences is demonstrated here.

In the *Bardo Thödol,* careful distinctions are drawn between the visions of lights that one sees in the after-death state, which signify the different realms of conditioned existence; and the clear light of Buddha-nature, or Spirit, that is "radiance from the seed of emptiness, the radiance in the realm of knowing and the light of self-generating wisdom."[16] The person experiencing the after-death (*bardo*) state is advised to stay with the clear light, to recognize it as the light of his own beingness, and to allow it to illuminate the *skandhas,* the thought forms and perceptual structures that make up our ordinary consciousness. All this suggests an infusion of light into the mind, altogether analogous to the infusion of light into the body.

In the New Testament there are many well-known sayings that refer to Jesus as the "light of the world"; yet there are an equal number that make it abundantly clear that according to Christ's teaching, every man and woman has, and is, a being of light within.

> Ye are all children of light, and children of the day . . . therefore let us not sleep, but let us watch and be sober.
> The light of the body is the eye; if therefore thine eye be single thy whole body shall be full of light.

The Gnostic Gospel of Thomas reinforces this interpretation of the Christ teaching. When the disciples ask Jesus to show them where he is, he answers: "Within a man of light there is light, and he lights the whole world. When he does not shine, he is in darkness."[17]

The significance of these passages is that they point unmistakably to light pervasive within and throughout the human being. They are consistent with many others in the Gospels and in Gnostic literature, where Jesus deflects the disciples' attempts to idealize him as the only enlightened one or as the only son of God. "Is it not written in your law, 'I said, you are gods'?"[18] Each human being is, in essence, a divine spirit of pure light. This light can come "down" or "through," into mind and body, into outward expression and manifestation.

Christian mystics and theologians make it abundantly clear that light is not an abstract symbol but an actual energy that is known in the mind, felt in the heart, sensed in the body, and that comes from, and is, Spirit. Saint Augustine writes: "I entered into the secret closet of my soul, led by Thee . . . and beheld the mysterious eye of my soul the Light that never changes. . . . It was not the common light that all flesh can see, but different. . . . It was higher because it made me, and I was lower because made by it. He who knoweth the truth, knoweth the Light: and who knoweth it, knoweth eternity."[19]

We noted earlier the Gnostic and Hermetic image of "light sparks," *scintillae:* they are called "germs" or "seeds" of the soul. Seeing with the eye of flesh and the light of nature, our first experiences of light are likely to be in the form of sparks, points of light in swarms, like fireflies in the night sky. Seeing with the eye of mind and the interior light, we understand these sparks to represent visions, flashes of insight, awakenings, moments of truth, and lucid awareness. Jung suggested we could think of ego-consciousness as "surrounded by a multitude of little luminosities." For him, as for Paracelsus, the unconscious, the "darksome psyche," was like "a starstrewn night sky"—a great, dark unknown, studded with brilliant gemlike points and stars of light. These are messages from the luminous realm of archetypes.[20]

In Gerhard Dorn, an eighteenth-century alchemical philosopher, we read of the illumined seeker: "Little by little he will come to see with his mental eye a number of sparks shining day by day . . . and a growing into a great light that thereafter all things needful to him will be made known. . . .

For the life, the light of men, shines in us, albeit dimly. It is in us, and not of us, but of Him to whom it belongs, who makes us his dwelling place. . . .

He has implanted that light in us that we may see.   Thus the truth is to be sought, not in our selves, but in the image of God within us."[21]

The sparks, or light seeds, or starlike flashes can be regarded as a visual representation of moments of discovery or insight. We speak of a "flash" of intuition, and comedic folklore has the lit-up light bulb above the head as an indicator of a "bright idea." Studies on the psychology of creativity and invention have documented that creative ideas are typically experienced as something that "came through" or "just happened." In other words, they are involuntary events, like sparks or flashes, that come from another, transpersonal dimension of consciousness.[22]

Some mystics have reported experiences of enlightenment coming after prolonged periods of intense inner struggle, analogous in many ways to the hellish and purgatorial experiences described in chapter 4. A classic example of such an experience is offered by the great seventeenth-century mystic Jacob Boehme, the shoemaker whose first illumination occurred when he was struck by the brilliant reflection of sunlight off a burnished copper plate. He described struggling for a long time with his "corrupting nature," trying to overcome his "evil will."

> Now while I was wrestling and battling, being aided by God, a wonderful light arose within my soul. It was a light entirely foreign to my unruly nature, but in it I recognized the true nature of God and man, and the relation existing between them.[23]

This kind of transition is characteristic of breakthrough experiences, where after a prolonged inner opposition of good and evil aspects of the psyche, there can occur a sudden opening to the light—a light that embraces both the polar opposites.

Often, the struggle of opposites is a struggle between fear and love. We want to love—others, ourselves, God—but we are afraid. The fear is experienced inwardly as a wall, an immovable block of resistance, or as a threatening force. When the power of love finally prevails and the light dawns in the heart, then the walls of fear are dissolved, the threat disappears, the heart opens. This is why it was said that Satan, who represents the principle of opposition and whose chief weapon is fear, is threatened when he sees the light in the heart. And this is why the Indian sages of the *Rig Veda* sang, "May I reach that light on reaching which one attains freedom from fear."[24]

When conflicting and depressing emotions prevail within the psyche, our experience is consistently one of darkness and gloom. The color and vibrancy may fade out of visually perceived objects; things may look foggy, gray, muddy, or obscure. This is the interior, or subjective, counterpart to the darkened visage, the lackluster eyes, that may be seen in people who are experiencing such heavy, oppressive moods. There have been many expressions and symbols to describe such a state. The alchemists called it *nigredo*, the "blackness," as well as *massa confusa*, a "confused mass." It was also represented as a "chaos of the elements," where "elements" symbolize psychological functions—thus a state where our psychic energies are in chaotic conflict and confusion.

This kind of experience also relates to "the dark night of the soul" that the Spanish mystic John of the Cross described. This is regarded by students of mysticism as an experience that typically occurs after an initial awakening but before the final illumination and union with God. It is, as Saint John expressed it, especially poignant for the soul that has already experienced some degree of illumination and already knows the intense ecstasy that is possible and promised. "What we call the dark night is the absence of pleasure in all things. For as night is the absence of light . . . so it can be said that the mortification of the appetites is night for the soul."[25] In order to understand this passage, we should remember that the word *soul* has undergone a number of changes in meaning over the centuries. The text makes clear that the frustration or mortification of "appetites," wishes, desires, cravings, and so on, is being described—and these are now not usually conceived of as components of the "soul." We are dealing with a personal, mind-created prison, hell, or chaos. For this reason, it has been suggested that the famous "dark night of the soul" could better be called the "dark night of the ego," for it is the *ego* that is frustrated, pained, and confused.[26] According to this view, which I share, the true soul is never in darkness; rather, it lives always in light, since it is light. This parallels the Gnostic conception of the soul as a self-luminous sphere.

A graphic description of an enlightenment experience is found in R. M. Bucke's *Cosmic Consciousness*, first published in 1901:

> I was in a state of quiet, almost passive enjoyment, not actually thinking, but letting ideas, images, and emotions flow of themselves through my mind. All at once, without any warning of any kind, I found myself wrapped in a flame-colored cloud. For an instant I thought of fire, an immense conflagration somewhere close by in that great city; the next I knew the fire was within myself. Directly afterward there came upon me a sense of exultation, of immense joyousness accompanied or immediately followed by an intellectual illumination impossible to describe. Among other things, I did not merely come to believe, but I saw that the universe is not composed of dead matter, but is, on the contrary, a living Presence; I became conscious in myself of eternal life.[27]

This account makes clear, once again, the consistent claim of the mystics: what they describe is not imagining or theory or philosophy or belief. It is, rather, the testimony of their direct experience: it is marked not by a character nebulous and obscure but by luminous clarity and irrefutable certainty.

The Self as a Being of Light

The basic feature of the experience of enlightenment appears to be a sensing, feeling, and knowing that one's body, heart, and mind are being infused, usually from "above," with inner light of a spiritual nature. Light coming in from above is a literal, direct perception in many instances of body enlightenment, and in some light-yoga practices, as noted, the light energy is channeled into the body from above the head. When speaking of mental or spiritual illumination, "light coming in from above" is a metaphorical expression. The spatial metaphor is based on the understanding that the light is of spiritual origin, that it comes from a part of our being, our totality, that is "higher" than the body or mind. Thus *Atman*, Spirit, which is Self, which is

Light, comes into and suffuses the body, the emotions, and the mind—the entire psyche. Thus it is transformation by illumination.

Sri Aurobindo describes the process as follows, using the word *enthusiasm,* which means, literally, "to be infused with god force" (*en-theos*):

> Into the consciousness, with a fiery ardor of realization . . . a downpour of inwardly visible light envelops the action . . . the vision of light accompanying inner illumination is not merely a subjective visual image, or a symbolic phenomenon: light is primarily a spiritual manifestation of the Divine Reality illuminative and creative. There is also in this descent the arrival of a greater dynamic, a golden drive, a luminous "enthusiasmos" of inner force and power which replaces the comparatively slow and deliberate process of the mind by a swift, sometimes vehement, almost a violent impetus of rapid transformation.[28]

Here Aurobindo makes the point that once the light of divine Spirit is received and perceived, the process of transformation takes almost a quantum leap forward in intensity and rapidity. This leap might occur spontaneously and unexpectedly, or it might occur after years of deliberate and purposeful practice, but with the dawning of the inner light of Spirit/Self, a new and higher phase is initiated. The individual is now "fired with enthusiasm" because connected to the divine source or ground of all life.

We saw (in chapter 4) how the mystics often perceive ultimate reality as a kind of fiery ground, preceding and subsuming all divisions, dualities, and opposites. Light and fire are always experienced as two aspects of the same basic energy. We know that on the level of physical reality, the sun and other stars are all massive spheres of both light and flame. Considered psychologically, when the fiery aspect of the primal life energy is emphasized, we have the fires of purification; when the luminous aspect is emphasized, we have illumined awareness.

That the innermost spiritual essence in humans is of light is emphasized again and again in the sacred literature of ancient India. "Like the sun when the clouds are removed—*Atman* is revealed shining when our ignorance is dispelled," wrote the Vedantist philosopher Shankara. And further, these texts affirm, this Self that is a "light in the heart" is one with the macrocosmic spiritual principle (*Brahman*). "The light that shines beyond this heaven, beyond all, in the highest worlds beyond which there are none higher, is truly the same light that shines within the person," according to the *Chandogya Upanishad*.[29]

The idea that the Light/Self/Atman is identified with, or unified with, the cosmic divine principle is consonant with the statements of the mystics. They declare that the light they sense is eternal and infinite, a light beyond the duality of light versus darkness—just as Boehme's fire ground is beyond all dualities. "It is an infused brightness, a light which knows no night, but rather it is always light, nothing ever disturbs it," says Saint Teresa of Avila.[30]

Gnostic and Neoplatonist writers referred to the soul as being *augoeides*—a word meaning "radiant," "brilliant," "shining," "possessing splendor," "raylike," or "lucid." G.R.S. Mead quotes the Gnostic philosopher Damascius: "In Heaven indeed our *augoeides* is filled with radiance, a glory that streams throughout its depths lends its divine strength. But in lower states, losing its radiance, it is dirtied, as it were, and becomes darker and darker and more material."[31] These expressions refer to what esoteric philosophies and transpersonal psychologies call a higher or subtle body. Because it consists of light, it is also referred to in some traditions as the "radiant body," "rainbow body," "body of light," or "diamond body."

Probably the hardest part of such teachings for a modern Westerner to accept is the claim that every human being has an inner light or a light body. Many people feel that such concepts, metaphors, or descriptions don't apply to them, because they may not have had any direct experience that corresponds to such descriptions. The accounts offered here have demonstrated, I hope, that such experiences are not at all rare and correspond very closely to the descriptions given in the literature of mysticism and religious experience, both Eastern and Western.

In the teachings of the mystics, the soul is regarded as the more individualized form of Spirit: "higher" than mind and body but not as cosmic or universal as Spirit. The "lower" levels of mind and matter, the several "bodies" that make up our personality, are regarded as sheaths, skins, or coverings for the soul. The enlightenment experience then involves light from the highest or innermost center of pure being, flowing down into and through soul, mind, emotions, and body. As Meister Eckhart wrote, "God pours himself into the soul, and the light at the core of the soul grows so strong that it spills out, even passing the outward man."[32]

The autobiography of Yogananda, one of the first of the Indian yoga teachers to bring the Indian spiritual teachings to the West, describes such an experience in his autobiography. It was triggered by a touch on the chest from his guru, Sri Yukteswar. He describes how his awareness left his body and his vision transformed to a spherical sight that saw everything in the environment as light and pure vibration, melting into a "luminescent sea." The ocean of light was interrupted at certain points by materializations of form. The experience continued, with an increasing expansion of awareness that included continents, the earth, planets, stars, and constellations: the outer cosmos become visible to inner sight. Yogananda saw "the entire cosmos, gently luminous, like a city seen afar at night, glimmering within the infinitude of my being."[33]

Here again, we find the identification of the individual self with the cosmic Self, which the Indian sages first discovered and described, and which came to be referred to as cosmic consciousness. In this state one sees and realizes that God stands in the same relationship to the universe as Self stands to the body and personality. One realizes, in the words of one of the aphorisms of the Gurdjieff student A. R. Orage, "God is the I of the universe."[34]

Such an experience, in which the individual Spirit realizes its identity with the macrocosmic Creator Spirit, is not, as might appear, an inflation of ego-identity. Such delusions of grandeur do occur in some kinds of psychosis: this would be the deluded assumption that "I am the god of the universe." In the mystic illumination, awareness shifts from the separated individual to the unified cosmic perspective: the objects of the outer world, including planets, stars, and galaxies, are then seen to be *within* one's field of consciousness. At this point, then, the sense of self, the sense of who "I" am, has also shifted. I am no longer just a separate human individual. At this level I am unified in consciousness with the divine being that sustains the universe.

Hildegard's mystical vision of a "sapphire-blue human figure, permeated and surrounded by brilliant light and flashing fire." The inner circle is golden light, the outer silver. (From *Scivias*, the illuminated book of visions by Hildegard von Bingen, 12th-century Germany)

Integrating the Inner Wild Animal   9

Behold, I send you like sheep among wolves;
be ye therefore wise as serpents and gentle as doves.

—GOSPEL OF MATTHEW (10:16)

The significance of animals in human consciousness and in the process of psychospiritual transformation can hardly be overestimated. The wisdom teachings of ancient times, encoded in the metaphors and symbols of ritual and myth, agree on the necessity for human beings to come to terms with their creature heritage. According to these teachings, we have both a human and an animal layer in our psyches. Indeed, the English word *animal* comes from the Latin word *anima,* meaning "soul." The human and the animal psyche are often either dissociated or in conflict with each other; and this dissociative condition is reflected in the abuse and exploitation of animal wildlife by "civilized" humanity. The philosophical traditions of transformation teach that this duality must be reconciled and brought into harmonious balance, both for the sake of our own health and spiritual well-being, and for the preservation of the world of nature.

Modern science sees animals simply as the predecessors of humans on the evolutionary tree of life. Our technological civilization regards animals (as well as plants and all other parts of the natural world) as resources to be managed and exploited for food, clothing, labor, or even, with the advent of genetic engineering, as biological factories for the production of biochemicals. Domestic pets, even when providing companionship or therapy, are basically the equivalent of slaves, with clearly defined "ownership" and control. In the popular mind of the modern era, animals are considered "lower" forms of life, with psychological associations of violence, aggression, or low intelligence.

Terms such as *bestial, brutish, beastly* express derogatory attitudes, and for most people, animal wildlife is "red in tooth and claw." In the Western rationalist humanist tradition, the essence of being human is seen as somehow transcending or rising above our animal heritage.

Therefore, the notion that one could or should integrate the animal component of our nature might seem strange indeed. However, a closer examination of the findings of evolutionary biology reveals that residues of animal evolution are very much present in our bodies, especially our brain and nervous system, with profound influence on our minds and behavior. To recognize ourselves, *homo sapiens,* as an animal species implies also that we recognize the other animals—primates, mammals, reptiles, vertebrates—as the evolutionary ancestors of the human species.

This new, much more respectful and egalitarian relationship between humans and animals that emerges from science is also present if we look at the symbolic imagery of animals in traditional folklore, mythology, and religion. There are myths reflecting the major stages of evolution and there are images of creator deities who have the form of animals. Wild animals were seen as friends and companions, as allies, protectors, and guides to healing and knowledge. Myths and legends the world over tell of humans transforming into animals and animals adopting human characteristics; of humans who can understand the language of animals, and animals who can speak the language of men. Shamanic traditions speak of humans who have gained wisdom and healing power from animal teachers.

Regardless of whether, in these myths, the animal is a real physical creature, a power, an image, or a vision, such stories reflect a very different inner relationship with the creature elements in our psyches: an attitude of respect, of gratitude, of companionship. Prior to the ascendancy of Descartes's mind-body dualism in Western thought, the general belief was that human beings had three "souls": a vegetative soul, which plants also had; an animal soul, which we shared with animals; and a rational soul, the peculiar human distinction. The human who speaks with an animal, who learns from it or is healed or helped by it, is one for whom a relationship with the animal soul is very much involved in the processes of transformation.

Remembering Our Evolutionary Ancestry

Classical evolutionary theory explains the emergence and development of species using the principles of adaptation and natural selection. Controversy exists over the interpretation of certain gaps in the evolutionary record (the so-called missing links) and over the apparent occurrence of major discontinuous jumps in evolution. The debates in scientific circles are especially intense in the area of humankind's immediate ancestors. Feelings run high around the questions of whether our inheritance from the animals is primarily territoriality and aggression, or cooperation and altruism.[1]

Perhaps nowhere in biological science is the intimate relationship of human consciousness with animal consciousness revealed more clearly than in the theory of brain organization developed by neurobiologist Paul MacLean. MacLean's theory is that the human brain is actually composed of three distinct layers, superimposed upon one another in evolutionary sequence. He calls this model the triune brain and compares it to a system in which there are three different drivers of a vehicle: the vehicle, in this analogy, is the lower brain-stem, the spinal cord, and the sensory-motor nerves, also referred to as the neural chassis.[2]

The lowest and oldest of the three brains is a group of ganglia at the base of the forebrain that MacLean calls the R-complex or reptilian brain; the second is the limbic system, which has strong connections via the hypothalamus to visceral and endocrine functions and is referred to by MacLean as the mammalian or old mammalian brain; and the third system is the neocortex, the latest layer, found in the higher mammals, in primates and humans (MacLean calls this system neomammalian).

The *reptilian brain* is involved in many of the self-preserving and species-preserving behavior patterns that are still observed in mammals, primates and humans. They include establishing and defending territories, ritualistic fighting, posturing and displaying, foraging, hunting, homing, hoarding, establishing dominance hierarchies, greeting, grooming, mating, courtship, and migration. Reptiles, however, are limited in their capacity to learn, and only rarely take care of their young. These two important functions are first noted in the mammals and are largely based in the limbic system.

The *mammalian brain* system organizes experience in terms of primary emotions such as fear, rage, sex-love, parental love, curiosity, sociability, joy, and excitement. The third component of our triune brain is what I call the *primate neocortex*. Found in the higher mammals, primates and hominids, it is concerned with the perception and interpretation of external reality and the making of decisions in anticipation of future events. This is the only one of the three brains that, in man, develops the use of language and other symbolic communication systems. However, as MacLean points out, the reptilian and mammalian brain systems provide the neural substrate for the basic personality.

In humans, clearly, the ability to reflect on experience, to examine inner perceptions, to observe one's own expression and behavior, and to empathize with others is highly developed. Yet one might well ask whether many of our difficulties in living successfully on this planet cannot be traced to unconscious repetition of behaviors that are genetically imprinted in these earlier animal brain systems. The three minds often do not coordinate very well with one another, as they vie for control of the body-vehicle. Much of the emotional reactivity that wreaks such havoc in interpersonal relations is traceable to the mammalian fight-or-flight patterns encoded in the limbic system.[3]

The worldwide prevalence of violence could be, in part, an unconscious residue of reptilian and mammalian predation and territoriality.

Nourishing and caring for live young is a mammalian invention; reptiles mostly don't seem to recognize their young (except for the birds) and will as soon eat them as feed them. Thus, physical abuse of children could be a stress-induced atavistic regression from mammalian to reptilian brain behavior patterns.

In states of consciousness induced by hallucinogenic plants and drugs, in dreams, and in certain forms of experiential psychotherapy, experiences often occur that seem to be representations of the older animal brain systems, something like evolutionary memories. Furthermore, it is possible in such states to differentiate these kinds of perceptions from images of animals that are purely symbolic in a personal way. Individuals sometimes report perceiving aspects of animal form or behavior of which they had no ordinary prior knowledge.[4] Such experiences can have a deeply transformative and integrative effect, enlarging our sense of who and what we are as humans.

Given these kinds of findings, the attitude of respect and mutuality toward animals that indigenous people express in their art, rituals, and shamanic practices makes perfect sense if we realize that the animals—their sensations, perceptions, feelings, and behaviors—are actually within us. The forms and functions of animal consciousness still live in us, interacting with our much-vaunted human consciousness in numerous complex, poorly understood ways. The English biologist Rupert Sheldrake has formulated a scientific theory that can account for experiences of evolutionary memory. In his *The Presence of the Past* and other books, he postulates that there are *morphogenetic* ("form-generating") fields, which determine the forms and patterns of perception, thought, and behavior at every level of life. Learning and memory, say in animals and humans, take place through the action of "morphic resonance" between fields of similar form.[5]

A striking mythological expression of evolutionary memory and continuity is found in the Indian myth of the ten incarnations or *avatars* (literally "descents") of the god Vishnu. The *Puranas,* where this story is found, were composed during the sixth to the twelfth centuries and contain in mythic form the cosmology and theology of classical Hinduism. Vishnu the All-Maintainer is one of the three forms of the supreme deity, the other two being Brahma the Creator and Shiva the Destroyer-Transformer. Of the three, Vishnu embodies the principle of continuity, as he incarnates again and again into life on this earth. There is a remarkable degree of correspondence between the sequence of incarnations and the Western scientific understanding of evolutionary stages. However, the underlying model of the evolutionary process is quite different: in each of his avatars the god performs a task that reestablishes the cosmic balance that had been lost or destroyed.[6]

Between his successive descents to recreate the harmony and balance of the cosmos, Vishnu sleeps on the cosmic water-serpent Sesha, who may symbolize our Milky Way home galaxy. Periods of rest, in which Vishnu dreams, alternate with periods of creative manifestation, in which Vishnu descends, over thousands of millions of generations. These enormous time scales provide another point of correspondence with Western science.

The first in the series of Vishnu's incarnations is Matsya the Fish. On the evolutionary scale this represents the arising of the first vertebrates, which allowed for much greater mobility than is possible for the marine invertebrates. The elongated vertebrate structure, with head at one end and tail at the other, provides what MacLean calls the neural chassis in all subsequent animal forms, including the human.

Vishnu's second incarnation is as a tortoise, representing the amphibian-reptilian breakthrough in evolution and the reptilian brain in the human. The story of the tortoise avatar is connected with the story of the churning of the cosmic ocean of milk, in which gods and demons collaborated to restore their waning powers. Following Vishnu's advice, they used the great axial mountain as the stick and the serpent as the rope, while the tortoise placed himself under the mountain-stick to stabilize it. The violent churning action led to earthquakes and massive destruction of animals, and to an outpouring of poisonous venom from the snake. It is possible to see these as images of violent cosmic upheavals, which we now know were associated with the end of the dinosaur age.

The next incarnation of Vishnu is as Varaha the Boar—corresponding to the mammalian stage of evolution, with its greatly expanded terrestrial mobility and the mammalian limbic brain-system in the human. Here again is a myth of flooding; Vishnu as the boar finds the earth submerged beneath waters and brings her to the surface.

Vishnu's fourth incarnation was as Narasinha, a creature half-lion and half-man in form, a reference perhaps to a period of time (and the layer of our psyche) in which transitional forms and images appear. There are many such in-between forms in the world's mythology: centaurs, mermaids, satyrs, sphinxes, and the like.

With Vishnu's fifth incarnation, Vamana the Dwarf, we come to hominid evolution. The myths of this avatar may be a reference to various protohominids and anthropoid apes that roamed the earth during the ten million years of evolution of humans from primates.

The sixth incarnation is as Parasurama, "Rama of the Axe," a type of heroic warrior who struggled against the excesses of a military caste that had become tyrannical and overbearing.

The seventh incarnation of Vishnu is as Rama, "Rama the Gentle," a noble warrior whose powerful expression of the virtues of courage, devotion, and perseverance inspired the loyalty and admiration of others. Rama had to battle the demon Ravana in order to win back his beloved wife, Sita—a story told at length in the epic *Ramayana*. In his adventures and battles, Rama was always accompanied and aided by the monkey-god Hanuman, the epitome of selfless devotion, loyalty, and courage. Rama and Hanuman symbolize the human and the animal in a relationship of mutual support and friendship.

The eighth incarnation of Vishnu is as Krishna, an avatar on the order of Jesus or Buddha, who performed miracles as a child, danced and made love with the cowgirls of Vrindavan as a youth, and counseled the prince Arjuna as his battlefield charioteer. Here also, he voiced the "Song of God," the *Bhagavad Gita,* the most revered sacred text in the Indian religious mystical tradition. Krishna symbolizes the immortal Self, the *Atman,* in relationship to the human personality symbolized by Arjuna. Krishna (Self) teaches and inspires Arjuna (personality). Both are riding in the chariot, which symbolizes the body, the "vehicle" of human life and consciousness. The myth of the Vishnu avatars implies a view of creation-evolution that starts with animals and goes on to humans and then gods. The ordinary human is midway between beasts and deities, having some characteristics of both. Some versions of the myth claim that Buddha was the next incarnation after Krishna. Other legends refer to Kalki, a form of the god that has not yet appeared but will manifest the divine powers of an avatar in a future age. This series of mythic images portrays not only a history of evolution but also a metaphor for the early human and prehuman layers of our psyche; and indicates the potential of the human being for attaining levels of enlightenment and mastery like gods.

Animals in Folklore, Mythology, and Religion

The pervasiveness of animal imagery and symbolism in our folklore, our mythology and religion, even our everyday thinking and speaking, is quite remarkable. The ecologist and naturalist Paul Shepard, in his extraordinary book *Thinking Animals,* argues that the development of our minds, our thinking, and our language is integrally involved with animals. Our hunter-gatherer ancestors (and children to this day) learned to categorize and name the world of reality through the use of animal imagery:

> As self-consciousness was facilitated by consciousness of the diversity of the world, our barely speaking ancestor found in animals the

tangible objects he needed to embody otherwise slippery ideas. . . .
The different animals not only represented usable images for social
categories and sensed experience, but evoked further thought
about them. . . . The analogical images carried whole trains of connection. . . . The intense drive of the child to learn animal names and
actions may be very old and persistent, even necessary in some way
to the development of speech.[7]

French anthropologist Claude Lévi-Strauss, in *The Savage Mind*,
makes the related point that tribal societies all over the world have
developed elaborate taxonomies of the natural world, classifying and
identifying their botanical and zoological environment. The argument
of this chapter, that we need to integrate wild animal and human consciousness, could be made equally well in terms of the "savage mind,"
the mind-set of the Paleolithic hunter-gatherers that we were for millions for years, and the "civilized mind," the mind-set of the domesti-
cated humans that we have been for a mere ten thousand years.[8]

To get a sense of the ubiquity of animal imagery in our consciousness, we need only consider this partial listing of the enormously varied animal verbs and expressions in everyday speech: *to buffalo, to
bug, to hound, to bullshit, to grouse, to hawk, to crab, to flounder,
to badger, to goose, to parrot, to rat, to duck, to ape, to lionize, to
chicken out, to pussyfoot, to outfox, to worm your way, to clam up,
to eat crow, to ram home, to pig out, to squirrel away, to smell a rat,
to play possum, to cry wolf, to get your goat, to turn turtle, to duck
an issue.* Then we also have *horseplay, bear hug, hangdog, copycat,
leapfrog, monkeyshines, cock and bull, busy bee, black sheep, lounge
lizard, cold turkey, cash cow, lame duck, scapegoat, eager beaver,
snail's pace, stool pigeon, underdog, white elephant, fox-trot, kan-
garoo court, swan song, bookworm, gadfly, red herring* . . . The list
is endless.[9]

For a better understanding of the role of animal imagery in the
process of transformation, we might consider what psychoanalytic

depth psychology has to say about animal symbolism. For Freud, wild animals in dreams usually symbolized passionate impulses of which the dreamer is afraid. Alternatively, the wild animal may represent a person of whom the dreamer is afraid: a wild stallion in a dream may represent the dreamer's feared father.

Western psychodynamic approaches mostly associate the imagery of wild animals with a frightening loss of rational control. However, there is another side of the picture, which suggests that animal imagery might be associated with positive psychological elements. Roberto Assagioli, in his work on psychosynthesis, mentions this possibility. In research carried out by by José Stevens, the occurrence of animal imagery was found to be associated with some aspects of self-actualization (Maslow's notion), especially "valuing" and "inner-directedness."[10]

Jung has also written eloquently of the presence of an "animal soul" in man, in a passage reminiscent of MacLean's theory of brain organization:

> For just as man has a body which is no different in principle from that of an animal, so also his psychology has whole series of lower storeys in which the spectres from humanity's past epoch still dwell, then the animal souls from the age of Pithecanthropus and the hominids, then the "psyche" of the cold-blooded saurians, and deepest down of all, the transcendental mystery and paradox of the sympathetic and parasympathetic psychoid process.[11]

Elsewhere in the same work, Jung speaks of the archetypal figure of the "Old Adam" as representing the primitive man and suggests that "the primitive man has his roots in the animal man (the 'tailed Adam'), who has long since vanished from our consciousness."[12]

Yet Jung never really developed the notion of an archetypal animal figure within us. This is surprising in view of the fact that his anima and animus archetypes derive their names from the Latin word for "breath" or "soul." Marie-Louise von Franz has made the point that "the urge toward individuation is a true instinct, probably the strongest of all. Therefore, it first appears as an animal, a spontaneous instinctual force in the unconscious."[13] Since individuation is an archetypal process, it seems clear we must recognize the archetype of the wild creature in the human psyche as a transpersonal complex on a par with the shadow, the animus, and the anima. This intrapsychic image may take the form of different animals in a person's lifetime, or even half-human, half-animal forms. It is a true alter ego, the animal soul of the ancients, the animal-headed deity, the shaman's "power animal."

The most ancient religious traditions in all parts of the world testify to the numinous charge that animal-spirits or animal-deities had for indigenous societies, whether they were nomadic hunter-gatherers or herders or village farmers. We need only recall the dynamic exuberance of animal imagery in the Paleolithic cave paintings at Lascaux and other sites to realize that identification and communion with the bison, the deer, the bear, the eagle, and other creatures was of central importance in the religious and artistic life of early humans for tens or perhaps hundreds of thousands of years.

Research in archaeomythology, the new discipline created by Marija Gimbutas, has amply documented the close association of the Goddess with animals in the religious imagery of the cultures of Old Europe.[14] Thousands of images have been found of the Great Goddess in mixed anthropomorphic and zoomorphic form: human (mostly female) features with parts of bees, butterflies, deer, bears, hares, toads, turtles, hedgehogs, or dogs. Particularly important in this zoological pantheon of Old Europe was the snake-and-bird goddess, often portrayed as a bird with a long, snakelike neck. This combination of animals is found again later in the Greek winged-serpent (*caduceus*) healing emblem, in the yoga symbolism of Hindu Tantra, and in medieval alchemy.

The creature archetype was expressed very prominently in the spiritual and religious teachings of ancient Egypt. The key to an understanding of the significance of the animal-headed deities is

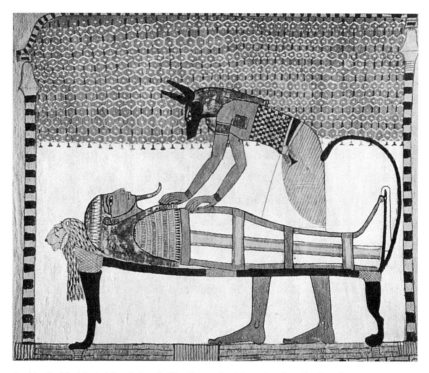

Anubis, the black jackal-headed god of healing and guide to the after-death realm, ministers to the mummy of a deceased pharaoh. (Wall painting, tomb of Siptah, Thebes, 12th-century B.C.E. Egypt)

the concept of the *neter*. According to the research of the French Egyptologist and esotericist R. A. Schwaller de Lubicz, the *neter* is "a principle or an agent of a cosmic law or function," comparable in some ways to the Platonic idea or the Jungian archetype. "All products of the earth, all plants and all animals, were symbols of a totality of vital elements crystallized in each one of them." This inner essence (*neter*) is symbolized by the animals, and also by the gods and goddesses with whom the animals are associated. Each individual human being, each place, also has its own *neter*, which it expresses in a sacred manner.[15]

For example, the qualities of the god Anubis, the guide of souls to the land of the dead, were perceived as manifestations of the same *neter* that is also expressed by the jackal: hence statues of Anubis show him as a man with the head of a jackal. The piercing sight, ferocious fighting spirit, and high-speed flight of the peregrine falcon were considered apt symbolic expressions of the nature and quality of the heroic god Horus, portrayed as falcon-headed. The animal sacred to Ptah, the creator god of artisans and builders, was Apis the bull, symbolic of the vital power of the material world. Those who worshiped Thoth, the scribe and keeper of records, the god of science and wisdom, portrayed him with the head of an ibis, as the original demiurge who hatched the world-egg. Similarly, the ram was associated with Amun; the cat with Bast; the scarab with Khepra, the god of transformations; and the scorpion with Set, who represented the searing heat-forces of the desert.

The significance of such zoomorphic iconography in these religious traditions is that the animal and the divine are linked. In ancient Egypt and in India, people would constantly be exposed to paintings, sculptures, and temple representations that integrate the three realms of animals, humans, and gods. One is reminded constantly of the continuity and interrelatedness of these three realms of beings. The symbols tell us that as humans, we have animal attributes *and* we participate in the divine.

In the mythology of the Judeo-Christian tradition, symbolic animals associated with the sacred also play an important role, though it is less recognized as such.[16] Scattered throughout the Bible are hints of a profound affinity between some of the great religious figures and various animals. Moses, for instance, is portrayed in folklore and some later art forms (such as the statue by Michelangelo) as having horns—a sign of initiatory status among ancient shamans and magi. Similarly, the story of Moses' rod turning into a serpent can be interpreted as a symbolic allusion hinting at Egyptian mystery teachings, involving the central axis, symbolized by the wooden rod, and transformative energy, symbolized by the serpent (kundalini).

Rod-turning-into-serpent parallels the Indian Tantric Yoga symbolism of serpent-rising-up-the-axis.

The story of Job involves a shamanic initiation of the ordeal type. When Job is "tested" by Yahweh, this is like an initiatory sickness, a psychotic dismemberment experience (as described in chapter 5): "My bones are pierced in me in the night season: and my sinews take no rest. I am a brother to dragons and a companion to owls. My skin is black upon me, and my bones are burned with heat." These are the animal visions of sickness, madness, and despair. Yet Job, in his patience and fortitude, knows the way of salvation and has always counseled his family and friends to study and learn from the animals and the earth: "Ask now the beasts, and they shall teach thee; and the fowls of the air, and they shall teach thee; or speak to the earth, and it shall teach thee; and the fishes of the sea shall declare unto thee."[17]

Turning to the New Testament, the story of Jesus being born in a stable, surrounded by animals, is a metaphoric allusion to the fact that each human spirit is born into the body of an animal. The story reminds us: the divine has been born into human form, and the human comes from and lives among animals. Animal, human, and god are synthesized in one sacred, archetypal image. As an adult, Jesus was to counsel his disciples to be "wise (or cunning) as serpents and harmless (or innocent or gentle) as doves" when they went out into the world, where they would otherwise be as "sheep among the wolves."

In later Christian folklore and legends of saints, animals again and again play a significant role. Best known, of course, are the stories of Saint Francis, who called to prayer on different occasions a sheep, a wolf, waterfowl, birds, and a cricket. The historian Lynn White, Jr., in a celebrated essay on the role of Christianity in supporting an exploitative attitude toward the earth, proposed that Saint Francis be declared the patron saint of ecologists. Saint Rose of Lima, a sixteenth-century mystic from Peru, had contests with birds, singing songs of praise to God; flowers turned toward her, insects and birds fell silent and listened when she sang in her garden.

When Job says, "Ask now the beasts, and they shall teach thee," he is echoing the shamanic traditions of indigenous societies. Such cultures, more attuned to the earth and to nature than we are, have always maintained the inner, psychic connection between humans and animals more than we do. Far from being a sign of "primitive" childishness or ignorant anthropomorphizing, this conscious connectedness actually represents a set of survival skills and life-enhancing qualities that we have lost to our detriment. Wise seers and elders of native cultures all over the world have repeatedly told us that our separation from, and neglect of, the animal and plant kingdoms has led to a dangerous and destructive imbalance in the entire biosphere.

American Indian and other native cultures regard animals as potential allies and protectors, to be respected and humbly learned from. Among the Pueblo Indians, for example, animal figures are curers, and the healing societies align themselves with animals such as Bear, Wolf, Eagle, or Mountain Lion. The healers take on names of these animals; they wear their masks and headdress; they dance and chant as these animals, invoking their strength, their healing knowledge. Some tribes refer to the "power animal" that the shaman contacts as a vital aspect of his or her training, with which he journeys in alternate states of consciousness, and that helps him in hunting, in healing, in combat, or in sorcery.

When the shaman goes into an altered state of consciousness and contacts his or her power animal, a definite inner communication takes place, which the trained and experienced shaman can bring back to ordinary reality-consciousness, and use and apply in the work being done. Joseph Epes Brown, discussing the spiritual beliefs and practices of the Lakota, writes:

> The component elements of either dream or vision in which the animals or birds appear may take a number of forms. Among the

> recurring patterns are associations of the animal or bird "spirit-form"
> with the powers of the four directions . . . or men may turn into
> animals, and vice versa, or one species of animals may shift into
> another, or an animal may take on some plant form, which is to
> become the sacred medicine herb. . . . The animal becomes the seek-
> er's guardian spirit, or else the animal entered his body and became
> part of his wakan, his strength.[18]

It is important to realize that when the shaman-healers pray to an animal, or the hunters ask for permission and forgiveness before hunting an animal, it is the spirit of that whole species that they invoke, not individuals—it is Bear, not a bear; Eagle, not a particular eagle. The animals that appear in the visions are spiritual, otherworldly beings, like gods. As they are the deities of the entire species, it is not surprising that they would have a vastly superhuman intelligence and knowledge.

Here, the shamanic traditions converge with the teachings of those esoteric philosophers who speak of the animals having a "group soul," guiding the behavior and destiny of the entire species, through what we call the inherited instincts. Humans appear to be comparatively less locked into instinctive behavior patterns, and the esoteric traditions say this is because we have in addition an individualized soul. However, it is not clear to me that indigenous people or shamanic traditions would go along with such a criterion for distinguishing humans from animals. To some it might seem too much like the same old human superiority complex toward animals, in disguise.

Tales of Animal Transformations

A story that speaks powerfully of the transformation of the human-animal relationship is the Sumero-Babylonian epic of Gilgamesh and his wild friend Enkidu, which dates from the second millennium B.C.E. In the first part of this story, we encounter the theme of the wild man, or savage, who is friend and ally of the human—a theme that has much later literary echoes in Rousseau's "noble savage," in Fenimore

Cooper's Indian stories, and in such inexplicably popular figures as Tarzan, as well as in the Indian myths of Rama and Hanuman. The wild man (or woman) represents the animal side of our nature, the archetype of the wild one within. In the psyche, this figure is our link to nature: when we are out of touch with it, our behavior is likely to be "unnatural" and separative.[19]

Gilgamesh was a legendary warrior king and culture hero of the Babylonians. He was said to be two-thirds god and one-third man—in other words, a powerful male leader in the time of the patriarchal city-states. At the outset, the myth tells us that he dominated and oppressed the people of Uruk, his city. His arrogant behavior so distressed the people of Uruk that they asked the gods for help. The gods in turn brought the request to the Creator Mother Goddess Aruru, who created Enkidu, "to be like him as his own reflection, his second self, stormy heart for stormy heart." This Enkidu had fur all over his body and "long hair like a woman." He was innocent of humankind and lived among the creatures in the field, helping to liberate them from the hunters' snares.

Gilgamesh had had premonitory dreams, so he was expecting his counterpart. When he heard of the strange wild man, he sent a priestess from the temple of Ishtar to initiate Enkidu into the ways of a man with a woman. The woman seduced Enkidu and he made love to her for nine days and nights, according to the story. After that, he could not return to his animal way of life: his former friends shunned him, and he could not keep up with their running. He was introduced to clothing, cooked food, and the ways of humans. He was brought to the city and waged a mighty and prolonged battle with Gilgamesh, in which neither could overcome the other.

This is the story of humankind's unique process of self-domestication: from the wild state to the settled, cultured, farming state. The roaming hunters and gatherers who lived in the wild came to live in the villages and towns. These were our ancestors—we were all wild men and women, and we all still have the wild man or woman within us. For hundreds of thousands of years before we were city-dwelling, farming, pastoralist, technological, literate people, we lived and moved in exquisite communion with the land and the wildlife on which we depended for food.

The story tells about the price that is paid for this separation from nature, for the separation from our own wild nature, our own instinctual nature—the loss of the communication and the communion that we had with the animals and of the knowledge of the land and the plants of the forest. Interestingly, here as in the much later Hebrew Genesis story, it is the woman who plays a key role in this transition, seducing the male into the ways of the world. In the latter story the departure from the paradise garden of oneness with nature is an unmitigated disaster, a "fall from grace," a punishment. But in the Gilgamesh story, the woman is not blamed for her role; rather she is honored, as occurs later in the story.

Enkidu, the wild man, the animal brother to Gilgamesh, comes into the story to prevent the male hero from being too overbearing. Psychologically, this is telling us that if the human (hero) ego is separated from its animal origins, it becomes dominating. When the wild creature, our instinctual nature, is brought into the picture, this minimizes the arrogance of the human, since the two are equally strong. The struggle between the human self and the animal self, we could say, as in this story, ends in a draw. The two men become fast friends and are henceforth inseparable. Psychologically, the human self and the animal self become allies.

Gilgamesh and Enkidu go on many heroic adventures together. The first of these involves cutting down a magnificent cedar forest to get wood for buildings in the city. Here, in the earliest written myth of Western civilization, there is an ominous story of ecological destruction arising from human arrogance. To cut down the cedar forest, they have to confront and battle the giant Humbaba, the guardian spirit

Transformation through the struggle of the wild and the domestic: "a wolf and a dog are in one house, and are afterwards changed into one." (From the alchemical text *The Book of Lambspring*, part of *The Hermetic Museum*, 16th century Germany)

of the forest, appointed by the gods. Gilgamesh wants to do it, saying Humbaba is evil and must be eliminated. Enkidu is reluctant to do so and warns his friend of the danger of upsetting the deities of nature. On the road to the forest, Gilgamesh has several mysterious dreams, which Enkidu interprets as further warnings not to persist in this dangerous venture. When they do fight the forest monster, Gilgamesh naively wants to let him go, but Enkidu's animal cunning saves them both from the consequences of this foolhardiness.

The story is filled with subtle insight into the complexities of the human-animal relationship. The human self, Gilgamesh, in his proud arrogance, projects evil onto nature and casts himself in a heroic conquering role. The animal self, represented by Enkidu, is more respectful and knowledgeable about the wild and more in touch with the spiritual forces of nature. He is also more intuitive and understands dreams and premonitory visions better than the human. The wild instinctual self tries to warn the human, but then he does go along because he has no choice, because he is one with the human—he is the same person. Enkidu has a better understanding of what the real issue is and what really needs to be done to accomplish the objective, whereas Gilgamesh is still more likely to be naively compassionate. This is not a black-and-white story. It's not as if Gilgamesh is all bad and Enkidu is all good. Enkidu is not the "noble savage" either. In comparison to the human, he is more cautious and canny. And because they are together, as one, they both suffer the same fate and consequences.

Sure enough, the cutting down of the forest and the murder of Humbaba, as well as some further gratuitous insults by Gilgamesh, result in the goddess Ishtar being furiously offended. She arranges, through her father the sky god, to send down the monstrous Bull of Heaven, who kills hundreds of people with each bellowing step. This could well be a mythic metaphor for the killer floods that ravaged Mesopotamia (the name means "Between the Rivers") from time to time, particularly after deforestation.

The two heroes kill this monster too, and then the gods decide one of the two has to die, and it is decided it has to be Enkidu, who goes through harrowing death-bed hallucinations. Gilgamesh is overcome with grief and sets out on a journey to find the meaning of life, the prototype of the classic hero's journey (see chapter 11). In the myth, Gilgamesh seeks to find his ancestor, Utnapishtim, called The Faraway, who survived the great flood and knows the secrets of life and death. The journey is long and arduous, like every journey of transformation, and it is a journey of discovery, from which Gilgamesh returns with only a partial answer but as a humbler, wiser, and more peaceful man.

In this magnificent story, Enkidu is the wild man within, the beast friend, the cunning wild one that lives inside the civilized man: he is a guide, an ally, a second self, a kind of double. The epic of Gilgamesh portrays a life of relationship and companionship between the civilized hero-ego and the natural wild man. In the alchemical tradition, this same duality is sometimes symbolized by a struggle between a wild and a domestic animal—for example, a wolf and a dog. The Gilgamesh story speaks of the problems that arise when the human is separated from its animal ancestry, as Gilgamesh was in the time before Enkidu; and how this split can be overcome. The animal, or wild spirit within, becomes a tremendous source of strength and wisdom. Enkidu, the wise and humble wild man, converts Gilgamesh from his posture of arrogant superiority to that of a humble seeker after truth. The mortality of the animal-man, of the instinctual creature-body itself (Enkidu) serves to awaken our spiritual inclinations, motivating us to embark, like Gilgamesh, on the great journey of transformation, the quest for vision and the meaning of life.

In the Chinese Ch'an (Japanese Zen) Buddhist tradition there is a famous series of allegorical images depicting ten stages on the path toward enlightenment, known as the Oxherding pictures, or also as the *Ten Bulls*. Based on earlier Taoist images, they have come down to us with commentaries by the twelfth-century Ch'an master Kaku-an.[20] The first six images in the series all involve the changing relationship of a young man with a wild ox. On one level the animal images can be read as symbolic of the human's unruly instinctual nature, which needs to be tamed and controlled through spiritual practice. Modern commentators often interpret the wild ox as a symbol of the intrinsic (or true) nature of consciousness, and the young oxherd as the ego. Kaku-an's original commentary (given below in italics) stays close to the image, avoiding abstractions. Unsuspected depths of meaning are revealed when we recall that a human being's original nature is actually that of an animal. The images show us the changing relationship between human and animal selves.

1—Searching for the Ox 2—Finding the Tracks

1. **Searching for the Ox.** In the first picture, the young man is shown wandering around in a wild landscape, looking for something. This is the phase of spiritual searching and seeking. The search begins with the perception that something is missing, one is disconnected in some way. *The ox has never been lost—so why search for it? Because the man has turned away from his original nature, he cannot find the animal. He is confused by his sense perceptions, confronted by a maze of crisscrossing paths. He is entangled by craving and fear, and by judgments of good and bad.*

2. **Finding the Tracks.** In the second picture, the young man finds tracks and begins to stalk the wild ox. This is the phase of a spiritual quest where we find useful traces and clues in the written and oral teachings of the spiritual traditions. We realize we are not alone and that there are guidelines. *By inquiring into the teachings, he has gained some understanding. He has learned that all phenomena are the projections of his own mind. He still cannot discriminate truth from illusion, but he has entered the gateway.*

3. **First Glimpse of the Ox.** In the third stage, the man sees the ox for the first time. He has the first direct perception, the first insight

into the true nature of reality. This is the stage of visionary, mystical experience, a fusion of sense perceptions. *When he hears the voice, he knows its source. Through the integrated senses he comes to realize the source and origin—within himself.*

4. **Capturing the Ox.** In this fourth phase, the human and the animal engage in a ferocious struggle (like Gilgamesh and Enkidu). The instinctual original nature pursues its own way with wild ("self-willed") strength. Because of the strength of the emotional reactions coming from the mammalian emotional brain, it is necessary to use disciplined practices to bring about concentration. *The animal has long dwelt in the wilderness and is easily distracted by various attractive stimuli. To overcome the animal's stubbornness, the man must use rope and whip.*

5. **Taming the Ox.** In this fifth phase, the man leads with a rope held gently and the animal follows docilely. As the intention of the human goes toward enlightenment, the rest of our thinking and reacting will also be true. The natural strength of the creature will go along, eventually even without the restraint. *Thoughts follow thoughts, so if the first are true the others will be also. Don't let*

3—First Glimpse of the Ox   4—Capturing the Ox

5—Taming the Ox   **6**—Riding the Ox Home

the animal nature wander off. Delusion and error arise only from subjective doubts.

6. **Riding the Ox Home.** Now the man is riding on the ox, playing his flute, enjoying the sky. He is no longer concerned over controlling his impulses or satisfying his desires. He lets his instincts carry him where he wants to go, naturally. *The struggle is over, there is no concern over gain or loss. He plays his flute, looks at the sky and clouds, and journeys serenely onward.*

With this stage the seeker has arrived at a stage of complete, harmonious integration of the human and animal selves. Original nature and the quest for enlightenment have become one and the same. This is the stage some writers refer to as the centaur stage, the integrated human-animal. The human is the rider, guiding the animal mount so effortlessly and serenely that the animal nature does not even feel controlled—it can go where it wants. Human spiritual intention and animal natural energy are smoothly and joyously fused.

Yet the Oxherding series of pictures continues. In the seventh picture, the man, now a sage, has returned home to his hermitage, and the ox is gone. Even the last distinction between the human and the animal has been dissolved. The last three pictures represent stages of transformation that come after the animal nature has been integrated, and we will discuss them further in chapter 12, "Returning to the Source."

With this, one of the most famous and oft-reproduced maps of the spiritual path, the integration of human and animal consciousness is the key metaphor for almost the entire process, in all its stages. In the Chinese Taoist and Buddhist tradition, from which this "map" stems, spiritual development is not seen, as one so often finds in both Eastern and Western texts, as a matter of overcoming the animal or conquering it. Here spiritual development is seen rather as a process of mutual understanding and support, which leads ultimately to a deeper, more inclusive wholeness.

Unfolding the Tree of Our Life

There rose a tree. O pure transcendence!
O Orpheus singing. O tall tree in the ear!
And all was silent. Yet even in the silence
There was new beginning, beckoning, change.

   —RAINER MARIA RILKE

The tree has been one of humankind's most ancient and universal symbols, appearing in myth, ritual, legend, shamanic initiation, sacred literature, art, and poetry, as well as in the dreams and visions of seekers and seers, both ancient and contemporary. The manifold branching form of the tree has symbolized protection, shade, nourishment, shelter, fertility, birth, regeneration, stability, and continuity. The seemingly miraculous, ever-renewing growth of the tree, from seed kernel to flowering or fruitladen giant, has been seen as a metaphor for the process of human life itself in its growth, development, extension, and unfolding. In relation to transformation, the tree symbolizes the ascent of the mind, or awareness, from the "earth" of matter-nature-body to the "sky" of spirit-god-consciousness. Like trees, we are "rooted in darkness and crowned with light": our being is grounded in the unconscious darkness of matter, grows and extends itself throughout life, and reaches upward into the "higher" realms of consciousness. The tree stands as the preeminent symbol of growth, renewal, and transformation.

Besides its symbolic or philosophical meanings, the tree has a personal emotional significance for many individuals. Most people have very positive feelings and associations connected with trees. In talks and workshops I have asked people to remember a tree that was significant to them growing up: almost universally, people have tree memories that they cherish. Perhaps there was a tree that they hugely enjoyed climbing and looking out from; a tree whose height, strength, color, and solidity they admired; a tree that sheltered them from the sun's heat or from the rain; or a tree whose delicious apples they gathered. Exceptions do exist, of course: for one man, the image of the tree reminded him of being forced by his father to cut down a switch for a beating; for another, there was a tree from which he fell and suffered painful injuries. But by and large, the image of the tree, whether remembered or imagined, is so powerful and numinous that we are clearly dealing with an archetype, in the Jungian sense.[1]

In connection with trees, some people have had experiences of emotional transformation so vivid that the idea of communing with trees or the spirits of trees seems very natural to them. I recall that when I was in the throes of intense grief over the death of my son, I walked under the dome-shaped canopy of a willow and felt a kind of comforting embrace enveloping me, offering solace. Another example is given in Victor Frankl's book on his experiences in a concentration camp. When he asked a mortally ill young woman in the camp how she was able to be so cheerful and positive even though she knew she was dying, she told him about a small tree outside her window that she was able to talk to. "This tree is the only friend I have in my loneliness," she said. Asked if the tree replied to her, she answered, "Yes, it says *I am here, I am here, I am life, eternal life.*"[2] The mythology, literature, poetry, and art of all cultures abound with stories and images of communication and emotional bonding between humans and trees. In shamanic practice, trees and other plants can be "helpers" in healing and therapeutic work.

The unfolding and growth of a tree is a metaphor for the unfolding and growth of an individual, physically, psychologically, and spiritually. It is a metaphor for a process in time, a life in progress. We sense our "roots" in the past and our "crown" as our full future potential. As Jung states, "If a mandala may be described as a symbol of the Self in cross-section, then the tree would represent a profile view of it: the self depicted as a process of growth."[3] We shall explore this metaphor, and the experiential meanings of seed, roots, trunk, branches, leaves, and fruit.

The tree is one of a number of symbols of ascent, a theme that will be discussed from the point of view of its role in shamanic "upper world" journeys. Climbing the tree is structurally analogous to climbing the mountain, the pillar, the tower, the pyramid, or the ladder—all are journeys "upward" in consciousness, to higher states of being. The tree, mountain, pillar, tower, pyramid, ladder, or staff represents the axis of travel, the interdimensional axis that connects ego with Self (in the Jungian terminology). Moving "up" and "down" along this axis is equivalent to changing one's state and level of consciousness. There is also the associated metaphor, from ancient Egypt, of "straightening the pillar"—which symbolizes straightening the axis, so that soul or consciousness can unobstructedly leave the body, or transcend the physical level.

The tree that is climbed in shamanic and mythic lore is not only the individual's axis that links ego to Self, the personal to the transpersonal. In accord with the Hermetic principle of macro/micro correspondence—"as above, so below"—the individual's axis and the world's axis (the *axis mundi*) are aligned or connected. There is a world tree, a world mountain, a world axis, which allows the shamanic or mystic traveler to move through the realms of being and consciousness that exist on the planetary and cosmic level. The image of a world tree axis also exists in a fascinating variant, that of the inverted tree, known in Hinduism and the Jewish Kabbalah.

The tree of life, along with its counterpart, the tree of knowledge, plays a central role in the Judeo-Christian account of the origin of humanity. There were said to be two trees in the Garden of Eden, one giving immortal life, the other giving knowledge of duality and opposites. We have an origin story that associates these trees of paradise with transgression, punishment, loss, and exile—the Fall.

The European alchemists treated this story in a characteristically different way, as a metaphor of transformation. What they called the philosophers' tree (*arbor philosophorum*), or the tree of truth or tree of wisdom, was to be sought *inside*. They taught that for a transformation of consciousness to take place, one had to seek and know this inner tree.

The Tree as a Symbol of Self-Unfoldment

The vision of man as a tree and of the world as a tree is a unitary vision in which all objects, events, processes, and structures are seen as interrelated, ramifying from a center, the axis or trunk of the tree. The historical origin of any process can always be traced to a single seed, whether we are speaking of a tree, a human life, the life of a group, of a culture, of the whole world—or the course of self-transformation. When we compare the seed with the fully grown tree, we are considering a process of unfoldment in time, as Jung stated. We can think of each of us as a tree, or as having a tree, that started from seed and grows and develops, each year adding another "ring."

Seen this way, a tree becomes a symbolic journal, a record of a journey of an individual's growth through time. Psychologists have even used tree drawings as a way of assessing a person's own internal, largely unconscious perception of the stage they have reached in their development. Jung, for example, collected many paintings of trees by patients; these paintings reflected the particular phase and characteristics of their individuation process. Along with mandala drawing, tree drawing is one of the most powerful integrative processes. The exercise of drawing this basic symbol appears to allow other parts of the mind (perhaps older parts of the brain) to express some inner knowing not normally accessible to rational intelligence.[4]

When people are asked to draw a tree, it is as if they are drawing a portrait of their life in process, in both its natural and spiritual aspects. In classes and workshops, I have guided structured imagination exercises based on this theme of the unfolding of the tree of our life. The results of this process, which may involve drawing, painting, and movement, are always highly revealing to the individual. The symbolic meanings that people discover in the tree and its parts—seeds, roots, trunk, branches, leaves, fruit—are also remarkably consistent.

Seed. What, then, is the meaning of the seed of our tree? Each man and woman, each plant and animal, grows from a single seed, as do all forms of life and all growing processes. In a manner that has always impressed the student of nature's ways as nothing short of miraculous, the potential of the entire tree is somehow present in the tiny seed, just as the potential of the fully developed adult human being is present in the fertilized ovum. Everything that we later become, develop, express, or create is present here in potential, in seed-form, in conception.

To tune into this seed-consciousness is metaphorically equivalent to the journey back to the source, to our point of origin. Remember the famous Zen koan, "What was your original face before you were born?" By seeing and holding the original face in mind, we may be able to come to a better appreciation of the wonder and complexity of our existence.

If the tree of our natural human life begins with the biological seed, fertilized in the moment of conception, the treelike process of self-transformation must also begin with a "seed." This seed has been variously called a spiritual seed, or *bindu* in Sanskrit yoga terminology, or the seed of enlightenment, or the seed of God. This seed is the initial idea, the *conception* or concept of transformation. It is the awakening impulse, the illuminating word or compassionate gesture of a teacher or master, that initiates the process of inner growth. For example, in a Buddhist Tantric text we read,

> From the seed of pure compassion
> Planted in the field of man
> Grows the Wish-Fulfilling Tree
> Of the openness of Being.[5]

The Sanskrit term *bindu* is used in both Hindu and Buddhist Tantric Yoga teachings to refer to the concentrated source seed, a kind of subtle psychophysiological essence, the point of origin from which the processes of self unfold. The *bindu* is usually represented pictorially in the center of a mandala, which represents the whole, unified field of consciousness. The *bindu* is the center from which the process of self-transformation is initiated, from which the intrinsic divine nature is manifested. Meister Eckhart expressed it in the following beautiful analogy: "The seed of God is in us. . . . it will thrive and grow up to God, whose seed it is; accordingly its fruit will be God-nature. Pear seeds grow into pear trees, nut seeds grow into nut trees, and God seeds into God."[6]

Roots. The roots of the tree symbolically represent the roots of our life in the genealogical sense: the parents, who provided the genetic base for the physical body, the grandparents, and more distant ancestors—familial, cultural, ethnic, and racial. Tracing our roots all the way back, we come eventually to Adam and Eve, the first ancestors, the original human parents. Our true ancestry goes much further back, however, as shamanic and native cultures know well. We have animal ancestors, evolutionary forebears, earlier branches on the tree of earthly life, branches from which we ourselves branched out— going all the way back through the evolution of species.

It is not uncommon, in such explorations of our origins, to experience another kind of roots: lives in other times and places, which we seem to be able to "remember" as vividly as this one. This strand is recognized as distinctly different from the ancestral one. Each of these past lives, with its joys and sorrows, has left imprints or traces, what Indian philosophers call *samskaras,* in our psyche. Thus the "roots" of our tree are the residues of our past history on this earth, in this lifetime and perhaps in others. In terms of the metaphors of transformation, tracing one's roots is analogous to retracing one's steps to return to the origin. This is the place within from which we originated, and it is the place from which, like trees, we draw strength and nourishment. In Jungian terms, we would say that the "roots" are our links to the creative unconscious, from which we draw up the sap of inspiration and insight.

Trunk. The trunk of the tree is symbolically the developing form and structure of our psyche and our life. The coming up through the ground, into the air and light, corresponds, in a plant or tree, to the moment of birth for animals and humans: for both, it is the first contact with breath and with light. Just as a tree grows in a spiraling fashion, each year adding a ring to the expanding trunk, so do we grow in recurring cycles. Each year's experiences add *samskaras*, memory traces, to the field of our psyche, which to varying degrees leave physical imprints in nerve synapse connections, muscles, blood vessels, tissues, sinews, and bones. The physical form, as the natural philosophers such as Paracelsus well understood, and as modern psychologists following the pioneering work of Reich have rediscovered, develops over time into a visible record of the individual's inner state, patterns of mood, or disposition.

In tree drawings used as projective tests by psychologists, characteristics of the bark of the tree are seen as indicative of an individual's sense of his or her periphery, the "skin" of the persona, as it were. Feelings of needing a tough or rough exterior manner might be expressed in rough, thick bark; or feelings of being exposed and vulnerable to penetration may be expressed in bark that looks faint and thin. It has even been observed that people drawing trees will indicate a physical abnormality of some kind, resulting from injury or accident, at a height on the tree corresponding to the age at which the injury or accident occurred.

The painter Paul Klee compared the artist to a tree, in language that applies equally well to anyone engaged in a process of self-transformation.

> From the roots the sap rises into the artist, flows through him and his eyes. He is the trunk of the tree. Seized and moved by the force

> of the current, he directs his vision into his work. Visible on all
> sides, the crown of the tree unfolds in space and time. . . . And
> so with the work. . . . In his appointed place in the tree trunk, he
> gathers what rises from the depths and passes it on. He neither
> serves nor commands, but only acts as a go-between. His position
> is humble.[7]

Here the tree is a metaphor of the creative artistic process and of the process of ex-pression, of bringing something forth from within. The individual is the medium, the bridge, the trunk that connects the matrix of the creative unconscious to the light of full expression.

Branches. The branches of the tree represent our self-extensions and relationships: the qualities, traits, characteristics, skills, and abilities we have developed, which serve to relate us to the world and to other people. With our branches we reach out, we extend ourselves; we make contact; we communicate and interact, both physically, socially, and interpersonally. A person's branching structure may be profuse, varied, and rich in associated meanings; or it may be sparse and simple, reflecting the relative simplicity of his or her personality structure and relationships.

The "branches," then, are our major "parts." Trees standing together seem to be relating and communicating through their branches. We can examine each of our "branches" and determine whether they are flowering and producing fruit or whether they have ceased to grow and have atrophied. A couple I know described to me a (physical) tree pruning operation they undertook in their yard. This event became metaphorical and psychological when they started to imagine that the dead branches they were pruning were the "dead" parts of their relationship that they desired to get rid of or change.

Leaves and flowers. The leaves and flowers of the tree are the thoughts and images of our mind. As the health and beauty of the leaves and flowers are a function of the nourishing sap rising up from below under the influence of light and warmth, so, we may suggest, the health and vitality of our thoughts and images are a function of how unobstructed their connectedness is to the instinctual nature "below," and of the mental and emotional acceptance and support they receive from "outside." The association of leaves and petals with the realm of ideas is also implicit in the Indian yoga symbolism of the "thousand-petaled lotus" chakra at the crown of the head.

In art therapy, using tree drawings, depressed individuals will sometimes draw bare, or even dead, trees, thereby reflecting an inner feeling of noncreative barrenness or spiritual impoverishment. Normally and naturally, ideas and concepts seem to arise, flourish, and drop out of our minds in much the same way as leaves grow, change colors, and drop off a tree. Here is another way in which both trees and humans practice "dying daily": it is good for us to remember and learn again and again that the little death of some idea of ours, of some project, plan, or vision, is not at all equivalent to the death of our identity. The tree in nature and the tree of the mind both have valuable lessons of nonattachment to teach us.

Fruits. The fruits of the tree represent the creative products that we bring forth, the results and output of our growing, self-extending activity in the world. They are the "fruits of our actions," by which we are known. They contribute to the nourishment, welfare, and delight of our fellow human beings and of all living creatures. The creative impulses begin deep inside the unconscious parts of the psyche; they then expand and develop and are eventually brought forth. "The apples in my mind are ripening," my eight-year-old son remarked one day to his grandmother apropos of nothing in particular. He was expressing a warm and exuberant mood.

Since the evolutionary function of fruit is that of a package of seed that will propagate the species, perhaps one of the functions of creative expression (symbolic fruit) is to carry the seed of enlightenment, the seed of growth and spirituality, to an environment that is receptive to these "seeds." A Buddhist text refers to "the perfect tree of unitary mind," whose "flower, compassion, bears the fruit of being-with-others."[8] Art, in other words, can be an inspiration to spiritual development and transformation: not only does it describe the process, it can stimulate and facilitate it. Artists and creative people, who "put out" a great deal of creative, inspirational energy, are involved in externalizing something of value to others. They correspond metaphorically to fruit-bearing trees.

Climbing the Tree, Straightening the Pillar

Stories of shamans and mythic heroes climbing trees are found in native cultures all over the world. In many of the shamanic societies, particularly in central and northern Asia, the shaman describes an ascent of a tree in a dream or in a vision; this ascent leads to his or her obtaining a leaf or fruit for healing or divination.[9] The wood of the particular tree seen in the vision is used to make the shaman's drum; this links the tree to the drumbeat that serves to induce the trance, or "journey." Hallucinogenic mushrooms, such as *Amanita muscaria,* which grow in association with birch trees in Siberia, were also used by some shamans as part of their initiation or practice.[10] "Climbing the tree" is a variant of the initiatory altered-state journey, in which the shamanic practitioner explores other realms of consciousness. "Tree climbing" is a type of upper-world journey and thus parallels magical flight and other ascensional metaphors (climbing the mountain, pillar, ladder, and so on).

The tree that is climbed in shamanism is variously said to have nine, twelve, sixteen, or (most often) seven notches or branches on which the vision seeker ascends. These "branches," which parallel the rungs of the ladder, the steps of the ziggurat pyramid, or the layers of cloud, symbolize the levels or planes of consciousness through which the shaman ascends—the various "heavens" of his or her culture's cosmology. The Altaic Siberian shaman sings:

I have climbed a step, . . .
I have reached a plane, . . .
I have broken through the second ground,
I have climbed the second level
See, the ground lies in splinters.[11]

This notion of levels that are separated by branches or planes is consistent with the idea, previously discussed, of veils, borders, or gaps between levels of consciousness.

The shaman's "tree," then, is the interdimensional axis that connects different levels or dimensions of consciousness. In Jungian psychology, this is also the axis that connects ego and Self. The shamanic ascent of the tree is a vision-seeking inner journey, undertaken while the physical body lies in a trance or coma. Like other mystical, shamanic, or mythic voyages, it has three main parts: the *departure* from the everyday plane of reality, and ascent to higher planes; the *arrival* at the top, crown, or summit, where a healing leaf or other substance is given or a vision offered; and the *return*, the descent back to the ordinary world.

Shamanic mythology describes the tree that is climbed as a world tree, heaven tree, or cosmic tree, at the top of which may live a ruling deity. This parallels the idea of the *axis mundi*, the world axis, and the Mount Meru, the central cosmic mountain of the Indian yoga tradition. These inner explorers are saying that the individual axis is aligned with the world axis, the microcosmic tree with the macrocosmic. As Eliade states,

By climbing up the seven or nine notches of the ceremonial birch tree, or simply by drumming, the shaman sets out on his journey to heaven, but he can only obtain that rupture of the cosmic planes which makes his ascension possible or enables him to fly ecstatically through the heavens because he is thought to be already at the very centre of the world.[12]

The individual and the world are linked by a relationship of micro-macro correspondence, by analogy and coincidence. By going to my center, my central axis or inner tree, I can also experience the central axis, pole, or pillar of the world—the cosmic hub, the navel of the world (*omphalos*).

In many cultures, in addition to this ritual ascent of the cosmic tree, there are myths that account for human birth as a descent, a coming down the tree, a traveling from higher realms to the physical world. In Sumatra, for example, there is the myth of *djambu baros,* the heaven tree, which has leaves of different personal qualities on it. The individual soul picks several of these leaves as it descends to earth for incarnation. In other Asiatic societies, the souls of unborn children perch on the branches of the cosmic trees—and shamans go there to find them, if necessary.

In pre-Christian Hawaiian mythology, when a person dies he or she comes to a tree, half of which is dead and brittle while the other is alive and green. Around the tree young children are playing; they instruct the deceased to ascend the tree on the dead side and then re-descend on the living side. This and similar myths point to the idea that the soul's initiatory ascent, at death and in special trance states (climbing the tree), is somehow a reversal of the descent into form, the birth into earth (descending the tree). The myth of Osiris as a metaphor for Spirit being first imprisoned and then released, as well as scattered, also has a profound connection with the tree of life motif. We remember that in that story, Osiris is tricked by his evil brother, Set, and locked in an intricately carved wooden coffer, which is thrown into a river. Floating down the river, the coffer eventually comes to land, where a tree grows through and around it. Finally the tree, with the god still in it, becomes the wooden framework of the house of a local king—until the goddess Isis releases her consort and brother from his vegetative imprisonment.

Straightening the djed pillar of Osiris: aligning the central vertical axis for the soul's passage into the land of the dead. (From the tomb of Seti I, Abydos, 13th-century B.C.E. Egypt; reproduced from *HerBak Egyptian Initiate,* by Isha Schwaller de Lubicz, Inner Traditions, 1978)

In chapter 3, I discussed the interpretation of this metaphor in terms of esoteric psychology. Spirit, symbolized by Osiris, becomes enveloped, on the way "down" into material incarnation, in four stages of form, or body: the mental body, represented by the wooden chest; the astral or emotional body, symbolized by the flowing river; the etheric or perceptual body, connected to the treelike sensory nervous system; and the physical body, the built house where we live most of the time. Thus, according to this myth, there is something akin to a tree inside and throughout the human psyche and nervous system.[13]

This tree inside the human psyche and body is represented in Egyptian sacred temple art: we find there the frequent portrayal of a secret ritual referred to as the "straightening of the *djed* pillar." This pillar looks like a tree trunk with its branches cut off—which makes it look like a human vertebral column as well. Sometimes two human figures (presumably priests) are shown pushing and pulling the pillar into an upright position. Sometimes ceremonial cloths are offered to or draped over the *djed*, and the face of Osiris may also be painted on the pillar. In some depictions, the head of the god is mounted on the top of the pillar.

Erich Neumann has pointed out that the *djed* pillar was composed of two segments: an upper segment, corresponding to a treetop and to the neck and head of Osiris; and a lower segment, corresponding to the trunk and base of a tree and to the back and sacrum of Osiris. When a person died a small golden *djed* replica was placed around his neck and the following prayer was uttered: "Rise up, O Osiris, thou hast thy backbone. O still Heart, thou hast the ligatures of the neck and head. Place thyself upon thy base."[14]

The straightening of the *djed* pillar, the alignment of its upper and lower segments, may be taken to symbolize the union and integration of the generative with the cerebral, the physical with the spiritual, the "lower" with the "higher." Straightening the physical vertebral axis, as in Rolfing or in osteopathic craniosacral alignment, is itself a healing process.[15] Moreover, since the *djed* pillar also represents the interdimensional axis, straightening it meant that the "lower" world of the material body could be connected with the "higher" worlds of spirit.

Within this framework of belief, placing the miniature *djed* on the dying person's heart center was believed to stimulate the straightening of the axis and thus the release of the soul from the body at the moment of death. In the Egyptian Book of the Dead, Horus the Sun-God, who is the son of Osiris and therefore represents his resurrection, rises from the *djed* pillar placed between the mountains of sunset (the past) and sunrise (the future). As Erich Neumann says, "The *djed* is therefore the material body that gives rise to the sun soul."[16]

The pillar, like the tree, symbolizes the physical body—specifically the vertebral-cerebro-spinal axis of the body—as well as symbolizing the energy-center axis that connects us with the subtler, "higher" dimensions of our being. In the Indian teachings of Tantra and Hatha Yoga, the vertical alignment, or straightening, of this double axis is regarded as essential to the processes of meditation and transformation. It provides the basis for the alignment of the "inner bodies" and for the "upward" and "downward" movement of awareness through the levels of our being.

Some colloquial expressions in current American usage appear to reflect the idea of an axis of some kind in our psyche—an axis that can be altered or distorted. For example, we may tell ourselves or another to "straighten up," to "get your act straight," or to "be straightforward"; these all refer to desirable psychological conditions or changes. By contrast, when we wish to refer to an unpleasant state, one that should be changed or corrected, we might speak of a "distorted attitude" or "twisted mentality." More temporarily, we could get "bent out of shape" by receiving some insult or offense; or someone could abruptly "be beside himself " with rage or emotional shock.

The latter expression in particular seems to imply that we can become "split" vertically, dissociated as well as misaligned.

The World Tree and the Inverted Tree

As already described, the individual tree that the vision seeker ascends is, in shamanic traditions, juxtaposed with the world tree, the world axis. The world axis is in the world, as the individual axis is in the body. And even though the world has the form of a rotating sphere and the human body has quite a different shape, they both have a central vertical axis. This is an example of the principle of macro-micro correspondence or isomorphism between person and world.[17] By ascending the levels of the individual dimensional axis, the shamanic traveler is simultaneously gaining access to other worlds.

Thus because the tree-climbing visionary is able to ascend the world tree, not just the individual tree, great visions that affect all of humanity have been recorded by such seers. This is how Black Elk, the great visionary elder of the Oglala Sioux, recorded his vision of the cosmic tree:

> Then I was standing on the highest mountains of them all, and round about me was the whole hoop of the world. . . . I was seeing in a sacred manner the shapes of all things in the spirit. . . . And I saw the sacred hoop of my people was one of the many hoops that made one circle, wide as daylight and as starlight, and in the center grew one mighty flowering tree to shelter all the children of one mother and father. And I saw that it was holy.[18]

Here the world tree is seen as the unifying center from which all forms of life on the earth, all humans of different races, all animals, plants, and elements, branch out: all of creation is held together through this *axis mundi*. The cosmic tree is often associated with a square-based pyramid or a mountain, such as the Indo-Tibetan Mount Meru. It is also associated with a circular or spherical form, such as a mandala.

Perhaps the shamans and seers of native cultures could perceive the spherical form of the planet Earth in their visions, even without the benefit of scientific information. The notion that the "world tree" is literally the axis of the globe is supported by the fact that in some mythologies it is called the "pole" and is seen as extending or attaching to the Sun or to the North Star. In ancient Chinese Taoism, it was called *t'ai chi t'u*, "the great ridge-pole" or "supreme beginning." It was regarded (accurately) as the rotational hub that lets the yang (daylight) and the yin (night darkness) appear in cyclic alternation.

A similar duality of the tree symbolism is found in Navaho sacred art, where there are sand paintings that depict the "giant corn plant." In the stalk of this giant corn plant is the "pollen path" or "blessing way," shown as the central axis of the corn plant. A male zigzag lightning stroke is shown descending on the right, and a female curved rainbow descends on the left. This parallels the left-female/right-male polarity of the yogic and alchemical traditions. At the top of the tree is a blue bird, symbolizing transcendence and the release of free inspiration and insight.

Eagles and other birds are found in association with the top of the world tree in many cultures. These birds are regarded as the observers and messengers of the gods; for the individual they symbolize insight, wisdom, and transcendence (flying). The other animal most frequently associated with the tree of life is the serpent or dragon, which is usually associated with the base, or root, of the tree. Tantra Yoga has the image of the kundalini serpent coiled around the root chakra, from which it rises in serpentine motion to the crown chakra. For the individual, the serpent symbolizes generation, regeneration, and the instinctual knowledge associated with the reptilian. Among mammals, the deer and the horse in particular have been found in association with the tree of life.

The most elaborate symbolism of the world tree is found in the ancient Nordic-Germanic myth of *Yggdrasil*. The name means "steed

249

of Odin," which points to its role in shamanic travel. Nine worlds are arrayed along this axis, of which the one in the middle, *Midgard,* is our ordinary world of humans, animals, and plants. Other worlds are the domains of the gods, the giants, the dwarves, and the elves. The roots of the tree descend into *Hel,* the underworld, where the dead reside. At the foot of the tree are found the three Norns, ancient goddesses who determine the fates of gods and humans. Also at the foot of the tree is Mimir's well, or the well of remembrance, which provides one who drinks from it knowledge of her or his origin and the origin of the world. In one key myth, Odin the knowledge-seeking shaman god hangs himself from the tree Yggdrasil for nine days and nights, in a voluntary self-sacrifice.[19]

The Nordic myth of *ragnarök,* the "twilight of the gods," is that the earth trembles as the tree shakes, and the roots come loose from the constant gnawing of the giant serpent coiled around its roots. This relentlessly gnawing serpent symbolizes the destructive forces of time, entropy, decay, and degeneration. The great tree, however, continues, ever renewing itself and nourishing all life. After one generation of gods dies, or fades away, a new generation of gods and humans will arise again, according to the visions related in the *Eddas.*

This kind of end-time vision, of a world falling apart and becoming uprooted, can occur in the course of a transformative process, as is shown in the following account written by me of an LSD experience, which also included interior yogic energy work:

> I felt as though deep-seated, very old complexes were being loosened, released, and discharged into open awareness, in a manner that felt like the uprooting of deeply tangled root systems. As these sick and decaying roots were being pulled up, analogously to a kind of weeding-out process, I felt my body shaking, going through mini-convulsions. Since my awareness and my sense of identity were "in" my body, it felt like the whole environment—my whole "world," in fact—was shaking and convulsing. I felt that in this upheaval, a

whole era in my life and in the life of the world was coming to an end. The rule of the old gods was ending.

This kind of experience suggests one possible psychological basis for the myth of the twilight of the gods: it represents the ending and dying of the old religious values and beliefs, including beliefs about the stability and continuity of the world.

A fascinating variant of the cosmic tree symbolism occurs in the ancient Indian Vedas and Upanishads and in the Jewish mystical Kabbalah. In both of these traditions, the tree is described as having its roots above, in heaven, in the Infinite, and extending its branches downward into the world of sense objects and matter.

> With the root above and the branches below stands this ancient fig tree. That indeed is the pure; that is *Brahman*. That, indeed, is called immortal. In it all the worlds rest and no one ever goes beyond it. (*Katha Upanishad*)[20]
>
> Now the Tree of Life extends from above downwards, and is the sun which illuminates all. (*Book of Zohar*)[21]

The symbolism of the inverted tree declares that the true origin, root, and source of our life is the One Spirit—called *Atman-Brahman* in the Vedanta, and *Ain Soph,* the Eternal One, in the Kabbalah. In this model, the downward-extending branches are our sense perceptions and emotional desires, through which we become attached to terrestrial nature. In India, the banyan tree, which sends down long aerial branches that form new roots in the ground, became a paramount symbol of the power of sense-based attachments. The idea that our source or origin is "above," in the "higher" world, agrees with previously mentioned myths describing birth as a descent from the world tree.

The Kabbalistic Tree of Life, also called the Sefirothic Tree, is pictured as an array of three vertical axes, with ten circles aligned on them: these represent the *sefirah,* the emanations, divine powers, that bring cosmic life energy from Infinite Source down into the world. The tree diagram is also applied to the human psychic constitution; and when it is laid over the human body, we have a close analog to the Indian chakra system. The Indian system, has one central channel (*sushumna*) and two serpentine side channels, one solar-right and one lunar-left. The Kabbalistic analogy with the yogic chakra system is seen further in the fact that the topmost *sephiroth* on the central axis, which is situated at the crown of the head in the human body, is known as *Kether* (Crown); this is also the place of the "thousand-petaled lotus," or crown chakra, in Indian yoga.

We can see that the idea of an inverted tree, rooted "above," representing the human body and consciousness situated in this world, is a natural and meaningful elaboration of the basic themes behind the Tree of Life symbolism. In the Kabbalah, as in Tantra Yoga, there exists a subtle and sophisticated psychology and technology for the transformation of human consciousness—and the tree or axis symbolism is central to both of these systems.

The Tree of Life and the Tree of Knowledge

Tree symbolism, of course, plays a major role in the Hebrew Old Testament, as well as in the Christian New Testament. In the Book of Genesis account, two trees stand in the center of the Garden of Eden, and four rivers flow out from the center. In the vision of the Book of Revelation, the "river of the water of life, sparkling as crystal," flows from the throne of God; a tree of life stands on either side of it, bearing twelve kinds of fruit and having leaves "for the healing of nations."

Other ancient cultures also have the image of two trees that play a central role in myths of the origin of humanity. Instead of the Judeo-Christian tree of the knowledge of good and evil, certain myths have a tree of wisdom or a tree of truth. The focus on the dualism of moral judgment that has literally "bedeviled" the Judeo-Christian

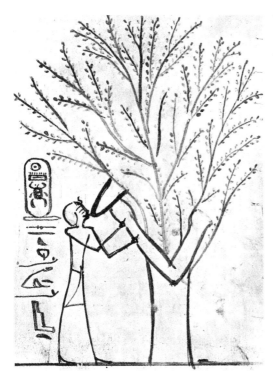

The Tree of Life giving nourishment: Isis as Tree Goddess suckling the human being. (From the tomb of Tuthmosis III, Thebes, 15th-century B.C.E. Egypt)

civilization is expressed in the original emphasis on "knowledge of good and evil." In other ancient religions, particularly those that worshiped the Goddess, the tree, the serpent, and the woman were regarded quite differently: it was through them that men were taught the mysteries of death, regeneration, and longevity. Only in the biblical account is the tree taboo and the serpent the instigator of sin.

It has long been recognized that the books of the Bible are actually composites of several different texts, written at different times. Recent research by feminist scholars have suggested that the earliest layers contain elements of a tree-serpent-Goddess religion, centering around the Canaanite goddess known as Astarte, Ashtoreth, or Asherah. Numerous biblical passages refer to *asherim,* goddess images set up in tree shrines, which the Israelites were exhorted to destroy.[22] According to these revised interpretations, the story of the woman succumbing to temptation by the serpent, then in turn leading the man into sin, is a priestly overlay, imposed in order to support the newly established monotheism and patriarchy.

We can surmise that in the original Canaanite Goddess-tree-serpent cult, as in other ancient Near Eastern Goddess religions, the tree of life had to do with nourishment, healing, and longevity. The woman is the priestess who provides the initiation into the evolutionary wisdom of the serpent, the knowledge of survival and regeneration. But in the account that has come down to us as the Bible, worship of or reverence expressed toward the Goddess, the tree, or the serpent was prohibited and punished by God.

God forbids Adam and Eve to eat of the tree of knowledge, because "on the day that you eat from it, you will surely die." The serpent, however, tells Eve that "of course you will not die . . . your eyes will be opened and you will be as gods, knowing both good and evil."[23] Thus, the fruit of the tree of knowledge causes Eve and Adam to awaken, to open their eyes, to gain awareness and insight into their true nature. The serpent, it turns out, is right—at least in part: Adam and Eve do not die from the fruit, but they do become aware of their sexuality, experience shame, and are subsequently expelled from Eden.

God is apparently concerned that they might now "take from the tree of life also, and live forever."[24] This strange statement, attributed to God, supports the connection of the tree of life with ancient teachings of regeneration and longevity. (The very long lives of the biblical patriarchs, including Adam, who reportedly lived 930 years, also support this notion.) After Adam and Eve depart from the Garden of Eden, they have to gain their bread "by the sweat of [their] brow," instead of being able to eat the abundant fruit of the garden effortlessly. In other words, they have to learn to survive in a much harsher physical world, with mortality an ever-present threat—"dust you are and to dust you shall return."

Origin myths such as these have many levels of meaning and are subject to widely divergent interpretations. At one level, as indicated,

The Inverted Tree of Knowledge: rooted above in the brain, the human nervous system extends downward and ramifies outward.

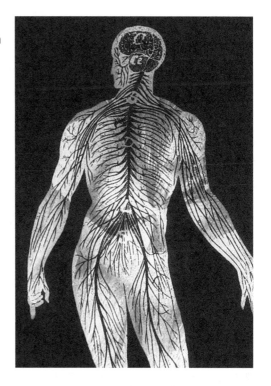

the story of the expulsion from Eden may reflect the historical impo-sition of Hebrew monotheism and patriarchy on the Goddess-cen-tered cultures of the Fertile Crescent. Going further back into the prehistoric past, the exit from paradise may reflect memories of the Neolithic domestication transition. Or even further back in the evolu-tionary archives, the myth may reflect the transition our aquatic ape ancestors made from a nutrient-rich wetlands environment to more demanding conditions on dry savannahs, where the hominid species finally established itself.[25]

In esoteric interpretations found in the Gnostic and Hermetic literatures, the descent or departure from Eden is a metaphor for the descent into physical incarnation, down from the spiritual level of being-consciousness called Eden (or Paradise, or the Garden, or Heaven, or the Pure Land).[26] According to such interpretations, the tree of life symbolizes the interdimensional central axis, with its energy centers and branching channels, that is our connection with the realms of spirit and hence immortal life. This would explain the reference in Genesis to the idea that by eating of this tree, Adam and Eve would "become like gods." The fruit of this tree is the divine energy essence, the "food of immortality," variously referred to in other traditions as the ambrosia of the gods, the divine soma juice, or the amrita, the "drink of immortality."

If the tree of life is the interdimensional axis connecting us with the angelic and spiritual realms, the tree of knowledge corresponds to the cerebrospinal nervous system, which connects us with the dualistic world of sense perceptions. The nervous system is clearly a treelike branching structure, the function of which is to give us knowledge of the physical world of matter. Sense perception ("eating the fruit of the tree") is inherently linked with dualistic judgments—of what is pleasurable and what painful, what is nourishing and "good" to eat

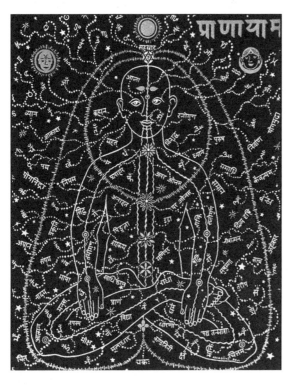

The Tree of Life: cosmic life-energy is earthed into the human form through the central vertical axis (*sushumna*), the energy centers (*chakras*), and the current lines (*nadis*). (From a Tantra Yoga diagram, 19th-century India)

and what is toxic and to be rejected as "bad" or "evil." Especially potent among the objects of the senses are of course sexual stimuli, which awaken the sex centers in the reptilian layers of the brain. The wisdom of the serpent includes, among other things, the "knowing" of sexuality, of reproduction and survival.

Each human being, following in the footsteps of Adam and Eve, descends into physical bodily incarnation from the higher, spiritual plane, and in doing so is plunged necessarily into the realm of dualities and of mortality. This is not, however, a punishment for disobeying God's word, in the esoteric interpretation. It is, rather, the inevitable consequence of the decision to incarnate, to descend into physical, human form.

Alchemical vision of the "philosophic paradise": Eve and Adam receive the fruits of wisdom from Melusina, the bird-serpent goddess descending from the Tree of Life. (From George Ripley's *Scrowles,* 15th-century England)

Jesus Christ spoke of the serpentine wisdom initiation when he counseled his disciples to "be wise as serpents and gentle as doves." According to Christian tradition, Christ was the "second Adam," who completed the cycle begun by the first Adam. The first Adam committed the "original sin," which brought us into mortality and separation from God; Christ, the second Adam, brings redemption, rebirth, and union with God. In developing these parallels further, we see that Christ's cross was identified with the original tree in the Garden. The legend of the Holy Rood arose; according to this legend, some wood from the tree of life was taken out of Eden and many generations later was used to make the cross of the crucifixion.[27]

The association of the tree of life with the processes of spiritual transformation and initiation—found in the mythic-sacred traditions of shamanism and of ancient Egypt, Mesopotamia, Scandinavia, and India, as well as in the world religions of Judaism, Buddhism, Islam, and Christianity—is continued and developed in the Hermetic-alchemical philosophy. Because the alchemists were concerned with nature as a living, divinely infused interrelated totality and with the transmutation and spiritualization of matter, their use of the tree symbol plays some interesting variations on the orthodox Judeo-Christian version.

There are alchemical drawings that depict the tree of life with Hermes Trismegistos, the sage and master, standing beneath it, instead of Adam and Eve; this Hermes is shown both as old man (*senex*) and as youth (*puer*). Here the symbolism points to the regenerative potency of the tree. Another alchemical text offers the following recipe for transformation: "Take the tree and place in it a man of great age. The old man does not cease to eat of the fruit of that tree, until he becomes a youth."[28] In other words, by tapping into our inner tree of life and eating its fruit, we can overcome or reverse the processes of aging and dying. Elsewhere, the fruit of the tree is likened to *manna*, the bread of life, and to the healing *panacea*, the divine tincture of immortality.

In George Ripley's *Scrowles*, an alchemical text quoted extensively by Jung, there is a picture of a tree with a tree-spirit figure known as a *Melusina*, who is part woman, part bird, and part serpent. The Melusina is descending from the tree, while a human male is climbing up the tree to meet her halfway. This image is in striking contrast, as Jung points out, to the biblical story of Adam and Eve, who are led into error and sin through the tree, the serpent, and the woman, and who try to hide themselves. The image is more consonant with the iconography of the ancient Goddess religions, in which the serpent-woman was revered and worshiped as the guardian and teacher of sacred natural wisdom.[29]

Sometimes the tree in alchemy is described as being "in the sea" and likened to a tree of branching coral. I suggest here that the "tree in the sea" refers to the vegetative (autonomic) nervous system— which is embedded in the fluid matrix of blood vessels and lymphatic and endocrine systems. These three systems together constitute what alchemists called our inner sea, the continuum of fluids within our organism. Here, alchemical symbolism communicates experiential physiology: organic processes and structures that were observed by the alchemical experimenters to be taking place in the "retort" of the human body.

In dreams, meditations, or visions, people not infrequently envision a treelike structure in their head or branches coming out of their head. Jung, in his essay "The Philosophical Tree," reproduced a number of paintings of trees done by patients, many of which showed a tree emerging out of a woman's head; this is an image also found in alchemical graphics.[30] It is suggestive of a tree of mind or of ideas and is congruent with the expression "to explore the ramifications of an idea."

Another alchemical inner-tree vision occurred in an altered state of consciousness induced by the empathogenic substance MDMA. A forty-year-old woman described her experience as follows:

> Strong sense that my head is expanding . . . feel like there's a small
> tree in my head. R [the guide] must see this tree. I am a tree and he
> sees it. Tree in my head expands . . . branches in my head and arm;
> torso becomes trunk; legs and feet become roots . . . combination
> of old roots and new branches . . . I'm attempting to integrate the
> old and the new.[31]

One gets a strong sense here of the tree image as an integrative psychic structure, a thought form or symbol that can hold the many diverse parts and aspects of the psyche, including ideas, feelings, perceptions, and sensations, in a unitive form or pattern.

For the alchemists, then, the tree of knowledge has little to do with the making of judgments—separating good and bad; it is more a symbol for inner "seeing," for insight into the inner structure of things, for seeing how everything hangs together. To them, and to those who follow their work today, the tree symbol is a vast reservoir of imagery and psychic energy. The "tree of the philosophers" is, to the alchemist, the axis of the transformational work, the unfolding *opus*. I find it highly significant that the Old English root word for "tree" and for "truth" is the same: *treow*. Perhaps this means that you are "straight" as a tree when you speak the truth.

From an elemental point of view, the alchemists' tree of truth and transformation is both watery and fiery: watery through its connection to fluids, to the humors and hormones, the emotional nature; and fiery through its expression of electrical life energy, vitality, and regenerative potency. Typically, the dual nature, as fire and water, was also portrayed in alchemical art as the sun-moon tree; sun was always above on the right of the tree, moon usually above on the left.

Alchemical experimenters, students of the art of transmutation of matter, observed the operations in their retorts—in both the outer and the inner retort (read "body")—the way a clairvoyant seer might observe a crystal ball or a geomantic pattern of lines. In the visions and images seen, they were advised to watch for the appearance of the tree in the retort and to contemplate its growth. The vision of the tree was considered a highly desirable and auspicious sign.

Instead of bearing conventional fruit, alchemical or vision trees are apt to be hung with many jewels and precious metals. These symbolize the gems of understanding and insight we have discovered, the pearls of wisdom we have been fortunate enough to find and express creatively. Hence, the seeming hyperbole of praise often showered on the tree in alchemical literature. A text attributed to the Jewish Gnostic adept Simon Magus, who was a contemporary of Jesus and his disciples, states, "Of all things which are both concealed and manifested, . . . the supercelestial fire is the treasure house, as it were, a great tree . . . from which all things are nourished."[32]

This is none other than the great, multidimensional tree of life energy and wisdom, the prime foundation and axis of our physical and spiritual life. This is indeed the tree of life and of truth, whose roots are nourished in the soil of our "earth," the physical ground of our being, the awakening darkness of matter; and whose crown reaches up to the heights and absorbs into itself the radiating energy essence of light, awareness, and Spirit.

Journey to the Place of Vision and Power

> Not I, nor anyone else can travel that road for you.
> You must travel it by yourself. It is not far, it is within reach.
> Perhaps you have been on it since your were born, and did not know.
> Perhaps it is everywhere—on water and on land.
>
> —WALT WHITMAN[1]

The sense of our movement through the ever-changing flux of life's events as a journey is certainly an almost universal human experience. Our life is a journey, with a beginning, middle, and end; it is a going out, extending into the world, and a returning, or settling down. The process of self-transformation is a journey within that journey, a branching out from the main trunk, a new growing. The literature of mysticism and mythology the world over speaks of transformation as a journey to another land, along a river, up a mountain, through a wilderness, into the depths of the earth, or searching for a hidden castle of marvels. The experience of change and the experience of wandering, of traveling, are very similar. In German, "to change" is *wandeln;* "to wander" is *wandern.* As we wander we change. The pilgrim who arrives at the sacred place is not the same person who left home. The seeker who returns to her family or tribe, bringing gifts of power, healing, or vision, is a transformed individual.

This metaphor is employed in all the spiritual traditions. The ancient Chinese sages spoke of *Tao* as "the way" or "the track." It is "the way that cannot be told," the way of heaven and earth, that humans are to follow. This Tao-way we cannot perceive; we can only see its tracks and traces in nature—in patterns of flowing water, in swirls of wood, lines of stone, curling smoke, the veins of leaves and

an involuntary journey, one for which he had no preparation and for which he finds no familial or cultural support. As R. D. Laing has written:

> In our present world, which is both so terrified and so unconscious of the other world, it is not surprising that when "reality," the fabric of this world bursts, and a person enters the other world, he is completely lost and terrified and meets only incomprehension in others. . . . Most people in inner space and time are, to begin with, in unfamiliar territory and are frightened and confused. They are lost. . . . They try to retain their bearings. . . . The person who has entered this inner realm (if only he is allowed to experience this) will find himself going, or being conducted—one cannot distinguish active from passive here—on a journey. The journey is experienced as going further "in," as going back through one's personal life, in and back through and beyond into the experience of all mankind, of the primal man, of Adam and perhaps even further into the beings of animals, vegetables and minerals. In this journey there are occasions to lose one's way, for confusion, partial failure, even final shipwreck; many terrors, spirits, demons to be encountered, that may or may not be overcome.[7]

Each of the many kinds of journeys, with its mythic variations, provides a recognizable symbolic description of a type of transformation experience. The completed journey always ends with a return, a homecoming, to the ordinary world of conventional reality that was left behind. This world has been transformed, if our journey has been successful, into a new world seen with fresh eyes. The end of the journey is the beginning of a new, empowered way of life.

This theme of returning home connects to an important variant of the journey metaphor: the idea that in ordinary life, we already are on a journey, that we come from a faraway place, that we are in exile. According to this metaphoric pattern, the mystical journey of enlightenment is actually a return to our original home, to a place we have forgotten. This metaphor will be discussed in the next chapter, "Returning to the Source."

The Myth of the Wanderer

The image of the human as a traveler or wanderer is an ancient one, perhaps rooted in ancestral memories of the hundreds of thousands of years our species spent wandering in nomadic bands of gatherers and hunters. People differ greatly in the quality of their experience of life's journey, and for each one of us, there may be differences in the type of journey at different stages of life. Some of us—probably all of us at some time—wander restlessly and aimlessly through life. At other times we may be seized by a sudden sense of destiny: we start off and aim for a destination, a definite goal. Perhaps our purpose is to escape some intolerable situation. Or the goal may be worldly: to attain power, wealth, fame, or love. Or it may be supernatural and mystical: a quest for meaning, a longing for God, a thirst for wisdom, a need to heal. The Islamic Sufi sage Ibn al'Arabi wrote, "Know that since God created human beings and brought them out of nothingness into existence, they have not stopped being travellers."[8]

The mythic wandering hero represents the human ego exploring and discovering the world of reality as he or she grows up to adulthood, traversing the rites of passage and the transitions and challenges of each phase. This journey of growth and development follows parallel lines for people in all cultures. The spiritual quest, the transformational journey, begins when the hero leaves home, leaving behind the familiar, conventional world in order to journey into the "far country," to the magical castle, the sacred city; to ascend the holy mountain; or to cross the great seas and deserts. A striking literary exposition of this theme is Lewis Carroll's *Alice in Wonderland;* the heroine's subterranean wanderings, initiated by her drop down a rabbit hole, lead her into a realm where the usual dimensions of time, space, and logic do not apply.

There are different types of wanderers on the pathway of transformation, having different purposes for their journeys. Some feel they have been instructed to wander. Like the biblical Abraham, whom God commanded to migrate from the city of Ur, they may hear an inner voice that directs them. Others may feel impelled to escape, to seek a "way out." These are the stories and myths in which one escapes from a prison or a labyrinth, or flees the threatening attacks of mortal enemies. In modern terms this corresponds to the story of a person who seeks to escape a career rut, a relationship trap, or a situation threatening bodily harm or legal difficulties.

Then there are those unfortunate souls, like Odysseus, who are doomed to wander because they have incurred the wrath of a deity. Wandering as a kind of divine punishment is the theme of the folktale of Ahasuerus, the Wandering Jew. The story, current in the European Middle Ages, told of a man who refused to help Jesus Christ when he stumbled while carrying his cross on the road to Calvary. For this, Ahasuerus was condemned to wander homelessly for centuries. These legends correspond to the situation of a person wandering restlessly, driven by guilt or remorse about some misdeed and unable to settle anywhere because of an uneasy conscience.

Often the death of a loved one or one's own illness and approaching death serves as the catalyst that propels one on a kind of existential quest to discover the meaning of mortality and loss. Gilgamesh, the warrior-hero of Babylonian myth, departs on his journey when Enkidu, his close friend and wild man companion, dies. "Bitterly Gilgamesh wept for his friend Enkidu; he wandered over the wilderness as a hunter, he roamed over the plains."[9] Three famous goddess myths express the same archetypal pattern: those of the Babylonian Ishtar, the Egyptian Isis, and the Greek Demeter, who all wander disconsolately over the earth, looking for their lost son, lover, or daughter. As they wander, the earth is barren; cold winds ravage animals and humans, and the forces of death and darkness hold sway. Until the life-giving goddess actually confronts death in the underworld, all of life is held in the balance.

These myths point to loss of love and grief over separation as a main theme of the journey: this loss and grief can be such a shock to the emotional nature that depression, despair, and even illness can ensue, symbolized in the myths by the barren lands and the cold winds.

We can understand from all this that the "path" or "journey" of both mysticism and mythology is a key metaphor for the process of self-transformation. The writings of the mystics are quite explicit about the interior nature of this journey: they tell us that the terrain to be explored and traversed is our own psyche. They give detailed landmarks for those who recognize they are on an inner journey and who need further guidance. They tell us that the "castle" is "interior," and that there is a "valley of detachment," a "swamp of despair." The mystics offer interpretations that reveal the psychological meanings of their symbols and metaphors.

On the other hand, the myths and legends that describe the hero's journey are not explicitly psychological: in myth the journey is described as an outer journey, carried out in real time and space. Therefore, the inner, psychological meaning of the mythic journey is not directly stated. Instead, it is communicated to the deeper, imagistic layers of our subconscious minds. The imagery of the path, the journey, the traveler's adventures, evokes in the psyches of the listeners or readers the recognition and remembrance of their own journeys of personal transformation, of their own life process. Because we identify with the hero or heroine, these stories awaken us to the process of transformation occurring in us. We can readily identify with the misadventures of Odysseus, seeking to return to his wife and family, and with Demeter, searching disconsolately for her lost daughter.

Just as the poetic imagery of the journey evokes ancient and personal resonances in us, an actual outer journey to a faraway land can have a similar effect—the outer stimuli perceived by the voyager can evoke corresponding inner experiences by symbolic resonance. For example, a thirty-five-year-old woman teacher found herself at a turning point in her life when she took a sabbatical leave from her job, dissolved a nine-year marriage, and began to plan a trip to Nepal. Months later she wrote, "I began to refer to my trip as a 'journey.' . . . Subsequently I realized that my outward trip was a mirror of my inward journey. My experiences . . . in Nepal and Europe reflected a personal transformation of equal magnitude—a spiritual awakening."[10] Later, while reading Joseph Campbell, she saw that she was getting the "call to adventure" and received "supernatural aid" in the form of visions: she started seeing mountains in her meditations, as well as a magic wand. In dreams and waking thoughts, she began anticipating both "treasures and dangers."

Some cultures have institutionalized such journeys of personal transformation. The vision quest of the American Indians is such a journey of self-discovery, in which the youth spends three days and nights alone in the wilderness, fasting and praying for a vision. On such a wilderness journey into terrain far removed from human society, not only is the inner journey evoked by analogy and mirroring, there are also profound alterations of consciousness induced by sensory deprivation and social isolation. The year-long "walkabout" practiced by some of the Australian aboriginal tribes, like the "year walk" among the Basques, extends the vision quest into a much longer journey, for the dual purposes of learning to survive in nature and finding the personal vision.[11]

In other cultures the journey may be ritualized as a group project. The Huichol Indians of Mexico go annually on the three-hundred-mile peyote hunt, in which they travel as a whole village to find the hallucinogenic plant that provides them with visions. While on that journey, through purification and meditation, they consciously engage in harmonizing their relationships with one another as a community.[12] Pilgrimages by groups of people to holy places—whether Chaucer's rowdy band of travelers on the road to Canterbury, devout Christian monks on the way to Jerusalem, or Muslim caravans on the road to Mecca—all share the same purpose: travelers seeking God, seeking to find the Self. In some traditions it is left deliberately ambiguous whether the goal of the pilgrimage is an actual outer place or is instead "only symbolic." The Tibetan Buddhist Lamaist teachings concerning the mythical kingdom of Shambhala, which may be hidden somewhere beyond the most remote Asian mountain ranges or may exist only as a state of consciousness, is an example of such an intentionally ambiguous metaphor.[13]

In medieval legends of the quest for the Holy Grail, it seems clear that both outer and inner journeys are being described. Knights definitely wandered through strange forests and wastelands, came to hidden castles, and fought actual battles. But the frequency with which the natural landscape in the tales changes to a magical one indicates that altered states of consciousness, visionary and meditative experiences, are also being described. King Arthur's fellowship of the Round Table may have been a military and political alliance, but in legend it was also a spiritual fraternity of mystical seekers. The Castle of Marvels that Gawain and Percival both visit, with its moving furniture and visible spirits, is clearly an inner place, a place in consciousness, something like Saint Teresa's "interior castle." On the other hand, Montsalvat, the supposed home of the Sacred Chalice, which was never found, is also an actual mountain in the Pyrenees.

The journey of transformation enters a crucial new phase when we realize that the journey is, in fact, interior; that the places we seek "out there," the dangers we fear "out there," are only within us. Recognize, says the Tibetan Book of the Dead to the traveler in the *bardo* realms, that both the peaceful and the wrathful deities are within your own mind. The demon that you meet and battle with is the shadow of your own ego. The damsel in distress that you rescue is your own anima, the knight in shining armor for whom you long, your own animus.

Closely associated with the theme of departure is the symbolism of doorway, threshold, gate, entrance, or passage. There is the "eye of the needle" through which the rich man cannot pass, and the "crack between the worlds" through which the sorcerer stealthily moves. Every time we make the transition from one state of consciousness to another, even when falling asleep or waking up, we cross a certain border or threshold. This is even more true in those prolonged changes of consciousness that are experienced as a journey. At these gateways or thresholds, there is often a special heightened sensitivity or receptivity. For example, the twilight stage before sleep is a fertile source of creative imagining. When we heed the call to adventure, our senses come into fine tuning—we don't, after all, want to miss any signposts or clues that might help us on our journey.

Sometimes the threshold may be a dangerous narrow passage, as between Scylla and Charybdis: here Odysseus found himself between a seven-headed serpent and a devouring maelstrom—caught between the "devil and the deep blue sea." The threshold may also be, as in many myths, a bank of fog or a cloudy, indistinct region where we feel confused and disoriented. This is the region that William Bridges, in his work *Transitions,* calls the "neutral zone": one phase of our life has ended, but the shape of things to come is not yet clear. In some traditions there are elaborate interior geographies that refer to these in-between states. The Tibetan Buddhist teachings refer to several bardos, the "intermediate states" between death and rebirth, where we have to negotiate many tricky and hazardous points of choice. And medieval theologians spoke of limbo, the in-between realm where the ghosts of the recently deceased hover. We feel we are in limbo when we are "neither here nor there," when we are not sure whether we are "coming or going."

The concepts of bardo and limbo imply that dying is a kind of departure. Indeed, death as a journey—the ultimate journey—is a nearly universal metaphor. In this context the threshold experience is often symbolized as the crossing of a river, like the Styx, which the dead were obliged to cross according to the Greeks. As dying is definitely the crossing of a threshold, so is being born the violent, tumultuous beginning of the long journey of our lives. Each phase of the journey has its passages and gateways. Each consciously guided new beginning is a threshold of initiation. Each threshold phase requires us both to see and to seize the opportunity for transformation and growth.

Many Eastern teachings, however, warn of too much striving, of the spiritual ambition so characteristic of the Western psyche. A poem by the Indian *bhakti* mystic Kabir tells us: "What is this river you want to cross? There are no travelers on the river road, and no road. There is no river, and no boat. There is no ground, no sky, no bank, no ford."[18] This seems to be a caution not to get caught up in the external trappings of transformation, not to make it an ego-achievement. Remember that everything is within you; all the old familiar structures of reality are being left behind.

Or, in the words of the Zen master Mumon,

The great path has no gates,
Thousands of roads enter into it.
When one passes through this gateless gate,
He walks freely between heaven and earth.[19]

The paradoxical phrase "gateless gate" captures perfectly the strange mixture of the familiar and the new that we find at these threshold crossings. There is "nothing to do," and yet, when we have come through this phase of transition, we are altogether transformed. We can move freely then between heaven and earth, between the spiritual realms of being and the worldly realms of existence.

Descent into the Depths

The lower world or underworld journeys that are so important in the shamanic traditions are clearly a kind of altered state of consciousness.

Most commonly they may be induced by hallucinogenic plants, rhythmic drumming, or prolonged dancing. They are referred to as "lower world" journeys because the shaman's experience while in the altered state is that of downward movement—walking, crawling, or falling (not physically—the physical body is lying on the ground). The sensation of downward movement may be accompanied by an image of a cave, a tunnel, a streambed, a well, or an opening into the ground— which then gives way, after a while, to an interior landscape of some kind.[20]

Psychologically, one is inclined to say that these lower world journeys represent experiences in the subconscious layers of the psyche, "below" normal waking consciousness; these are the layers that are plumbed through dreams and "depth" analysis. These levels of consciousness are often (thought not invariably) experienced as more constricting, arduous, painful, and frightening than either "middle world" or "upper world" journeys or states of consciousness.

Lower-world, or underworld, journeys also have a significant place in mythology: many a hero or heroine, god or goddess has to descend to the inferior regions for the purpose of healing and salvation or to obtain some vital piece of knowledge. Typically in mythology, both hell and the land of the dead are found in the lower region, beneath the surface of the earth. Odin, the Nordic shaman-god, descends to Hel, the underworld land of the dead, riding on his magical horse, in order to consult a seeress about the ominous dreams of his son Baldur. Religious heroes, including Jesus and Muhammad, generally have to traverse an underworld hell at some point in their initiatory career. The prototypical Christian mystical journey, as portrayed in Dante's *Divina Commedia,* begins with a descent through the nine layers of the Inferno.

The lower-world journey may be a descent into the depths of the ocean. In psychological terms, the ocean symbolizes the vast collective emotional unconscious, since the element of water is associated with affect and feeling. In dream journeys we may find ourselves descending into the watery deep, following the way of many a mythic hero. Gilgamesh has to descend to the bottom of the sea to find the herb of immortality. Theseus goes into the sea depths to obtain from the ocean goddess Thetis the gift of a crown of gold, which he uses to illuminate his travels through the labyrinth. Jonah is drowned and swallowed by the whale: "The waters compassed me about, even to the soul—the depth closed me round about . . . yet thou has brought my life up from corruption, O Lord my God."[21] The stories suggest that while experiences of descent into the fluid depths of the emotional psyche may be arduous, they are also potentially healing and liberating.

In some instances, lower-world altered states may actually be excursions into the interior geography of the body. This is especially evident in the markedly physiological imagery found in many myths and shamanic accounts. For example, we are told the Siberian Yakut

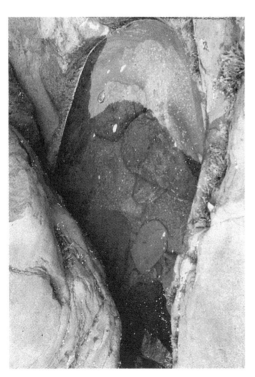

Descending into the Earth:
Entrance to the Lower World.
(Photo by Ralph Metzner, Joshua
Tree National Park, California)

shaman must travel through the throat and body of a serpent monster, whose gullet and bowels are lined with sharp spikes. As Joan Halifax has documented in her book *Shaman: The Wounded Healer,* on lower-world journeys "the shaman and the soul must brave icy winds, burning forests, stormy rivers, and bloody streams."[22] These and related images, such as the river of blood, the inner sea or swamp, the heaps of bones, the wind-swept caves (lungs), the sloping, gullet-like tunnel, are suggestive of symbolic visualizations of internal physiological structures and functions. This idea is consistent with what we know of the material and organic preoccupations of shamans and alchemists. It is furthermore highly appropriate, from a common-sense point of view, that healers, or heroes on a self-healing quest, would need to tune their awareness to the biological processes occurring within their own bodies.

Besides healing, the other main objective of a lower-world journey, as described in countless myths, is to find the land of the dead and contact dead relatives or ancestors. Orpheus journeys down to Hades to find and recover his lost love Euridice, pacifying the beasts and monsters of this world with his soulful music. Odysseus visits Hades in order to speak to his dead mother and to consult the seer Tiresias for prophecy concerning his fate. The Sumerian Inanna and the Babylonian Ishtar descend to the land of death to find and bring back their lost son or lover. The girl-child Kore is forcibly abducted into the nether world by Hades, Lord of Death: the involuntary lower-world experience of this story, marked by violence and terror, might be a metaphor for the altered state of consciousness induced by a near-fatal injury or illness.

The myth of Demeter, who wanders disconsolately over the earth searching for her lost daughter Persephone and causes the world's vegetation to wither and decay, has been interpreted as a metaphoric account of vegetative seasonal cycles. Barren winter alternates with fruitful spring and summer, these seasons corresponding to Persephone's alternating sojourns, first in the cold underground of Hades, then in the warmth of the Earth Mother's blooming valleys and fields. Demeter and Persephone/Kore are two aspects—mother and virgin—of the ancient great goddess of grain and nourishment.

Yet the myth has another, more interior dimension: it concerns transformation-individuation as well, particularly of the way of women. Seen from this perspective, Demeter and Persephone are two aspects of the feminine psyche—the mother and the girl-child (the Jungian *puella*). Demeter's disconsolate wanderings in search of her lost daughter, while earth's vegetation withers and decays, is a metaphor for a woman's shock at the physical and psychic loss of fruitfulness, the longing for a lost youth, as fear and grief overtake the soul. Support for this interpretation exists in a poignant detail of the myth: as the wandering Demeter calls her daughter's name in the mountainous wilderness, only her own name is echoed back—as if to say, "It is your own Self, your own identity that you seek."

In the myths of the Sumerian Inanna and the Babylonian Ishtar, the descent into the land of death has the same connection to seasonal vegetative cycles and rituals, but it is also motivated by the longing search of the woman for her lover or son, who has died. In the ancient Near East, the priestesses of these Goddess cults imitated their divinity in the rites of lamentation, crying and calling the name "Tammuz, Tammuz" in the cold darkness of the midwinter season. In such rites of lamentation, they not only evoked the grief and loneliness of women who had actually lost sons or lovers, but also gave expression to the eternal longing for the soul companion who will complete us. These myths embody the quest for the alchemical conjunction of the king and queen, the sacred marriage with one's own internal counterpart, which has "died"—that is, become separated or dissociated.

The story shows the initiatory character of the descent of the goddess by the requirement that Inanna remove seven garments and ornaments from her body before confronting, in nakedness, the death goddess Ereshkigal. The stripping of the ornaments at the seven gates on the way into the lower world represents the process of stripping the psychic energy centers (the yogic chakras) of obstructions and superimposed coverings and distortions, to reveal the naked truth about oneself.[23]

The lower-world journey of the goddess is a metaphor for the often painful and laborious self-examination and self-confrontation that accompanies the quest for inner unification. Inanna does not succeed in regaining her lost lover-son until she has hung as dead for three days and until the great god Ea, Lord of the Sacred Eye, intervenes. This means, psychologically speaking, that the woman must die to her old self and open herself to the guidance of higher wisdom (the god Ea) in order to be restored. Again, for modern women and men, such an opening up might be catalyzed by an experience of near-fatal illness or deathlike depression, in which one learns to give up all attachments to past identities in order to reconnect with one's other half in the union that restores love and regenerates life.

"Flying" and the Upper Realms

What shamanism calls upper-world journeys or magical flight are altered states of consciousness with the general theme or experience of ascent, rising, climbing upward, or gliding effortlessly through space. Flying dreams also fall into this category of states of consciousness, as do experiences we describe as "highs." Milder versions might be states in which we feel "uplifted" or "elevated" in moods of ecstatic reverie. Sometimes one has the experience of ascending through several layers, steps, or rungs of a ladder—which would correspond to the several levels, or planes, of consciousness that are known and described in both Eastern and Western esoteric spiritual traditions. Rising upward in space is a metaphoric image for the process of raising the vibratory frequency of consciousness—analogous to the raising of a musical tone to a higher frequency or pitch.

Dreams of flying are everyone's upper-world journey. We have already noted that waking up, as well as other kinds of heightening of awareness, are almost always experienced and described in metaphors of upward motion. In flying dreams we usually feel exhilarated, "high," exceptionally lucid, and observant—we seem to have the vision of eagles or of hawks. This kind of dream can be regarded as a simple, involuntary version of states pursued intentionally by shamans, yogis, and mystics. These are states especially valuable for "seeing," for clairvoyant perception, and for prophetic and prognostic visions. They are akin also to the states of consciousness studied by parapsychologists under the categories of out-of-body experiences (OBEs) and "remote viewing" experiments.[24]

Many mystics and poets have described spiritual visions metaphorically as being like the flight of birds. Recall, for example, the words of Black Elk, "For you see the birds leave the earth with their wings, and we humans may also leave this world, not with wings, but in the spirit."[25] His words echo those of the fourth-century Christian theologian Gregory of Nyssa, who wrote, "The human soul has but one vehicle by which to journey heavenward, that is to make itself unto the flying dove."[26] Gregory goes on to say that the same "dove" is what Scripture calls the Holy Spirit. A poem by Rilke evokes the feeling of a life in which there are cycles of visionary spiritual states:

> I live my life in growing orbits which move out over the things of the world. . . .
>
> I am circling around God, around the ancient tower, and I have been circling for a thousand years.
>
> And I still don't know if I'm a falcon, Or a storm, or a great song.[27]

The shaman, mystic seer, or dream flyer typically finds himself or herself flying through the air *like a bird*; riding *on a bird*, such as an eagle or a giant goose; or, transformed magically, flying through the air *as a bird*. To the ancients, the intentional pursuit of this path was known as sky magic, in contrast with the earth magic involved in lower-world journeys. Mircea Eliade recounts the ritual of the Altaic Siberian shaman, who speaks while in a trance of his experience flying on the back of the great goose that is his vehicle: "Under the white sky, over the white cloud, under the blue sky, over the blue cloud, rise up to the sky, bird!"[28] North American Indian stories tell of vision seekers who become a crow or a raven and fly thus, unrecognized, in conscious journeys of "seeing." Tibet's great yogi Milarepa writes in his autobiography of learning to transform himself into any shape desired and flying through the air: "By night, in my dreams, I could traverse the universe unimpededly... and I saw everything clearly as I went."[29]

Other modes of ascent are also found: one may find oneself riding a winged horse (this metaphor is often used to describe the powerful LSD-driven "trips") or flying a plane or a spaceship. I have heard of dreams and visionary states in which the person feels as if rising up through a chimney or curling upward on the smoke of a fire. The latter sensation is reminiscent of the idea taught by Native American

Ladder to the Sky World: Looking upward from the kiva. (Photo by Ralph Metzner, Pecos Pueblo, New Mexico)

elders that when one smokes the sacred pipe, one's prayers rise up with the smoke to the Great Spirit.

Other variants of the ascensional journey are climbing the world tree (with seven or nine branches), a pillar, a ladder (for example, Jacob's ladder), or a vertical rope (as in the famous Indian "rope trick"). In the *Maitri Upanishad*, the spider's upward movement on a self-generated thread is a metaphor for the heightening of awareness practiced in mantra meditation: "As the spider moving upward by the thread obtains free space, thus assuredly does the meditator, moving upward by means of the *aum*, obtain liberation."[30]

The upper-world traveler may ride great clouds, where ancient people envisioned the gods and goddesses living and moving. The biblical psalmist wrote, "O Lord, my God, thou coverest thyself with light as with a garment; . . . who maketh the clouds his chariot, who walketh upon the wings of the wind."[31] The North American Indian theme of the "windwalker" and the modern film hero Luke Skywalker are other versions of this mythic image. The sixteenth-century Chinese Taoist master T'u Lung wrote:

> One who travels does so in order to open his ears and eyes and relax his spirit. He explores the eight states and travels over the eight countries, in the hope that he may gather the divine essence and may eat of the plant of eternal life, and find the marrow of the rocks. Riding upon wind and sailing upon aether, he goes cooly wherever the wind may carry him.[32]

For someone involved in a transformative journey, such visionary flying experiences are particularly valuable. They tend to be experiences in which we are granted a preview or vision of our life or of some aspect of the world. They are usually accompanied by insights, intuitions, and new images; and they often instigate a mood of playful and euphoric creativity. On the other hand, the immoderate or egotistical pursuit of high states and visionary phenomena can be distracting

Upper-World flying journey: female warrior spirit on winged mount.
(Bicycle advertising poster, 1895, France)

hubris; so the ancient teachings tell us. Some traditions, including Zen Buddhism and Christian Protestantism, tend to disparage visions as "illusions" or "the devil's work." The possibility of a flying journey that leads to a fatal mistake is shown in the myth of Icarus, who flew too high and burned his wings in the sun's fire. We enact the tragedy of Icarus when we get "carried away" by our narcissistic moods of self-aggrandizement, by pride and vanity, or by "flights of fancy"—or ego-inflation, as the Jungians call it.[33]

Collective expressions of misguided sky magic also exist. The prevalence of UFO cults whose members believe in a superior race of advanced beings who will descend from the skies to save us, can be seen as a collective example of this kind of grandiosity. The technology of nuclear missiles is perhaps another manifestation of the Icarus complex on a mass scale: phallic weapons rape the sky, impelled by reckless ambition and suicidal arrogance.

Journeys into Nonordinary Reality

We turn now to the third of the three great "cosmic zones," as Eliade calls them: the regions of consciousness in which transformational travelers may find themselves. Shamanism, alchemy, and yoga, which have mapped out these various inner domains, situate one between the upper and lower worlds: it is the intermediate world, or Middle Earth, in which things and presences have a human scale. Ordinary men and women live in this world, and on our journeys in this world, in dreams and visions, we see and meet one another, converse, and relate as humans do. This middle world, like the upper and lower worlds, does have strange and magical qualities, which is why it is also called (in the Celtic tradition) the Otherworld.

I have come to believe that the transformative potential of such experiences is a function of intention: if we explore these states with respect and openhearted attentiveness, we begin to discover all sorts of valuable pieces of knowledge. If we wander in aimless curiosity or unconsciously flit about without awareness or attention, we experience "spacey" trips. "Things are not always what they seem" is a useful motto or mantra for these realms and states. An aura of unreality may surround ordinary objects: there are enchanted forests, interior labyrinths, castles of marvels, hallucinatory deserts. When we have an intention of self-transformation, these sequences of nonordinary images we perceive are symbolic representations of the lessons we are to learn. They show us the interior landscapes of the mind.

As mentioned before, there are often intriguing synchronicities between inner altered-state journeys and outer geographical journeys. The external journey may serve as a catalyst for definite inner changes. Conversely, an inner psychic transformation may be symbolized in dreams and visions by a space-time journey. Our perception of outer-reality places may be transformed in certain hypersensitive states: an ordinary landscape may suddenly assume an aspect of mystery or numinosity or have unexpected personal significance. The nineteenth-century Indian yogi-saint Ramakrishna once said, speaking of such states, "Meaning seems to leap out of matter, like a tiger out of a dark cave." The hidden glow in the landscape paintings of the old Dutch masters reflects such numinous vision, as does the swirling exuberance of Van Gogh's fields, trees, and skies. When we see a landscape in this light, whether internally or externally, we are moved to walk with wonder and respect, "in a sacred manner," as American Indian elders teach.

Holy Mountain. The theme of the holy mountain is both a middleworld journey experience as well as a variant of ascension imagery. Some of the sacred mountains have been actual geographical mountains that are believed to have supernatural power: Mount Fuji, Chomolingma (Everest), Mount Ararat, Mount Olympus, Mount Sinai—all play a central symbolic role in religious mythology. In other cases, such as the Indian Tantric Mount Meru, we are dealing with a symbol of the world axis, the central pivot or pillar of the world. On the microcosmic, or individual, level, the corresponding central axis, which has the chakras (energy centers) on it, is referred to as the "staff of Meru" (*merudanda*). Climbing or approaching the holy mountain is a pilgrimage to the center of the world—psychologically speaking, to the center of our existence.

The French philosopher René Daumal, a disciple of G. I. Gurdjieff, traced the mountain-climbing metaphor with literary elegance in his *Mount Analogue*, subtitled *A Novel of Symbolically Authentic Non-Euclidean Adventures in Mountain Climbing*. This so-called novel is actually a thought-provoking guidebook for those who would find and climb the interior mountain.

> You cannot stay on the summit forever; you have to come down again.... So why bother in the first place? Just this: what is above knows what is below, but what is below does not know what is

During this aimless wandering in the wilderness, we endure many hardships and sufferings; but we are also saved and rewarded with God' s gift of "manna from heaven"—the unexpected blessing that nourishes both body and soul. The voice of God, speaking through Hosea, another of the great Hebrew prophets, proclaims: "That is why I am going to lure and lead her [Israel] out into the wilderness and speak to her heart. I am going to give back her vineyards, and make the valley of Achor [misfortune] a gateway of hope."[37]

The mythic hero Gilgamesh, on his journey to discover the meaning of life and death, has to cross vast steppes and pass through a mountain fastness guarded by monstrous scorpion men. The knights of the Arthurian legend, on their quest for the Holy Grail that would give salvation, wandered dejectedly through the "gray lands," finding in the desolate wilderness of dim light and sparse vegetation no clues and no hope for their search. The mystic visionary Hildegard von Bingen wrote of the human soul's quest to escape from the dungeon of sinful life, finding "narrow paths" through stoney wilderness, hiding in small cracks in the rock, climbing through thorns and thistles, and avoiding poisonous snakes and scorpions.[38]

All these are images of our psychological condition, our state of consciousness when we are in the midst of a transformative process but have lost our way. We are trying to leave behind our past, highly unsatisfactory way of life, with its sufferings and insults, "the slings and arrows of outrageous fortune," but we have not yet found the promised land. We have not fully healed the ancient wounds, and we have lost hope and heart. T. S. Eliot captured the haunting feeling of this kind of experience in his poem "The Wasteland":

What are the roots that clutch, the branches grow
Out of this stony rubbish? Son of Man,
You cannot say, or guess, for you know only
A heap of broken images, where the sun beats,

And the dead tree gives no shelter, the cricket no relief,
And the dry stones no sound of water.

Perhaps one reason why this theme is so stirring to the modern psyche is that the wasteland symbolizes the modern Western condition of alienation, discouragement, and existential despair. We all at times feel ourselves to be wandering dejectedly through a life journey devoid of meaning and beauty. Since water is the great symbol of emotional and spiritual nourishment, the absence of water, as in a desert wasteland, is suggestive of emotional deprivation and lack of spiritual inspiration or enthusiasm.

This kind of experience of despair and hopelessness, symbolized by being lost in a barren wilderness, is represented somewhat differently in the Eastern traditions. In Buddhism, for example, we have the analogy of life as a senseless round, a repetitive wheel of existence (*samsara*). This endlessly turning wheel, fueled by greed, anger, and desire, symbolizes the ordinary human condition, lost in utter unconsciousness (*avidya*). From this we are to escape by practicing the ways of meditation, by turning inward to the source of light within.

Mysterious Castle. The theme of finding and exploring a mysterious castle is also widespread: in folktales ("the castle of no return"), in myth ("Castle Merveil"), and in mysticism ("The Interior Castle"). The latter work, by Teresa of Avila, is considered a classic of Western mysticism. In it, the human soul is likened to a crystalline castle surrounded by seven concentric "mansions." The innermost circle is that of the King of Glory, the indwelling Spirit who is the Sun, the Light that is at the center of our Being.

Each mansion has many rooms, many doors, passages, gardens, mazes, fountains: these are the many aspects and facets of our nature, which, according to Teresa, the soul must be permitted to explore. The outermost mansions, which symbolize the surface personality, the masks and roles that we act out, are uncared for and dark—in other words, there is quite a discrepancy between the outer form and

Returning to the Source

12

To return to the root is to find the meaning,
but to pursue appearances is to miss the source.
—SENGTSAN, HSIN HSIN MING[1]

In the previous chapter we discussed the journey as a metaphor for the experience of transformation. You leave your home in the ordinary, familiar world; travel to a faraway place, or to a magical Otherworld, where you are changed; then you return to the place of your family and friends, your tribe, your people, to live in a new way. The metaphor we are now considering conveys the quality of transformation as a homeward journey rather than an outbound journey. It sees human life as a kind of exile, an alien environment in which you feel like a stranger and from which you return to your true home, to the place where you came from, your source and origin.

In accounts of profound transformative experiences, whether mystic, psychedelic, cosmic, or spontaneously ecstatic, it is not uncommon to read or hear such expressions as: "a feeling of having been here before," "this is like coming home," "I've been away from here so long," "this is my true home." People often feel their usual state of consciousness to be one of alienation, especially in comparison with this new, changed state of "being found." An example of this kind of experience is described in the following account by one of the contributors to the *Common Experience* anthology:

> When I was sixteen I had an experience I can only describe as mystical. . . . The feeling was that I suddenly, that very moment, became aware of the answer to the mystery of life, and the knowledge of it made me want to shout with joy. As if I had been dead before that moment, and suddenly I was alive. . . . Always this same feeling

leaving me weeping with great joy and feelings of deep reverence, and feelings of worship and love, I think best described as a sort of homesickness, a nostalgia for some-other-where, almost as if I had known an existence of such great beauty and indescribable happiness, and am yearning and homesick for it again.[2]

This contemporary account is indistinguishable from similar experiences described in many mystical writings. The Chinese and Japanese Taoist and Buddhist masters frequently use the imagery of returning to the origin, to our true home, to the primordial beginning, in describing the experience of enlightenment.

Another example is provided by the following dialogue, which occurred in the deep phase of an empathogenic psychotherapy session.

client:	This feels like before.
therapist:	You mean in previous psychedelic experiences?
client:	No, earlier than that.
therapist:	Like in childhood?
client:	No, before that.
therapist:	You mean like in the womb?
client:	No, before . . . —this is where it all starts.[3]

This woman later described having felt somehow connected back to her source, the center from which her ordinary personality and behavior are created and expressed. As a matter of fact, this type of experience is somewhat characteristic of the particular empathogenic substance she had ingested—MDMA, which has acquired the code name Adam. The name seems apt for the sense of primordial beingness, ancestral wisdom, and groundedness often reported with this substance. The experience is reminiscent, too, of the Zen koan: "What was your original face before you were born?"

When this kind of experience occurs during a prolonged journey-like transformative phase, the traveler may feel as if on a homeward journey, returning to his or her roots. Life itself is seen as a great outward journey, initiated at birth, for learning and exploration. The path of spiritual evolution then is one of turning inward, returning to the world of spirit and light from whence we came. In the Gnostic Gospel of Thomas, Jesus says, "Blessed are the single ones (*monachos*) and elect, for you shall find the Kingdom; because you came from it, and you shall go there again. If they say to you—'from whence have you originated?'—say to them 'we have come from the Light, where the Light has originated through itself.'"[4]

An associated image is that of ordinary life as a kind of exile, where we are separated from our true spiritual home. The great Flemish mystic Jan van Ruysbroek wrote: "Knowledge of ourselves teaches us from whence we came, where we are and where we are going. We come from God and we are in exile." The transformation to a new way of being is compared to the process of one who leaves exile or leaves imprisonment and slavery (a closely related metaphor) and returns to the place of origin. This experience is consonant with the idea of "recollection," the regathering of scattered pieces that have been lost; and with *anamnesis,* the "overcoming of forgetfulness." The New Testament parable of the prodigal son who returns to his royal parents, after wasting his talents in debauchery and forgetting his mission, also fits this pattern.

We are all prodigal sons and daughters, insofar as we forget our origin and lose our sense of purpose and our vision of life. When we finally awaken and begin the process of self-transformation, much of the journey seems like a retracing of our steps, an undoing of knots tied before, or an escape from a prison we had inadvertently created, to rediscover a long-lost treasure.

In a remarkable essay on "The Awakening of a New Consciousness in Zen," the Buddhist philosopher D. T. Suzuki unites several of these metaphors:

> The awakening is really the rediscovery or the excavation of a long-lost treasure ... [The awakening] is no other than consciousness

becoming acquainted with itself.... Consciousness itself turns inwardly into it-self. This is the homecoming. This is the seeing of one's own "primal face" which one has seen even before birth. This is God pronouncing his name to Moses. This is the birth of Christ in each of our souls. This is Christ rising from death. The Unconscious, which has been lying quietly... now raises its head and announces its presence through consciousness.[5]

The return journey of transformation here is compared to an awakening and to a death-rebirth; it is described also as a raising of consciousness. In both Western and Asian traditions, the theme of return is an essential component of spiritual teachings.

The image is so pervasive and so consistent across many traditions that we may safely conclude that we are dealing with an archetype. We find the image associated with a model for the development of consciousness, in which there are two phases: an outward movement, a descending arc (often called involutionary), and an inward movement, an ascending arc (called evolutionary). In the latter we return to the paradise state we had left. The evolutionary path of the mystic involves a going back to Spirit, to the ground of being, to *Brahman*, to the Tao, to *Ain Soph*, to the Godhead.

Often in such experiences of "return," the person may feel that he or she has contacted some special inner companions, who seem to be one's "true family," a kind of spiritual family. Sometimes these may be perceived as deceased relatives or ancestors. This sensed inner family, these beings with whom we have a special spiritual rapport and communion, may be quite different from those we call family in the "real," everyday world. These inner-world companions may not even have a physical incarnation, and we may know them only in these special states of mystic vision, dreams, or meditations; we might call them "guide," or "ally," or "muse," or "inner voice."

Shamanic cultures and traditional societies that cultivate an openness to the spirit world believe that you can communicate with deceased ancestors just as readily as with an animal spirit or the spirit of a particular place. In such cultures there is the widespread custom of addressing spirit beings as "father," "mother," or "grandparents." In such practices, sometimes erroneously referred to as "ancestor worship," members of the tribe communicate with ancestral and other spirit beings for the sake of obtaining guidance in living.

The mythic hero Gilgamesh, when he goes forth to find the answer to the questions of life and death, searches for Utnapishtim, the ancient one called The Faraway who survived the great flood, and when he finds him, addresses him as "Father." Likewise, Black Elk addresses the Powers of the World that he sees in his vision as the "Six Grandfathers." American Indians pray to Mother Earth, Grandfather Fire, Father Sky, Grandmother Ocean, and so forth. In this kind of spiritual homeward journey, we come home then not only to a place, but to our great and original family as well.

Man as Stranger, Life as Exile

In a typical transformation process, after one has an awakening vision or breakthrough, the everyday world of family and society may be experienced as strange and *unfamiliar*—literally "not of the family." Having obtained even a glimpse into higher realms of consciousness, having seen the daytime sun outside the Platonic cave, the seeker may feel lost because he or she can no longer relate to the old, illusory shadows within the prison-cave. The seeker becomes a wandering stranger, filled with longing for a faraway home, the memories of which lie in the heart. Generalized, this feeling becomes one of life on earth as exile, banishment, or expulsion from a paradise state, of being lost and abandoned.

Becoming aware of the exiled or alienated condition we are in is, as always, the necessary first step to returning on the homeward journey. Thus, paradoxically, the closer we come to the source from where we originated, the more acutely we sense our estrangement. But then we may also find the solace and support that comes from finding ourselves in a *sangha*, or community of like-minded seekers. This is a transformation of our sense of belonging. It is beautifully expressed in the following paradoxical saying by the great thirteenth-century Chinese Zen master Ekai, also called Mumon:

> When you understand, you belong to the family;
> When you do not understand, you are a stranger.
> Those who do not understand belong to the family,
> And when they understand they are strangers.[6]

The first line refers to our ordinary situation—accepting conventional social reality and experiencing the acceptance of belonging to a "normal" family. But, as the second line states, one who awakens, who experiences inner realities and questions previous beliefs, will feel like a stranger in the conventional world. The third line tells us that those who seek and question, searching for knowledge and enlightenment, find then that they are part of another family, the family of other alienated seekers, others "who do not understand." They are for him or her what Goethe called the *Wahlverwandschaften*, the "chosen relations." As the fourth line states, these alienated seekers understand only that they are strangers in this world, and because they understand this, they do, in fact, in the eyes of the unawakened, become strangers. This is why in so many cultures there are traditions of the "holy fool," the "wise idiot," the eccentric, quirky person who turns out to be the wisest and most enlightened one of all.

Undeniably, many sensitive individuals come to feel at a certain point in their lives that a mistake has somehow been made: they are in the wrong place, or born in the wrong era, or banished into exile, or lost in a wasteland, or adrift on an ocean of illusions. This theme occurs in many contemporary works of mythological fiction, testifying to modern humanity's condition of profound existential alienation. We need only think of books such as Albert Camus's *The Stranger,* Colin

Wilson's *The Outsider,* or Robert Heinlein's science fiction classic *Stranger in a Strange Land* (which even provided the doctrinal basis for a neopagan religious community).[7] Films also express this theme: Nicholas Roeg's *The Man Who Fell to Earth* gave a vivid, affecting portrait of an alien, whose story has all the features of the classic exile myths. The popularity of these stories attests to the deep, essential nature of the myth they embody.

Because the feeling of alienation is so widespread, when a powerful, affecting story about it is told in fiction or film, it often touches deep chords and may even on occasion have healing effects. The mother of a twenty-year-old autistic "child" wrote to the producers of the enormously popular film *E.T.* to say that her son, who normally talked with nobody and never cried or laughed, "in the darkness [of the theater] came out of himself. He screamed, he clapped, he laughed, and then he cried—real tears . . . and talked, nonstop." She said that her son had always liked movies about spacecraft and aliens, and that seeing *E.T.* had changed his life. "It has made him relate to something beyond himself. It's as though Tommy has also been an alien life form and trying to find his way home, just like *E.T.*"[8] The psychoanalyst Otto Rank, who was one of Freud's closest disciples, wrote a classic analysis of the exile motif in *The Myth of the Birth of the Hero.* In this book he pointed out the striking parallels between the fantasies of neurotic patients, who may often imagine that their parents are not their real parents, and the pattern found in many myths of a hero (for example, Moses) who is born of royal parents but raised in exile by foster parents under conditions of early poverty and anonymity. This suggests that the neurotics, who are among society's most sensitive individuals, are experiencing a highly personalized and distressing version of this stranger/ exile motif. A transpersonally oriented psychotherapy would focus on transforming the sense of abandonment and exile so it can provide motivation for the spiritual homeward journey.

of attention became fixated on external things, the soul laments: "I am imprisoned, deprived of my sight and the joy of knowing. My garment is torn. I am driven out of my inheritance. I have been abducted into alien territory, where there is no beauty and no honor. I have been delivered into degradation and slavery."[12] The main difference between the mystic and the psychotic, in terms of this metaphor, is that the former has a sense of where he needs to turn—inward to God—whereas the psychotic is totally lost.

It is among the Gnostics that we find the strongest expressions of the theme of alienation and estrangement. There is even a key text among the Nag Hammadi scrolls, entitled *Allogenes,* which means "Stranger" and refers to the author of this tract. According to the editors, this appellation, which literally means "of another race," was a common one in this period for semidivine revealers of higher wisdom.[13] To the Gnostics, the whole process by which this world was created was fundamentally flawed: humanity was a mistake perpetrated by demiurge creators who misplaced us into this gloomy world, which they called a "circle of dark fire." To quote Jacques Lacarrière, "We are exploited on a cosmic scale, we are the proletariat of the demiurge-executioner, slaves exiled into a world that is viscerally subjected to violence; we are the dregs and sediment of a lost heaven, strangers on our own planet."[14]

The Gnostics taught that all humans suffer this fate of exile. *Gnosis* ("knowledge") is the aware recognition of this state of affairs—"and when they understand they are strangers." The sense of alienation, so widespread in Western culture and so particularly acute in twentieth-century consciousness, can be seen as the inevitable and perhaps necessary starting point for personal transformation. Estrangement leads to questioning, searching, and wondering. The quest or search may lead, if we are graced, to an awakening; the journey homeward may lead to the source of our beingness.

The Outgoing Path and the Returning Path

The spiritual and mystical traditions of both East and West have consistently distinguished between two phases of the process of transformation. Using the metaphor of a path or journey, these can be expressed most simply as the outgoing journey and the returning journey. The outward journey is our ordinary life in physical form, our worldly existence from birth to death. The return journey is the inner quest for our origins, the quest to remember our purpose and to find again the light within, from which we became separated. In a text by the first-century Neoplatonist philosopher Philo Judaeus, we read of this twofold journey:

> All whom Moses calls wise are represented as sojourners.... Their way is to visit earthly nature as men who travel abroad to see and learn. So when they have stayed a while in their bodies, and beheld through them all that sense and mortality has to show, they make their way back to the place from which they set out at first. To them the heavenly region, where their citizenship lies, is their native land; the earthly region in which they become sojourners is a foreign country.[15]

The metaphor of the return journey for the process of transformation implies, therefore, that an outward journey, into the alien world of conventional and social reality, precedes this inward turning toward spiritual reality.

C. G. Jung drew a similar distinction between two kinds of development, relating them to two major phases of the life cycle. In the first phase, which normally lasts from childhood to middle adulthood, we are becoming individuals, in the sense of learning the ways of the world and involving ourselves in the demands of family, work, and society. In the second phase, which begins, according to Jung, with the midlife crisis, when we may find ourselves, like Dante, "lost in the middle of a dark forest," we begin the process of individuation, which involves a turning inward, to reconnect with the Self, the center of our being. One could say in the first phase you build and develop your ego and in the second phase you transcend it. Of course, there are always exceptions to the general pattern; there are certainly individuals who begin the return journey of inner transformation in earlier adulthood, sometimes even in youth or childhood.

In the ancient philosophies of India, these two paths of human development are seen against the backdrop of two parallel cosmic processes, interweaving cycles of nature, inherent in every form of life. They are both sequential and simultaneously coexisting. One is called *pravritti,* literally "out-turning"—the unfolding, externalizing process of emanation and creation, also called the "out-breath of *Brahman.*" For us humans, *pravritti* is the outflowing of attention, desire, and impulse into matter and form. The other, complementary process is called *nivritti,* literally "back-turning"—the enfolding, internalizing process of transcendence and transformation, also called the "in-breath of *Brahman.*" At the human scale, *nivritti* is the inward orienting of meditation and spiritual practices, the releasing of attachments to matter and form, a returning from the manifest world back to unmanifest, invisible essence.[16]

The reader may, with some justice, protest that these philosophical distinctions are abstract and seemingly of little relevance to us today. However, the pervasive metaphor of the two types of paths is found in many myths and allegories both contemporary and historical. The underlying cosmic duality posited by ancient Indian philosophy is also a widespread contemporary theme, as for example in the cosmological theories of the universe expanding from a Big Bang and collapsing into a Big Crunch. Becoming aware of and interested in the wider cosmic or universal dimensions of life is not at all uncommon for individuals who are passing their midlife transition, even for those who have had no prior interest in ultimate questions.

Theories concerning a twofold process of consciousness transformation are also found in other ancient spiritual traditions, in occult systems such as theosophy, and in the writings of mystics and those of a very few modern scientists. Such theories usually suggest that the second phase, the return path, in some way leads back to the beginning of the first phase, although in a new way. People in this phase of the process may feel that they have returned to a place they knew before, but that they now know it with a new and different quality of awareness. Much has been learned, they may feel, on the outward journey, and these insights and lessons learned about the external world now form the background for a new transition.

In the writings of mystics and visionaries, the home or origin or source we return to is often described as "behind," "within," "underneath," or "above" the usual world of phenomenal appearances. To call it "behind" suggests that our original home is veiled from our knowing by perceptual screens and filters. Calling it "within" points to an external orientation as having brought us into the state of exile. "Underneath" suggests that the source of our existence is a kind of ground, the ground of being, of which the existentialists speak. "Above" suggests that we have come into the world of limits and forms from higher realms, from God, the Infinite, the Absolute.

Some teachings speak of the outgoing phase as *evolutionary* and the return phase as *involutionary*.[17] To *evolve* is literally to "roll out" or "unroll"; so in this phase, Spirit or consciousness is turning outward, unfolding, developing, into matter and form. To *involve* is literally to "roll up" or "envelop." Therefore, in this second phase there is an inward turning, enfolding, enveloping, of external matter and form back into formless infinity.

A modern scientific theory that fits this general paradigm is David Bohm's theory of implicate and explicate orders. According to Bohm, the explicate order is the world of our time-space oriented sense observations; and an implicate order exists that is more "subtle" and cannot be reached through reasoning or thought, only through direct insight. The implicate order is concerned with the whole; it is a *holomovement*—a dynamic flux that is the unmanifest ground of the manifest world. "What is manifest is, as it were, abstracted and floating in the holomovement. The holomovement's basic movement is folding and unfolding."[18]

Other teachings seem to say the opposite: in theosophical and other esoteric formulations, the movement from spirit into matter is described as involutionary, a "descent" into form, into embodiment, a building and inhabiting of form, the clothing or wrapping of the Spirit into bodies, the Logos into flesh. In such a model, the evolutionary movement is an unfolding of the spiritual essence within material and biological forms: a series of successive self-transcendences that lead us, over countless aeons, to the divine home from which we came.

Among modern scientists, Arthur Young with his theory of the "reflexive universe" gives a rational, considered, and elegant version of this theme. He posits a downward, involutionary arc from photons, to particles, to atoms, to molecules, each step involving more constraints and fewer degrees of freedom. There is a "turn," and then an upward, evolutionary arc, from molecules through plants, animals, and humans, with each step generating more possibilities and degrees of freedom. "To throw off compulsive embodiment, to disconnect from specific function, to become universal, a total being, is the role of man."[19]

The apparent contradiction between these two interpretations of the evolution-involution process, can, I suggest, be resolved if one regards them as each describing different aspects of a twofold process. There are two pairs of movements, involutionary and evolutionary, occurring simultaneously. Sri Aurobindo has expressed this paradox as follows: "In a sense the whole creation may be said to be a movement between two involutions—Spirit in which all is involved and out of which all evolves downward to the other pole of matter, Matter in which also all is involved and out of which all evolves upward to the other pole of Spirit."[20]

There is the evolution of spirit into matter: the *pravritti*, out-turning, unfolding, explicating. There is also the involution of spirit into matter: form building, creating, embodying. There is an evolution of matter toward spirit: enlightening, spiritualizing, transcending. And there is an involution of matter toward spirit: the *nivritti*, turning inward, internalizing, implicating.

The homeward or returning path is an evolutionary transformation, because through an unfolding of latent capacities the individual becomes personally aware of his or her unity with the original source-Self. The return path is an involutionary transformation also, in the sense that it is a retracing, a refolding of personality back into the vast, all-embracing, allcontaining context or ground of pure being. The homeward journey always returns us to Spirit; this is both an *un*folding, developing process and an *en*folding, *en*veloping process, depending on our point of view.

The Gnostic text *Allogenes* ("The Stranger") makes it clear that it is describing the vision of one who has turned within: "I was very disturbed and I turned to myself. Having seen the light that surrounded me and the good that was within me, I became divine." The seeker received instruction: "O Allogenes, behold your blessedness, . . . in silence, wherein you know yourself as you are, and seeking yourself, ascend to the Vitality that you will see moving."[21] This passage is typical of the kind of experience modern seekers often report: a growing sense of awe at the sacredness and numinosity of the inner realms of spirit that they are entering, coupled with a recognition that this is the true Self.

To recognize is to *re-cognize*, to "know again," to discover again that which was in the beginning. On the return path we get the "shock of (self-) recognition." The homeward journey is one of self-revelation, in which we gain insight into our true nature and awareness of the

The *tenth* and final picture is titled either "In the World" or "Entering the City with Bliss-Bestowing Hands." It shows the man, now an enlightened sage, walking, smiling, meeting others. This portrays the situation of one whose personality is completely transformed and who gives freely of his energy now, for the healing and enlightenment of others. *Inside my garden gate, even the wise do not know me. There is no need to follow the steps of the ancient sages. I go to the marketplace with my gourd, and I return home with my staff. Everyone I touch, even trees, blooms with enlightenment.* This represents the ideal of the compassionate bodhisattva, dedicated to the enlightenment of all sentient beings. No longer attached to the results of his actions, he is freed from the limitations imposed by ego concerns. It is also akin to the ideal of the adept of *gnosis*, who was said to be "in the world, but not of the world."

The myth of Odysseus is the story of the hero on the homeward journey toward wholeness. Odysseus is the archetype of the lover-warrior, seeking both to return home and to reunite with his wife-consort. The psychologist William Bridges has written perceptively on the meaning of the Odysseus story for the midlife transitions of the modern individual.[23] Odysseus is separated from his wife, Penelope, who symbolizes the anima, the inner counterpart with whom he wants to reunite. Thus, this is a journey toward androgyny, the inner union of the male and female sides of our nature, as well as the return journey to the origins. Odysseus experiences numerous difficulties and obstacles on the way back. Metaphorically, the myth portrays the tests and challenges that confront anyone, man or woman, on the homeward journey toward wholeness.

The journey of Odysseus begins "far from home"; he is in a "foreign land," waging war. He incurs the wrath of Poseidon for injuring one of the god's offspring, and then gets lost and embroiled in various dangerous situations. This represents the psychic situation of a person (man or woman) who has become so involved and entangled in various external activities and battles that he or she loses contact with his or her inner being, or soul; the way of return seems blocked off. The obstacles encountered are the direct karmic consequences of one's injurious and destructive actions. It is one's fate to have to deal not only with dangerous monsters and strong opponents but with the temptations and distractions of erotic pleasure as well; these are portrayed in the myth in the form of a siren, a nymph, a goddess, and a princess. Odysseus represents the person who has turned away from his true inner nature in reacting to the attractive and engaging sense objects of the external world.

The longing of Odysseus for return to his true home, his wife and family, keeps awakening him out of forgetfulness and motivating him to find his way home. In the meantime, his palace at home is overrun by Penelope's suitors, who try to persuade her to forget Odysseus and marry one of them. These suitors symbolize the intrusive thoughts, images, and impulses that usurp and distract our consciousness. We may feel then (and may dream) that alien forces have invaded our minds. Alchemical texts refer to this mental condition as having "enemies in the house." Their recipe for overcoming this divisive condition was to merge the male and female, the alchemical *coniunctio* of opposites—which is what Odysseus attempts to do when he returns.[24]

The final test Odysseus must pass in order to regain his kingship, metaphorically his selfhood, is probably a symbolic allusion to a yogic concentration process. It will be remembered that the climactic contest challenge was to shoot an arrow through twelve ax heads that had been lined up. The foreign suitors could not do this—only Odysseus could. This can be seen as a metaphoric description of the process of aligning the energy centers and piercing them with enlightened awareness, a process that allows the ego to reconnect with Spirit or Self and to eliminate the degrading and usurping influences (symbolized by the suitors) that have kept separate the royal pair, the inner male and female.

The Gnostic parable variously known as the Prodigal Son, the Hymn of the Robe of Glory, or the Hymn of the Pearl speaks eloquently of the return journey, which in theistic traditions is a journey back to God. The account given in the Gospel of Luke is a truncated version of a much longer verse narrative, dating from the Hellenistic period, with many interesting details.[25] I have combined elements from the different versions for this discussion.

The story tells of a royal couple who send their son out into the world. We are told the son "wasted his substance with riotous living." The "royal couple" are symbolically the divine inner parents, the Mother-Father Self from whom we "descend"—going forth into the world. The "son" (or daughter, or child) is the human ego, the personality, that grows up forgetting its origins.

In the longer versions, the son is actually on a mission to obtain a pearl from a venomous dragon, and he forgets that mission also. The pearl symbolizes the shining nugget of wisdom and insight that is contained in the instinctual, animal consciousness. The dragon represents the instinctual nature, especially the reptilian sexual and aggressive drives; but also the "wisdom of the serpent." The son was given a robe of many colors (hence the title of one of the versions) to protect and inspire him; but he forgets this as well. Instead, he dissipates himself among the Egyptians, who symbolize the stimuli of the sensory-material world. He eats of their food—that is, follows the dictates of greed and lust—until he is groveling in the field with the swine, totally oblivious to his purpose.

Then comes the turning point: asleep, drunk, and stupefied (all favorite Gnostic metaphors for our ordinary condition of unconsciousness), he receives a letter from his father, sent at the urging of "Princes

from the East." The letter urges him to "rise up and awake out of sleep
. . . and remember that thou art a son of kings; thou hast come under
the yoke of bondage." He is reminded of the pearl, of the robe, and of
his agreement to return to the kingdom that he left. Rousing himself,
overcome with guilt and shame, the son-hero takes the pearl from the
dragon while it sleeps, then directs his way homeward.

Miraculous things happen on this return path—a sure indication
that we are dealing with a sacred story of transformation, a mystic
journey. The letter that had awakened the son-hero turns into a light
that guides his way; the multicolored robe he'd lost sways before him
in a vision, also encouraging him along his journey. "At once, as
soon as I saw it, the Glory looked like my own self. I saw it all in all
of me, and saw me all in all of it—that we were twain in distinction,
and yet again one in one likeness." This is probably an esoteric reference to the inner "light body," or "garment of light," an illumined,
transpersonal form of the self. "And I stretched forth and received it
and adorned myself with the beauty of the colors thereof and in my
royal robe excelling in beauty I arrayed myself wholly."

The homebound voyager moves on, learning and making discoveries at each step of the way. He is ecstatic, as are all those who
have knowingly embarked on the journey of returning to source. He
is finally received into the palace of his parents, "the brightness of
the Father which had sent me." He has fulfilled his promise: he has
obtained and brought back the pearl of great price, which is the pearl
of the wisdom of nature (the dragon).

The Father then fulfills his promise: to receive the prodigal son who
has wasted himself but has now returned; to receive him with gladness
and rejoicing into the palace, "which was from the beginning." In the
Gospel version, the father says, "For this my son was dead, and is alive
again; he was lost and is found." The divine inner parents rejoice when
the personality finally returns, recognizing the true Self.

In the beautiful Navajo prayer "I Was Lost and He Found Me,"[26] the Divine Elder or Ancestor (*Hasji-Alte*) moves up out of the Emergence Pit, conversing with the grandchild. This is a symbolic dialog between the Great Inner Spirit, represented by the grandparent, walking and talking with the small, personal self, symbolized by the grandchild. The Great Spirit reminds the small self of the return journey to be undertaken, provides him with the "rainbow cloak" (here also!) of protection, and leads him into the land where all is beautiful. This is clearly a reference to a state of consciousness where one's perceptions have been cleansed and purified to such a point that everything wears the vestments of beauty.

"I came searching for you—
You and I will begin our return, my grandchild;
We two are leaving now, my grandchild,"
Hasji-Alte says to me. . . .

Encircling me sunwise with a rainbow,
He turns me, sunwise, toward himself,
And shows his compassion for me. . . .

"This is your home, my grandchild,"
He says to me as he sits down beside me.
"I have returned with you to your home,"
He says to me as he sits down beside me.
"Your home is yours again.
Your fire is your fire again.
Your food is yours again.
Your people are your people again.
Your parents are your parents again.
Your sacred mountains are yours again.

Your creatures are yours again.
The beauty of nature is yours again to enjoy, my grandchild,"
He says to me as he sits down beside me.

"From the dwellings of the Holy Ones
Kind feelings will come to you as you go about in life,"
He says to me as he sits down beside me.
"Guided by these things, you shall find protection,
In all places as you live on, my grandchild,"
He says to me as he sits down beside me.

All is beautiful behind me
All is beautiful before me
All is beautiful below me
All is beautiful above me
All is beautiful all around me.

For I have been found and everything is beautiful.

In this serene and simple song of the heart, we find expressed in an incomparable fashion all the themes of the spiritual homeward journey: the emergence-awakening out of the darkness of the external world; the guidance and protection of the Ancient One, the Grandparent, the Spirit; the perception of a new-old familiarity in all things and people around one; the multicolored garment of light; the feeling of being lost in the world, transmuted to being at home in the world; the overflowing of feelings of love and compassion toward others; and the exaltation and delight at finding oneself again in the shining presence of inner family and in the realm of beauty from which one originated.

(p. 82). Govinda goes on to spell out how, for example, perception of form (*rupaskandha*) is transformed into transcendent awareness of emptiness (*sunyata*). In each case, a previously ego-centered, limited mode of functioning changes into a relational, interdependent, interconnected mode.

5. Michael Murphy and Rhea White, *The Psychic Side of Sports*. Murphy's book *The Future of the Body* presents an astonishing compilation of documentation and evidence for psychophysiological changes in extreme situations and as the result of transformative practices. Another work, based on personal experience, that describes and discusses the potential for physical transformation is *The Mind of the Cells* by Satprem. This book, whose subtitle is *Willed Mutation of Our Species,* presents the transformational experiences of Sri Aurobindo's partner, The Mother.

6. Freud's analogy of the oceanic unconscious and Reich's idea of the character armor are scattered widely throughout their writings. Jung's night-sky metaphor is perhaps less well known. In his essay "On the Nature of the Psyche" (*The Structure and Dynamics of the Psyche*), he writes, "We would do well to think of ego-consciousness as being surrounded by a multitude of little luminosities" (p. 190); further, referring with obvious affinity to the views of Paracelsus, he says, "He beholds the darksome psyche as a star-strewn night-sky, whose planets and fixed constellations represent the archetypes in all their luminosity and numinosity" (p. 195).

7. Lakoff and Johnson, trained in linguistics and philosophy, do not say much about the psychological aspects of metaphors. They do, however, include in their discussion some speculations about what they call the experiential basis of metaphors. "We feel that no metaphor can ever be comprehended or even adequately represented independently of its experiential basis" (p. 19).

It is interesting that psychologists studying artistic development in children have become convinced of the importance of metaphoric processes in the life of the individual. Howard Gardner, in *Art, Mind, and Brain*, writes, "We can discern metaphor in the very first forms of learning, in which the child searches out commonalities in objects or situations known to be different, and then proceeds to behave in a similar fashion toward comparable elements" (p.166). See also *Metaphors in the History of Psychology,* ed. David Leary.

Classic discussions of metaphor from a literary point of view can be found in *Metaphor and Reality* by Phillip Wheelwright. He writes: "What really matters in a metaphor is the psychic depth at which the things of the world, whether actual or fancied, are transmuted by the cool heat of the imagination. The transmutative process that is involved may be described as semantic motion; the idea of which is implicit in the very word 'metaphor,' since the motion (phora) that the word connotes is a semantic motion—the double imaginative act of outreaching and combining that essentially marks the metaphoric process" (p. 72). See also my paper "Resonance as Metaphor and Metaphor as Resonance" in *ReVision* 10, no. 1 (1987): 37–44.

8. Evelyn Underhill, *Mysticism*, p. 79.

9. In her 1984 doctoral dissertation at the California Institute of Integral Studies ("Goddesses and Gods as Vehicles for Self-Development: An Application of Jungian Theory in a Group Process"), Sandra Lewis showed that a group process in which men and women worked imaginatively with the myths of Greek gods and goddesses had a significant effect on their perception of their own identity.

10. The following are useful general reference books on symbolism: Hans Biederman, *Dictionary of Symbolism*; J. E. Cirlot, *A Dictionary of Symbols*; and J. C. Cooper, *Symbolism: The Universal Language*. Funk and Wagnall's *Standard Dictionary of Folklore, Mythology, and Legend* is an invaluable source for the cross-cultural exploration of symbols.

11. Jung, *Structure and Dynamics of the Psyche*, pp. 336, 409.

12. Buckminster Fuller, *Synergetics*. In his inimitable style, Fuller says, "Omnidirectional means that a center of a movable sphere of observation has been established a priori by the Universe for each individual life's inescapably mobile viewpoint; like shadows, these move everywhere silently with people" (p. 613).

13. William James, *Varieties of Religious Experience*, p. 157.

14. Mircea Eliade, *Ordeal by Labyrinth*, p. 154.

15. James, *Religious Experience*, p. 319; Underhill, *Mysticism*, p. 81.

16. C. G. Jung, "Concerning Rebirth," in *The Archetypes and the Collective Unconscious*, pp. 113–147.

17. R. Gordon Wasson, Carl A. P. Ruck, and Albert Hofmann, *The Road to Eleusis: Unveiling the Secret of the Mysteries*.

18. A. K. Coomaraswamy, "On Being in One's Right Mind," in *Selected Papers of A. K. Coomaraswamy*, ed. Roger Lipsey. This important essay has been reprinted in *ReVision* 5, no. 2 (1982): 63–67.

19. Ken Wilber, *The Atman Project*. Wilber says he is extending the stages of development, as laid out in Western child psychology, to the transpersonal realms described in Asian psychologies. Another way of saying this is that he is describing spiritual development with the analogy of child development, or using child development as a metaphor for transpersonal development. Wilber also states that we die at each level and are reborn at the next higher level—an application of the death-rebirth metaphor.

20. William Bridges, *Transitions: Making Sense of Life's Changes*.

21. Satprem, *Sri Aurobindo*, p. 316.

22. Adolf Portmann, "Metamorphosis in Animals: The Transformation of the Individual and the Type," in *Man and Transformation*, ed. Joseph Campbell, pp. 297–325.

23. Julian Huxley, "On Psychometabolism," *Journal of Neuropsychiatry* 3 (August 1962); also in *Psychedelic Review* (Fall 1963): 183–204.

24. Underhill, *Mysticism*, p. 179. Using the imagery of liberation that we discuss in Chapter 3, Underhill adds, "The deeper mind stirs uneasily in its prison, and its emergence is but the last of many efforts to escape."

25. Cognitive psychologists have concerned themselves with this distinction of

lasting versus temporary changes by differentiating "states" from "traits." For example, a widely used test designed by Charles Spielberger measures "state anxiety," the current level of anxiety; and "trait anxiety," the relatively stable tendency to be anxious. William James concerned himself with the same issue by asking whether a conversion experience or a religious experience, though positive in itself, would necessarily lead to the development of "saintliness"—that is, enduring personality traits with similar qualities.

26. Descriptions of the miraculous features of the Buddha's "body of transformation" (*nirmanakaya*) abound in the Buddhist literature. One early text, quoted by Govinda in *Foundations of Tibetan Mysticism,* refers to the Lord's form, "adorned with eighty minor signs and thirty-two major signs of a great man, . . . full of splendor and virtue, incomparable and fully awakened" (p. 216). Another text describes with great wealth of detail the many kinds of multicolored radiance issuing from the body of the Teacher.

The description of the Taoist sage, who corresponds in the Western tradition to the hermit "hiding his light," is found in verse 15 of the *Tao Te Ching:* "Tentative, as if fording a river in winter/Hesitant, as if in fear of his neighbors/Formal, like a guest/Falling apart, like thawing ice/Thick, like an uncarved block/Empty, like a valley/Obscure, like muddy water. Who can be muddy and yet, settling, slowly become clear?"

27. Under the category diminution of personality, Jung discusses the primitive's "loss of soul" and Pierre Janet's term *abaissement du niveau mental:* "It is a slackening of the tensity of consciousness, which might be compared to a low barometric reading. The tonus has given way, and this is felt subjectively as listlessness, moroseness, and depression." This can occur as a result of fatigue, illness, violent emotions, shock, and, modern psychologists would add, stress. Elsewhere in the same essay, "Concerning Rebirth," Jung writes of changes of internal structure that are neither enlargement nor diminution. Possession is an example, which is "identity of the ego-personality with a complex." Identification with the persona, the social mask; with the inferior, unconscious function; with anima or animus; with deceased ancestors; or with a group or a cult hero are all listed by Jung as examples of this kind of transformation (pp. 120–128).

28. Jung, in "Concerning Rebirth," describes "transcendence of life" experiences, either induced by ritual or occurring "in the form of a spontaneous, ecstatic, or visionary experience." These are experiences "in which the spectator becomes involved though his nature is not necessarily changed. These more aesthetic forms of experience must be carefully distinguished from those which indubitably involve a change of one's own nature."

Ken Wilber, in his writings on transpersonal developmental theory, seems to confuse the two processes. Developmental transformation, for him, is a series of transcending movements of consciousness, from lower to higher levels. For example, in *A Sociable God* he writes, "As we turn to transformative or vertical development, in order for an individual to transform to the next higher level, he or she has, in effect, to accept the death of the present level of adaptation. It is only when the self is strong enough to die to that level that it can transcend that level, that is, transform to the next higher level of phasespecific truth, food, manna" (p. 53).

29. These classic sayings are given in many books on alchemy—for example, C. A. Burland, *The Arts of the Alchemists,* pp. 2–3.

30. *Chuang Tsu: The Inner Chapters,* trans. Gia-Fu Feng and Jane English, p. 136.

Chapter 1: Awakening from the Dream of Reality

1. Quoted by permission from an unpublished account by James Mahood, California Institute of Integral Studies.

2. The Gospel of Truth is one of the relatively recently discovered Gnostic texts, published in *The Nag Hammadi Library,* ed. James M. Robinson. The "nightmare parable" reads, in part, as follows: "They were sunk in sleep and found themselves in disturbing dreams. Either there is a place to which they are fleeing, or, without strength they come from having chased after others, or they are involved in striking blows, or they are receiving blows themselves, or they have fallen from high places, or they take off into the air though they do not even have wings. When those who are going through all these things wake up, they see nothing, they who are in the midst of all these disturbances, for they are nothing. They leave them behind like a dream in the night" (p. 43).

   Excellent discussions of Gnostic thought are found in Elaine Pagels, *The Gnostic Gospels,* and Jacques Lacarrière, *The Gnostics.* The passage quoted from the latter work continues: "Hermes is one of their favorite gods, because he is the personification of 'The Wide Awake,' the god to whom Homer attributed the power to 'awaken, with his golden wand, the eyes of those who sleep.'. . . There is a quest for an asceticism and a specific power: for the ability to keep one's eyes open, to refuse sleep, to awaken to a true consciousness of oneself " (pp. 22–23).

3. The *Diamond Sutra* and the *Heart Sutra* are published, in translation by Edward Conze, in *Buddhist Wisdom Books.*

4. Nagarjuna's commentary is quoted in Conze, *Buddhist Wisdom Books,* pp. 6870.

5. Selections from Gregory of Nyssa's writings are published in a volume entitled *From Glory to Glory.* The passage on Angelic Vigilance is found on p. 243.

6. An excellent brief introduction to modern sleep and dream research is *Some Must Watch While Some Must Sleep* by William Dement.

7. The association of awakening with "up" and of going to sleep with "down" seems to hold in several different languages, although there are some interesting variations. This would provide a fascinating study in linguistics, illustrating both the pervasiveness of metaphor and some aspects of the structure of human consciousness. In German, one says *einschlafen,* literally "to sleep

inward," and *aufwachen,* literally "to awaken open." Here we have an associated metaphor of closing inward and opening outward. In French one says *s'endormir,* literally "to insleep" (comparable to the German expression); and *se reveiller,* literally "to reveal oneself "—again the notion of closing and opening. The latter expression we shall encounter again in the next chapter in connection with the symbolism of veils and reveiling (= revealing).

8. A large amount of interesting work has been published in recent years abut lucid dreaming. Stephen LaBerge has done research on learning to voluntarily enter and control lucid dreaming; see his book *Lucid Dreaming,* and, with Howard Rheingold, *Exploring the World of Lucid Dreaming.* Some useful books on dreaming are *Creative Dreaming* by Patricia Garfield, *Dream Reality* by James Donahoe, and *Living Your Dreams* by Gayle Delaney. There are dream research networks, as well as a lucidity network, with their own journals and newsletters.

9. In Carlos Castaneda's books, lucid, consciously controlled dreaming is referred to as *dreaming,* or "dreaming," and several techniques are used for learning to become lucid in a dream, such as looking at one's own hand in the dream. Flying dreams play a major role in many shamanic cultures and are analogous to what are called "upper-world journeys"—that is, altered states of consciousness in which one appears to be moving upward. Mircea Eliade, in his book *Shamanism,* writes: "The shaman's instruction often takes place in dreams. It is in dreams that the pure sacred life is entered and direct relations with the gods, spirits, and ancestral souls are re-established. It is in dreams that historical time is abolished and the mythical time regained—which allows the future shaman to witness the beginnings of the world, . . . the primordial mythic revelations" (p. 103).

10. Tibetan dream yoga teachings and practices are described in W. Y. Evans-Wentz's *Tibetan Yoga and Secret Doctrines.* Evans-Wentz writes: "As a result of these methods, the yogin enjoys as vivid consciousness in the dream-state as in the waking state. Thereby the content of the dream-state is found to be quite the same as that of the waking state, in that it is wholly phenomenal, and therefore, illusory" (p. 216 n.). Mutual dreams, which present the strongest challenges to the conventional view of reality, are described and discussed in *Dream Reality* by James Donahoe.

11. Mark 13:33–36.

12. A very useful collection of articles on kundalini was published as *Kundalini, Evolution, and Enlightenment,* ed. John White. In this work, Swami Rama quotes the eminent nineteenth-century authority on the Indian Tantras, Sir John Woodroffe: "When kundalini sleeps in the *muladhara,* man is awake to the world; when she awakes to unite, and does unite, with the supreme consciousness which is Shiva, then consciousness is asleep to the world and is one with the Light of all things" (p. 33). The kundalini energy is always conceived of as female, the Mother, Shakti, full of enormous power; and she is said to unite in the crown center with her consort Shiva, who represents pure consciousness but without energy or power.

13. Daniel Goleman, *Varieties of Meditative Experience,* p. 116.

14. The clearest exposition of Gurdjieff's ideas regarding the sleeplike characteristics of ordinary consciousness are in P. D. Ouspensky's *In Search of the Miraculous,* especially pp. 142–145. Gurdjieff says: "Man can be a self-conscious being. Such he is created and such he is born. But he is born among sleeping people, and, of course, he falls asleep among them just at the very time when he should have begun to be conscious of himself." Charles Tart has written a book entitled *Waking Up* that integrates the teachings of Gurdjieff with modern psychological research on transpersonal states of consciousness.

15. The passage by Saint Teresa is quoted from William James's *Varieties of Religious Experience,* p. 314; the one by Ramakrishna is from *The Gospel of Sri Ramakrishna,* p. 257.

16. Studies of the physiological and psychological changes occurring in meditation have demonstrated two quite different kinds of responses, depending on the type of meditation, which correspond to the distinctions made here. The book *Altered States of Consciousness,* edited by Charles Tart, contains accounts of these studies. In one study of Indian yogis, it was observed that when they were absorbed in deep meditation (*samadhi*), their brainwave recordings did not show the usual kind of response to outer stimuli, such as lights, sounds, and so on. In other words, they had become oblivious to the external world; they had transcended it. A different study used Zen meditators and noted that habituation—which is the normal diminishing of brain response to outer stimuli—did *not* occur. This suggests that while meditating, these meditators were not absorbed but rather more alert and attentive to all kinds of stimuli than normally. Several interesting reviews of meditation research have appeared: one is by G. Boals, "Toward Cognitive Reconceptualization of Meditation," *Journal of Transpersonal Psychology* 10, no. 2 (1978): 143–182; another, by D. H. Shapiro, "Meditation as an Altered State of Consciousness," *Journal of Transpersonal Psychology* 15, no. 1 (1983): 61–81.

17. The story of Black Elk is told in John Neihardt's *Black Elk Speaks,* pp. 271–272.

18. Gopi Krishna's account of his kundalini experiences is in his book *Kundalini: The Evolutionary Energy in Man.* See also the book by Lee Sannella, *Kundalini: Psychosis or Transcendence,* for examples of the kundalini syndrome.

19. *Katha Upanishad* 1.2.8. *The Principal Upanishads,* ed. S. Radhakrishnan, p. 638.

20. 1 Cor. 15: 51–52. In the New English Bible, the word *sleep* has been replaced with *die;* which omits the metaphor of sleep and simply conveys the straightforward idea that we are totally changed at the moment of death.

21. D. T. Suzuki, "The Awakening of a New Consciousness in Zen," in *Man and Transformation,* ed. Joseph Campbell, pp. 179, 185.

and in *The Time Falling Bodies Take to Light* by William Irwin Thompson. Concerning the relation of Inanna's seven garments and the chakras, Thompson says, "If indeed the seven laws are the seven chakras, then the untying of knots which bind the physical body to the subtle would remove the etheric and astral body to wander in hell in the out-of-the-body state" (p. 178). In other words, Inanna's descent and the removing of her veils and garments can be regarded as a metaphoric description of an initiatory experience, which involves stripping the chakras of obstructions, and an altered state of confrontation with disease and death, followed by rebirth.

28. R. A. Nicholson, *The Mystics of Islam,* p. 15.

29. The passage by Eckhart is found in *Meister Eckhart,* trans. Raymond B. Blakney, p. 77. The complete passage reads, "That to which the soul inclines tends always to become like a cover or hood; but in being lifted up, the soul is made naked before the idea of God, for God's begetting; the image of God is unveiled and free in the open soul of the aristocrat."

30. 2 Cor. 3:15–18.

Chapter 3: From Captivity to Liberation

1. The Swiss psychoanalyst Alice Miller wrote a book, *Prisoners of Childhood,* that was subsequently reissued under the title *The Drama of the Gifted Child.* In this book she eloquently demonstrates how the unspoken expectations of parents create a subtle yet powerful set of limits and inhibitions for the child, especially the sensitive gifted child. *Man in the Trap,* by Ellsworth Baker, is an exposition of Wilhelm Reich's theories.

2. Plato's cave parable and the passages cited here are from books 6 and 7 of *The Republic.*

3. Shri Ramamurti Mishra, *Self Analysis and Self Knowledge,* sutra 49. In Sanskrit, *moksha,* or *mukti,* is the process or state of liberation, and *jivan-mukta* (from *jivan,* "living") is one who is "freed while living"—that is, a liberated being.

   "Being-consciousness-joy" (or bliss), *sat-chit-ananda,* is the Vedanta term for the kind of consciousness of someone who has attained enlightenment or liberation.

4. Jacques Lacarrière, *The Gnostics;* Evelyn Underhill, *Mysticism.*

5. In Saint John's symbolism, the body is the prison for the soul, which knows nothing except what it can see through the windows of its cell, which are the senses. Perhaps the imagery of life in material form as a kind of imprisonment was heightened by lifelong residence in cloisters and monasteries.

6. Herbert V. Guenther, *The Life and Teachings of Naropa,* pp. 25–26.

7. The Harvard Prison Project, as it was called, was written up in a technical research report by Timothy Leary, Ralph Metzner, et al., "A New Behavior Change Project Using Psilocybin," in *Psychotherapy: Theory, Research and Practice* 2, no. 2 (1965): 61–72. It is also described, less formally, in Leary's autobiographical *Flashbacks,* Chapter 11.

8. John Milton, *Samson Agonistes,* 1.40.

9. From "The Dove and the Darkness in Ancient Byzantine Mysticism," by Jean Daniélou, in *Man and Transformation,* ed. Joseph Campbell, p. 282.

10. Wilhelm Reich, *The Function of the Orgasm,* pp. 206–207. See also his *Character Analysis.* An excellent psychological biography of Wilhelm Reich is *Fury on Earth* by Myron Sharaf.

11. Alexander Lowen, *Bioenergetics,* pp. 183 ff. Other useful books on body "reading," or diagnosis from body structure, influenced by Reich's work, are Ken Dychtwald's *Bodymind;* Hector Prestera and Ron Kurtz's *The Body Reveals;* and Stanley Keleman's *Somatic Reality.*

12. Don Johnson, *The Protean Body,* pp. 20–21. Johnson's most recent book, not as closely based on the work of Ida Rolf, is called *Body.*

13. T. S. Eliot, from "Burnt Norton," in *Four Quartets.*

14. Used by permission from an unpublished account by Alan Levin.

15. The parapsychological research on out-of-body experiences (OOBEs, as they are called) is well summarized and reviewed in *Psi, Scientific Studies of the Psychic Realm* by Charles Tart. Also, *With the Eyes of the Mind* by Glen Gabbard and Stuart Twemlow gives a lucid discussion of research on OOBEs and other unusual states of consciousness.

16. Shirley MacLaine, *Out on a Limb,* p. 329.

17. Stanislav Grof, *Realms of the Human Unconscious,* pp. 116–121. Grof 's theories and findings on the importance of the birth experience, which, as he says, sets up "perinatal matrices" for the experiencing of subsequent life-and-death traumas, was anticipated in the work of Otto Rank on the birth-trauma. The experience of being trapped or enclosed, as part of the birth-trauma, was also discussed in *Endeavors in Psychology* by Henry Murray, who identified a "claustral complex," derived from the birthing process.

18. The phrase "the imprisoned splendor" is from Robert Browning's poem "Paracelsus." Raynor Johnson's book *The Imprisoned Splendor* presents a synthesis of findings from the natural sciences, psychical research, and classical mysticism.

19. My interpretation of the Osiris myth, though independently arrived at, is similar to the one put forward by William Irwin Thompson in *The Time Falling Bodies Take to Light.* "When we come to the coffin that has become embedded in a tree, we are, as any student of yoga would recognize, clearly in the realm of the esoteric physiology of the central nervous system" (pp. 218 ff.).

20. *Katha Upanishad* 2.3.15; *Mundaka Upanishad* 2.2.9.

21. Mircea Eliade, "The God Who Binds and the Symbolism of Knots," in *Images and Symbols,* p. 112.

22. The "double-bind theory of schizophrenia" was first enunciated by Gregory Bateson and is described in several of his books and articles, including *Steps Toward an Ecology of Mind* and *Mind and Nature.*

23. See the essay by Eliade cited in note 21. The Fata were the Roman goddesses of fate who enunciated the word, or decrees, of Jupiter; *fata* means literally "that which has been spoken." The Moirae were the Greek goddesses of fate: Clotho, the spinner of the thread of life; Lachesis, the one who determined its length; and Atropos, the one who cut it at the end. The Norns are the Scandinavian goddesses of fate, who inscribe our fates on runic tablets. They all resemble the threefold goddess of Celtic mythology and the three fairy godmothers of many folktales.

24. P. D. Ouspensky, *In Search of the Miraculous*, p. 30.

Chapter 4: Purification by Inner Fire

1. From *Sonnets to Orpheus*, II, no. 12. The original German reads: "Wolle die Wandlung. O sei für die Flamme begeistert, drin sich ein Ding dir entzieht, das mit Verwandlungen prunkt." I interpret these lines to mean that as we surrender to the fires of transformation, as we will them, intend them, there will be so many rapid and profound changes that any thing we might want to hold on to (like a self) will elude us.

2. Agni Yoga, or light-fire yoga, as taught in the school of Actualism, is described in my books *Maps of Consciousness* and *Know Your Type*. The Actualism lightfire yoga system was founded by Russell Paul Schofield. The Actualism website can be found at http://www.Actualism.org. The Actualism version of Agni Yoga is quite unrelated to the Agni Yoga teachings formulated by the Russian painter-philosopher Nicholas Roerich, who traveled in the East and in America extensively during the 1920s and wrote a number of books on the subject.

3. From the anthology of the *Rig Veda* selected and translated by Wendy Doniger O'Flaherty, pp. 99–117. See also Satprem, *Sri Aurobindo*, pp. 322–327.

4. Lama Anagarika Govinda, in his *Foundations of Tibetan Buddhism*, writes, "The fire of spiritual integration which fuses all polarities, all mutually exclusive elements arising from the separateness of individuation, this is what the Tibetan word *gTum-mo* means in the deepest sense. It is the all-consuming incandescent power of that overwhelming Inner Fire which since Vedic Times has pervaded the religious life of India: the power of *tapas*" (pp. 160–161). The statement on *tapas* is from the *Rig Veda*, 10.190.1.

5. Rudra embodies the warrior fury and demon-conquering aspects of Shiva, and the black Kali personifies the destructive, devouring aspect of the life-goddess Shakti. In his book *Shiva and Dionysus*, Alain Danielou argues that Shiva was originally a Dravidian vegetation and fertility deity, worshiped in the form of the phallic *lingam*. The Brahmins turned him into an ascetic, and the Tantrics revived his erotic dimension. See also *Asceticism and Eroticism in the Mythology of Siva* by Wendy O'Flaherty, and *The Presence of Siva* by Stella Kramrisch.

6. Ps. 68:2.

7. Luke 12:49–50; Matt. 3:11; Gospel of Thomas, no. 82.

8. Extensive discussions of alchemy in general and of the symbolism of fire in particular can be found in C. G. Jung's *Alchemical Studies* and *Mysterium Coniunctionis,* and in *Anatomy of the Psyche* by Edward Edinger. In addition, there is a chapter on alchemy in my *Maps of Consciousness.* The alchemical texts *The Glory of the World* and *The Sophic Hydrolith,* from which several quotations are drawn, are found in the collection entitled *The Hermetic Museum,* ed. A. E. Waite. The original was published in Frankfurt in 1678.

9. An excellent introduction to Taoist mysticism is the book *Tao: An Eastern Philosophy of Time and Change* by Philip Rawson and Laszlo Legeza. An extraordinary compilation of dragon lore from all over the world is Francis Huxley's *Dragon.*

10. An outstanding compilation of art and literature on the theme of hell and paradise is *Visions of Heaven and Hell* by Richard Cavendish. Another book that contains much valuable material on these themes is *Beyond Death* by Stanislav and Christina Grof.

11. Huxley writes: "The Inferno is psychologically true. Many of its pains are experienced by schizophrenics, and by those who have taken mescalin or lysergic acid under unfavorable conditions" (*Heaven and Hell,* p. 109). Interesting personal accounts of schizophrenic experiences, which illustrate many of the points made here, have been collected in the book *Exploring Madness: Experience, Theory, and Research,* ed. James Fadiman and Donald Kewman.

12. Stanislav Grof, *Realms of the Human Unconscious,* p. 131.

13. For a discussion of the role of suffering and sacrifice in shamanic traditions and practices, see Joan Halifax's *Shaman: The Wounded Healer.*

14. The *Treatise on Purgatory* is quoted from Evelyn Underhill, *Mysticism,* p. 204. The passage continues: "The more it is consumed, the more they [the souls] respond to God their true Sun. Their happiness increases as the rust falls off and lays them open to the divine way."

15. From Boehme's *Supersensual Life,* quoted in *Treasury of Traditional Wisdom,* ed. Whitall Perry.

16. See note 8 above.

17. Account used by permission from the author's files. Empathogenic substances, such as MDMA and 2-CB, differ from the classical psychedelics, such as LSD and mescaline, in that the perception of reality is not altered, only the emotional center is opened, producing a state of profound empathy for self and others. See *Through the Gateway of the Heart,* ed. Sophia Adamson, for a collection of accounts of experiential therapy with these substances.

18. Edward Edinger's book *Anatomy of the Psyche* explores many aspects of and variations on the alchemical themes and images in much greater depth than I am able to in the present work. The symbolic transformative processes he discusses are *calcinato, solutio, coagulatio, sublimatio, mortificatio, separatio,* and *coniunctio.*

19. For a comprehensive summary of current research and thinking on subtle energy healing, see *Vibrational Medicine* by Richard Gerber.

20. Sri Aurobindo, *The Life Divine*, p. 907.

21. The picture of the wolf and the king is one of a series of alchemical emblems published in 1617 under the title *Atalanta Fugiens* (*The Fleeing Atalanta*) by the alchemist Michael Maier.

22. Lee Sannella, *Kundalini: Psychosis or Transcendence?* Sannella's book is concerned with establishing the diagnostic criteria for distinguishing a kundalini process, which he regards as basically a healthy, powerful transformation, from the misguided and chaotic manifestations of energy psychosis. The underlying physical or physiological mechanism of the kundalini process is still totally unknown. Itzhak Bentov, in his book *Stalking the Wild Pendulum,* proposed a theory involving resonating circuits in the brain that is capable of accounting for some aspects of this phenomenon. At this point, about all that can be said about the phenomenon, in terms of Western science, is that it involves some aspect of bioelectricity, or what Russian researchers refer to as "bioplasmic" or "psychotronic" energy. A volume edited by John White, *Kundalini, Evolution, and Enlightenment,* contains experiential accounts of kundalini phenomena, as well as extracts from the Indian literature and from modern research studies. See also the book by Bonnie Greenwell, *Energies of Transformation: A Guide to the Kundalini Process.*

23. Gopi Krishna, *Kundalini: The Evolutionary Energy in Man.*

24. For Aurobindo's view on Agni Yoga and for Actualism, see the references cited in notes 2 and 3 above.

25. Taoist yoga principles and practices are detailed in *The Secret of the Golden Flower,* ed. and trans. by Richard Wilhelm, with commentary by C. G. Jung; and in *Awakening Healing Energy Through the Tao* by Mantak Chia.

26. Used by permission from the author's files.

27. From *The Glory of the World,* in *The Hermetic Museum,* ed. A. E. Waite.

28. From "O llama de amor uiua," in *The Poems of Saint John of the Cross,* trans. J. F. Nims, p. 23.

29. *Treatise on Purgatory,* quoted from Underhill, *Mysticism,* p. 221.

30. The passage from Richard Rolle is cited in *Silent Fire,* ed. Walter H. Capps and Wendy M. Wright. Rolle's reference to "we exiles" touches on the metaphor of alienation and homecoming, discussed in Chapter 12.

31. T. S. Eliot, from "Little Gidding," *Four Quartets.*

32. The passage cited is from Boehme's work *Clavis* (The Key), first published in 1624; translation by the author.

Chapter 5: From Fragmentation to Wholeness

1. Used by permission from the author's files.

2. Quoted in Aldous Huxley, *The Perennial Philosophy,* p. 96.

3. William James, *Varieties of Religious Experience,* p. 143.

4. Roberto Assagioli, *Psychosynthesis*, p. 75. The analogy of the Self as an orchestra with its conductor is suggested by John O. Beahrs, in his book *Unity and Multiplicity*.

5. For a description and discussion of the humoral and other earlier somatically based typologies of personality, see my *Know Your Type*, Chapter 2. See also *Psychiatric Dictionary*, ed. Robert J. Campbell, under "type."

6. Georg Groddeck, *The Book of the It*, p. xiv.

7. P. D. Ouspensky, *In Search of the Miraculous*, p. 59.

8. David Bohm, *Wholeness and the Implicate Order*, p. 7.

9. Dissociative disorders such as post-traumatic stress disorder (PTSD) and multiple personality disorder (MPD) are being diagnosed much more frequently, though it is not known whether this is due to an increase in the actual occurrence of such disorders or to improved recognition of conditions previously misunderstood. Dissociation is a normal and natural cognitive function, the opposite of association. Even the simple act of focusing or concentrating attention clearly involves some degree of dissociation, some screening out of awareness anything that is not in focus. In the Freudian view, psychic material (thoughts, images, feelings, etc.) in the repressed unconscious (also called the id) is disorganized, primitive, and childish, functioning according to the "pleasure principle"; whereas the conscious mind (the ego) functions according to the "reality principle" and is capable of adjusting or adapting to the demands of reality in a rational, organized manner. The dissociationist view, as originally put forward by Freud's contemporary Pierre Janet and in the neodissociationism of Ernest Hilgard and others, is that dissociation involves a "vertical" separation of strands of consciousness that may be equally well organized, rational, and in touch with reality. See Ernest Hilgard's *Divided Consciousness*, and *Dissociation*, ed. S. J. Lynn and J. W. Rhue, for excellent reviews of theory and research in this area.

10. Numerous examples of shamanic dismemberment visions are cited in Mircea Eliade's monumental study *Shamanism: Archaic Techniques of Ecstasy*, especially in Chapter 2. The extraordinary experiences of Australian aboriginal medicine men are vividly recounted in A. P. Elkin's *Aboriginal Men of High Degree*. The case for the similarity between shamanic initiations and psychotic experiences was first made by Julian Silverman in an article entitled "Shamans and Acute Schizophrenia," in *American Anthropologist* 69 (1967): 21–31.

11. From an unpublished account by the author.

12. W. Y. Evans-Wentz, *Tibetan Yoga and Secret Doctrines*, pp. 277–333.

13. The mystery cults involved an elaboration and collectivization of earlier individual initiations. Tests were staged for the initiates, consisting of a sequence of experiences. For members of the public, they were instructive ritual dramas, akin to later morality plays. Initiates and observers were sworn to secrecy, to maintain a "closed mouth" (Greek *mustes*). The purpose of keeping the secret was to ensure that the meaning and power of the initi-

repressed, though in all essentials the repression persists." S. Freud, *General Psychological Theory,* pp. 213–214.

10. Wilhelm Reich, *Ether, God and Devil,* p. 120.

11. The English word *devil* comes from the Latin *diabolus,* which in turn is derived from the Greek *diaballein,* "to slander or lie," literally "to throw (*ballein*) across (*dia-*)." In English folk speech we have the interesting phrase "to put something over" on someone, meaning to lie to or trick them—which still reflects this etymological origin.

12. "Fusion, inner unity, is obtained by means of 'friction,' by the struggle between 'yes' and 'no' in man. If a man lives without inner struggle, if everything happens in him without opposition, if he goes wherever he is drawn or wherever the wind blows, he will remain as he is." P. D. Ouspensky, *In Search of the Miraculous,* p. 32.

13. Paul Ricoeur, in his study *The Symbolism of Evil,* sees in the Christian tradition three main themes or experiences involving evil: one is the feeling of guilt, accusation, and unworthiness; a second is the notion of sin as deviation or missing the mark; and third is the idea of defilement, the sense that some stain or blemish infects us.

14. W. D. O'Flaherty, in *The Origins of Evil in Hindu Mythology,* discusses Indian myths that see humans as emitted from the anus of Brahma, the Creator. Stanislav Grof, in his *Realms of the Human Unconscious,* has described excremental visions in LSD therapy that derive from memories of the birth experience. In his paper "Perinatal Origins of Wars, Totalitarianism, and Revolutions," *Journal of Psychohistory* 4, no. 3 (Winter 1977): 269–308. Grof applies his LSD findings to the phenomenon of the concentration camps. The folklorist Alan Dundes, in his book *Life Is Like a Chicken Coop Ladder,* has examined German folklore and literature for evidence of anality as a trait of the German national character—with implications for an understanding of the Nazi holocaust.

15. Michael Flanagin, "Putrefactio: Death and Decay in the Alchemical Imagination," in *Transcendence and Transformation,* ed. Vern Haddick.

16. James 4:1.

17. *Treasury of Traditional Wisdom,* ed. Whitall Perry, p. 410.

18. Ibid., p. 397.

19. *Bhagavad Gita,* 6.6.

20. Quoted in A. K. Coomaraswamy, "Who Is Satan and Where Is Hell?" in *Selected Papers,* Vol. 2.

21. Paul Shepard, *Thinking Animals,* pp. 11–13.

22. See Mircea Eliade, *History of Religious Ideas,* Vol. 1, pp. 302–333, for Zoroastrianism, and Vol. 2, pp. 387–395, for Manichaenism.

23. The Buddhist Wheel of Life, which plays a particularly important role in the Tibetan Buddhist tradition, shows a circle divided into six sections, or "worlds." (See *The Tibetan Book of the Dead,* trans. Francesca Freemantle and Chogyam Trungpa, pp. 3–10). These worlds may be regarded as symbolizing (1) different incarnations or lifetimes of human beings, or (2) dif-

ferent personality types, or (3) different states of consciousness that anyone could find himself or herself in. See also my article entitled "The Buddhist Six Worlds Model of Consciousness and Reality," in *Journal of Transpersonal Psychology* 28, no. 2 (1996): 155–166.

24. Lama Govinda, *Foundations of Tibetan Mysticism,* p. 198 ff.

25. "*Agathos* and *kakos* daimons, fair and foul selves, Christ and Anti-Christ, both inhabit us, and their opposition is within us. Heaven and Hell are the divided images of Love and Wrath *in divinis,* one in God, and it remains for every man to put them together again within himself." Coomaraswamy, "Who Is Satan and Where Is Hell?" An excellent discussion of the concept of *daimon* in classical antiquity, and how this may be understood in terms of depth psychology, is in Marie-Louise von Franz's *Projection and Re-Collection in Jungian Psychology.*

26. The history and meaning of the figure of the devil has inspired numerous studies, among which are the following two books by Jeffrey B. Russell: *The Devil: Perceptions of Evil from Antiquity to Primitive Christianity* and *Satan: The Early Christian Tradition.* An interesting Ph.D. dissertation was written by Eliot Isenberg at the California Institute of Integral Studies (1983) on "The Experience of Evil: A Phenomenological Study."

Chapter 7: On Dying and Being Reborn

1. William Bridges, *Transitions.*

2. From *Zen Flesh, Zen Bones,* ed. Paul Reps.

3. Cited with permission from an unpublished account by John Prendergast.

4. C. G. Jung, "Concerning Rebirth," in *The Archetypes and the Collective Unconscious,* p. 115.

5. John 12:23–24 New English Bible.

6. 1 Cor. 15:36 NEB.

7. Meister Eckhart, in *Treasury of Traditional Wisdom,* ed. Whitall Perry, p. 208.

8. Plato, *The Phaedo,* quoted in Edward Edinger's *Anatomy of the Psyche,* pp. 169170.

9. An interesting compilation of European folklore on death is Edgar Herzog's *Psyche and Death.*

10. *Katha Upanishad,* in *The Principal Upanishads,* ed. and trans. S. Radhakrishnan, p. 607.

11. Ibid., p. 648.

12. *Rumi: Poet and Mystic,* trans. Reynold A. Nicholson, p. 103.

13. *Chuang Tsu: The Inner Chapters,* trans. Gia-Fu Feng and Jane English, p. 114.

14. Quoted in Evelyn Underhill, *Mysticism,* p. 217.

15. P. D. Ouspensky, *In Search of the Miraculous,* p. 218.

16. For an account of shamanic "killing" rituals see Mircea Eliade's *Shamanism* and A. P. Elkin's *Aboriginal Men of High Degree.*

17. Edinger, *Anatomy of the Psyche*, p. 25.

18. Raymond Moody's book is *Life after Death;* Karlis Osis's is *Deathbed Observations by Physicians and Nurses;* Kenneth Ring's is *Life at Death.* In Kenneth Ring's latest work, *Heading Toward Omega,* he makes the startling claim, based on the reports of survivors, that "near-death experiences may be part of an evolutionary thrust toward higher consciousness for all humanity They may foreshadow the birth of a new planetary consciousness as we head toward Omega, the final goal of human evolution" (from the jacket).

19. Stephen Levine, *Who Dies?*, p. 157. Levine founded, with Ram Dass, the Dying Project, which conducts seminars for the terminally ill and their families, in which attitudes toward death are examined and transformed. Levine's book *Who Dies?*, subtitled *An Investigation of Conscious Living and Conscious Dying,* is a profound and moving description of this work, with many meditation and guided imagery sequences given for self-work.

20. Joan Grant's most powerful and vivid story is *Winged Pharaoh,* one of three she wrote about different periods in Egyptian history; they contain detailed accounts of death-rebirth and other initiations and trainings. Joan Grant claimed to remember these as "far-memories" of past incarnations. The work by Elizabeth Haich, *Initiation,* is also based on past life recall. Of the several books describing the theories and research of the Egyptologist and esoteric philosopher R. A. Schwaller de Lubicz, *Her-Bak: Egyptian Initiate* by Isha Schwaller de Lubicz gives a good account of mythic initiatory training.

21. The W. Y. Evans-Wentz version of the Tibetan Book of the Dead (1960) is the one used by Leary, Metzner, and Alpert to prepare their adaptation *The Psychedelic Experience* (1964). Since then, there have been new translations: one by Francesca Freemantle and Chogyam Trungpa, published in 1975; and one by Robert Thurman, published in 1994.

22. The work by Pahnke, Grof, and others on LSD psychotherapy with cancer patients is described in *The Human Encounter with Death* by Stanislav Grof and Joan Halifax.

23. Lewis Thomas, "A Meliorist View of Disease and Dying," in *Journal for Medicine and Philosophy* 1, no. 3 (1976).

24. Catatonia is characterized by "plastic immobility of the limbs, stupor, negativism, and mutism" (*American Heritage Dictionary*). Literally, the term means "lower" or "downward" (*cata-*), "tone" or "tonus." Catatonia could thus be said to be a condition of lowered psychic tonus.

25. See Robert J. Lifton, *The Life of the Self,* especially pp. 43–45. See also R. D. Laing, *The Divided Self.*

26. Otto Rank, who was one of Freud's most brilliant students, made fear of death one of two central motives in human nature (the other being fear of life). In his book *Beyond Psychology,* he proposed that throughout history, human beings have pursued immortality in various ways: through the creation of "other world" religious beliefs (the "historic" solution); through identification with heroes who conquered monsters (the "heroic" solution); through idealized love relationships (the "romantic" solution); or through

the accumulation of objects (the "philistine" solution). Rank's own preferred, and hoped-for, solution was the "creative" one: achieving immortality through works of art.

27. David Bakan makes this suggestion in *The Duality of Human Existence,* pp. 157–158. In this book, Bakan quotes from a letter Freud wrote to a friend after he discovered he had cancer: "From that time on the thought of death has not left me, and sometimes I have the impression that seven of my internal organs are fighting to have the honor of bringing my life to an end." One could argue that the perception of death processes going on in one's own body is perhaps quite common. The crucial question to look at, considered in connection with healing transformation, is: What is my attitude toward these processes? Is it fear, repugnance, avoidance; or is it acceptance, affirmation, release?

28. In part, the resistance to Freud's ideas may be explained by errors in the English translation of some of Freud's terms, as Bruno Bettelheim has argued in his book *Freud and Man's Soul.* The German word translated as "instinct" was *Trieb,* which would be much better rendered as "drive" or "urge." The notion of a "death instinct" has a kind of inherent implausibility that "death drive" or "death urge" do not. Apart from this semantic confusion, it would seem that the well-known fear and denial mechanisms with regard to death have played a role in the nonacceptance of Freud's ideas.

29. Sigmund Freud, *Beyond the Pleasure Principle,* p. 47.

30. See Edinger, *Anatomy of the Psyche,* pp. 147–180.

31. *Treasury of Traditional Wisdom,* ed. Whitall Perry, pp. 203–244.

32. For discussions of Chinese Taoist alchemy, see *The Secret of the Golden Flower,* ed. and trans. Richard Wilhelm, and *The Forge and the Crucible* by Mircea Eliade.

33. C. G. Jung, *The Psychology of the Transference,* p. 102. It can be stated that *coniunctio* is the alchemical operation that corresponds to eros; and *mortificatio* the alchemical operation associated with thanatos.

34. C. G. Jung, "The Psychology of the Child Archetype," in *The Archetypes and the Collective Unconscious,* p. 164. Jung continues: "In the psychology of the individual, the 'child' paves the way for a future change of personality. In the individuation process, it anticipates the figure that comes from the synthesis of conscious and unconscious elements in the personality. It is therefore a symbol which unites the opposites; a mediator, bringer of healing, that is, one who makes whole."

35. The reader is referred also to the accounts of modern shamanic journey experiences in Michael Harner's *The Way of the Shaman.*

36. The quote from Eckhart is in *Meister Eckhart,* trans. Raymond B. Blakney. The Islamic Sufi quoted is Najm ad-din al Kubra, from "The Transformation of Man in Mystical Islam," by Fritz Meier, in *Man and Transformation,* ed. Joseph Campbell. The New Testament quote is John 3:3. A parallel passage is 1 Corinthians 15:44: "It is sown a natural body, it is raised a spiritual body. There is a natural body, and there is a spiritual body."

37. Jung, "Concerning Rebirth," p. 121. Edinger, in his writings and talks on the encounter with the Self, has emphasized, somewhat one-sidedly it seems to me, the overwhelming, shattering kinds of Self-confrontation, as symbolized in the story of Job. See his *Creation of Consciousness.*

38. *The Nag Hammadi Library,* ed. James M. Robinson, p. 53.

39. Jung, "Psychology of the Child Archetype," pp. 151–181.

40. William Shakespeare, Sonnet 146, "Poor soul, the centre of my sinful earth."

41. Lao Tsu, *Tao Te Ching,* trans. Gia-Fu Feng and Jane English, verse 55.

Chapter 8: From Darkness to Light

1. Ken Wilber, *Eye to Eye,* pp. 2–4.

2. Modern research on subtle energy phenomena is summarized and discussed in a number of different works: *Vibrational Medicine* by Richard Gerber; *Rainbows of Life: The Promise of Kirlian Photography* by Mikol Davis and Earle Lane; *Orgone, Reich, and Eros* by Edward Mann; and *The Fields of Life* by Harold S. Burr. *Breakthrough to Creativity* by Shafica Karagulla, M.D., is a particularly careful and impressive collection of first-person accounts by "sensitives"—that is, clairvoyants and psychics. A recent excellent compilation of light-energy techniques from Hindu, Buddhist, and Taoist traditions is *The Body of Light* by John Mann and Lar Short.

3. The experience of the German traveler with Ramana Maharshi is quoted in Lama Govinda's *Foundations of Tibetan Mysticism,* p. 164. All the biographies of Ramakrishna mention the luminescence phenomena, as reported by eyewitnesses. Several other similar enlightenment transfigurations are described in Mircea Eliade's essay "Experiences of the Mystic Light." This excellent compilation of materials from many sources is found in his book *The Two and the One.*

4. Matt. 17:2–10; Mark 9:2–10.

5. *Meister Eckhart,* ed. Raymond Blakney, p. 104.

6. J. M. Cohen and J-F. Phipps, *The Common Experience.*

7. "Light is not an objective thing that can be investigated as can an ordinary object. Even a tiny snow crystal, before it melts, can be photographed or seen by more than one person. But a photon, the ultimate unit of light, can be seen only once: its detection is its annihilation. Light is not seen; it is seeing." (Arthur Young, *The Relflexive Universe,* p. 10.)

8. From the *Brihadaranyaka Upanishad* (4.3.7), which was probably written in the eighth century B.C.E. *The Principal Upanishads,* trans. S. Radhakrishnan, p. 256. The quotation from Shankara is sutra 67 of his *Atma Bodha,* in S. R. Mishra, *Self Analysis and Self Knowledge,* p. 266.

9. Quoted in Fritz Meier, "The Transformation of Man in Mystical Islam," in *Man and Transformation,* ed. Joseph Campbell, p. 54.

10. Quoted in Stephen Larsen, *The Shaman's Doorway,* p. 77.

11. See C. G. Jung's essay "Paracelsus as a Spiritual Phenomenon," in his *Alchemical Studies,* pp. 109–189.

12. See the book by John Mann and Lar Short, *The Body of Light*, for an excellent overview of these different but similar approaches.

13. Emanuel Swedenborg, *Heaven and Hell*, no. 130.

14. *Tibetan Book of the Dead*, trans. Francesca Freemantle and Chogyam Trungpa, p. 37.

15. See Mircea Eliade, *The Two and the One*, p. 34.

16. *Tibetan Book of the Dead*, Freemantle and Trungpa, p. 43.

17. 2 Thess. 5:5; Matt. 6:22; Gospel of Thomas, no. 24.

18. John 10:34.

19. From Saint Augustine, *Confessions*, quoted in Evelyn Underhill, *Mysticism*, p. 250.

20. C. G. Jung, "On the Nature of the Psyche," in *The Structure and Dynamics of the Psyche*, p. 190.

21. Ibid., p. 192.

22. The following are excellent surveys of psychological knowledge about creativity: Silvano Arieti, *Creativity: The Magic Synthesis;* C. W. Taylor and F. Barron, eds., *Scientific Creativity: Its Recognition and Development;* and Arthur Koestler, *The Act of Creation*.

23. Franz Hartmann, *Jacob Boehme: Life and Doctrines*, p. 50.

24. *Rig Veda* 2.27.

25. See Underhill, *Mysticism*, Chapter 9, pp. 380–412.

26. I owe the suggestion that this would be a more accurate phrase to Salvador Arrien and Angeles Arrien.

27. R. M. Bucke, *Cosmic Consciousness*, p. 8.

28. Sri Aurobindo, *The Life Divine*, p. 944.

29. Shankara is quoted in Mishra, *Self Analysis and Self Knowledge*, p. 28; *Chandogya Upanishad* 3.13.7.

30. Saint Teresa, quoted in Underhill, *Mysticism*, p. 78.

31. G.R.S. Mead, *The Doctrine of the Subtle Body in the Western Tradition*, p. 59.

32. *Meister Eckhart*, ed. Blakney, p. 104.

33. Paramahansa Yogananda, *Autobiography of a Yogi*, pp. 166–168.

34. A. R. Orage, *On Love*, p. 52.

Chapter 9: Integrating the Inner Wild Animal

1. For a good overview of post-Darwinian evolutionary biology, see *The New Biology: Discovering the Wisdom of Nature* by Robert Augros and George Stanciu. An audiotape guided meditation by Ralph Metzner on "The Evolutionary Journey of the Human Animal" is available from the Green Earth Foundation.

2. See Paul MacLean, *A Triune Concept of Brain and Behavior*.

3. Daniel Goleman, in his book *Emotional Intelligence*, traces the emotional reactions of fear, rage, and so forth to the limbic system, without specifically mentioning MacLean's triune brain model. "Emotional intelligence" would

consist in being able to consciously monitor and modulate these reactions, thereby minimizing their destructive impact.

4. Stanislav Grof, in his book *The Adventure of Self-Discovery,* writes: "The experiential identification with various animals can be extremely authentic and convincing. It includes the body image, specific physiological sensations, instinctual drives, unique perception of the environment and emotional reactions to it. In the holotropic mode of consciousness, it is possible to gain experiential insight into what it feels like when a cat is curious, an eagle frightened, a cobra hungry, a turtle sexually aroused, or when a shark is breathing through the gills" (p. 53).

5. See Rupert Sheldrake, *A New Science of Life, The Presence of the Past,* and *The Rebirth of Nature.* His theories of morphic resonance and similar approaches are discussed in *ReVision* 10, no. 1 (1987), a special issue entitled *The Resonating Universe: Explorations of an Integrative Metaphor,* edited by Ralph Metzner, with essays by Sheldrake, Ralph Abraham, Terence McKenna, Jill Purce, Nick Herbert, Ralph Metzner, and others.

6. For the Vishnu myths, see the *Standard Dictionary of Folklore, Mythology, and Legend* and the *New Larousse Encyclopedia of Mythology.*

7. Paul Shepard, *Thinking Animals,* pp. 26–28. Shepard was an outstanding philosopher and critic of the relationship between human culture and nature, especially animals. His other books include *Nature and Madness, The Others,* and *Traces of an Omnivore.*

8. Claude Lévi-Strauss, *The Savage Mind,* pp. 135–160, 191–216.

9. See Shepard, *Thinking Animals,* and the engaging discussions of animal colloquialisms in Christine Ammer, *It's Raining Cats and Dogs,* and Robert Hendrickson, *Animal Crackers: A Bestial Lexicon.*

10. José Stevens, "Power Animals, Animal Imagery, and Self-Actualization," Ph.D. dissertation, California Institute of Integral Studies, 1983. Stevens used Shostrom's Personal Orientation Inventory (POI) to assess levels of self-actualization.

11. C. G. Jung, *Mysterium Coniunctionis,* pp. 212–213.

12. Ibid., p. 417.

13. Marie-Louise von Franz, *Shadow and Evil in Fairy Tales,* pp. 259–260.

14. Marija Gimbutas, *The Language of the Goddess.*

15. Isha Schwaller de Lubicz, *Her-Bak: Egyptian Initiate,* p. 304 ff. According to Schwaller de Lubicz, who devoted his life to decoding the esoteric meaning of Egyptian temple structures and paintings, the *neter* differs from the *totem* in that the latter is a matter of belief in a kind of natural affinity between an individual or clan and an animal species. The *neter,* on the other hand, is a cosmic principle, operating invisibly but with its own inherent meaning.

16. Particularly striking is the contrast between the human-animal relationship portrayed in Eden, the paradise state, in which animals live at peace with one another and with man, and the relationship as it developed subsequently, after the Fall. Humanity has carried out Adam's mandate to name the animals; but apart from that, the "dominion" Adam was supposedly given

over the animals has been taken as divine license to exploit them, rather than to care for them in wise stewardship. For a more extensive discussion of the contrary biblical attitudes toward nature, animals, and the environment, see my "The Split between Spirit and Nature in European Consciousness," in *Noetic Sciences Review* (Spring 1993); also in *The Trumpeter* 10, no. 2 (Winter 1993) and in *ReVision* 15, no. 4 (Spring 1993).

17. The first passage, on his sickness and despair, is at Job 30:17, 29–30. The second passage, with the ecospiritual vision, is at Job 12: 7–8.

18. Joseph Epes Brown, "The Bison and the Moth: Lakota Correspondences," in *Parabola* 8, no. 2 (May 1983—special issue on animals).

19. The archetypal image of the wild human, a figure covered in hair and/or with horns, is discussed in my essay "Mythic Images for Remembering the Earth," in *The Green Man* 1, nos. 1 and 2 (Summer/Autumn 1993). The Gilgamesh story is discussed by me in an unpublished manuscript, "The Hero, the Wildman, and the Goddess: The Story of Gilgamesh, Enkidu, and Ishtar," and in an audiotape available from the Green Earth Foundation. A basic version of the myth can be found in *The Epic of Gilgamesh*, trans. N. K. Sandars. A fascinating Jungian study of the myth has been published by Rivkah Schärf Kluger, *The Archetypal Significance of Gilgamesh*.

20. Several versions of the Zen Oxherding pictures and commentaries exist. The ones drawn on here are in *Zen Flesh, Zen Bones*, ed. Paul Reps, pp. 130–155; *Coming Home* by Lex Hixon, pp. 77–107; and *The Hero: Myth/ Image/Symbol*, ed. Dorothy Norman, pp. 180–191.

Chapter 10: Unfolding the Tree of Our Life

1. C. G. Jung's important essay on "The Philosophical Tree," originally published in 1954, appears in *Alchemical Studies*. An earlier version of the present chapter was published as "The Tree as a Symbol of Self-Unfoldment," in *The American Theosophist* 69, no. 10 (Fall 1981). An audiotape guided meditation on the theme of the tree is available from the Green Earth Foundation.

2. Victor Frankl, *Man's Search for Meaning*, p. 37.

3. Jung, "Philosophical Tree," p. 253.

4. The tree paintings of Jung's patients are presented and analyzed in the abovementioned essay on the philosophical tree. In psychological assessment by "projective drawing," drawings of persons, houses, trees, and animals are frequently used. A very detailed and comprehensive examination of tree drawings as projective test devices is presented in a book by Karen Bolander, *Tree Drawings*.

5. Herbert V. Guenther, *The Tantric View of Life*, p. 120.

6. *Meister Eckhart*, trans. Raymond B. Blakney, p. 75.

7. From a lecture by Paul Klee, published in 1924 under the title On Modern Art. Quoted in *The Tree of Life* by Roger Cook, p. 31. This book is an excellent compendium of art and symbolism related to the theme of this chapter.

8. Guenther, *Tantric View of Life*, p. 119.

9. Mircea Eliade, *Shamanism*, Chapter 4, pp. 110–144, and Chapter 8, pp. 259–287.

10. See R. Gordon Wasson, *Soma: Divine Mushroom of Immortality*; and Peter T. Furst, *Hallucinogens and Culture*, p. 89 ff.

11. Quoted in Cook, *Tree of Life*, p. 37.

12. Mircea Eliade, *Images and Symbols*, p. 46.

13. William Irwin Thompson, in his *The Time Falling Bodies Take to Light*, writes: "The coffin is the causal body (an alternate name for the mental body); the movement down the river of time is the descent through the intermediate realms, the astral plane; and the beaching upon the earth where it becomes embedded in a tree is the final process of incarnation in a physical body. The trunk of the tree is the spinal column of the animal, physical form" (pp. 218219).

14. Erich Neumann, *The Origins and History of Consciousness*, pp. 230, 232. Additional information and interpretation concerning the Egyptian *djed* pillar can be found in Wallis Budge's *Egyptian Religion*, and in *Her-Bak: Egyptian Initiate* by Isha Schwaller de Lubicz.

15. Rolfing is a type of bodywork, also called structural integration, invented by Dr. Ida Rolf. Craniosacral alignment refers to a type of bodywork practiced by some osteopaths, in which the pulsation of the cerebrospinal fluid up and down the spinal axis is amplified and unblocked. See Andrew Weil, *Natural Health, Natural Medicine*, for further information about these procedures.

16. Neumann, *Origins and History of Consciousness*, p. 234.

17. For a more extensive discussion of the Hermetic principle of macro-micro correspondence in relation to the development of ecological or Gaia consciousness, see my essay "Gaia's Alchemy: Ruin and Renewal of the Elements," *ReVision* 9, no. 2 (1987): 41–51. Reprinted in *The Sacred Landscape*, ed. F. Lehrman.

18. John G. Neihardt, *Black Elk Speaks*, p. 43.

19. For a discussion of the Yggdrasil world tree complex and the Odin myths, see my *Well of Remembrance*, pp. 191–214.

20. *The Principal Upanishads*, trans. S. Radhakrishnan, p. 641.

21. Quoted in Cook, *Tree of Life*, p. 18.

22. Persuasive reexaminations of the Bible in light of the evidence for earlier Mother Goddess religions are offered in *When God Was a Woman* by Merlin Stone: "Many Bible passages report that idols of the female deity, referred as *asherah* (in lower case), were to be found on every high hill, under every green tree and alongside altars in the temples. They were a symbol identified with the worship of the Goddess as Asherah and may have been a pole or a living tree, perhaps carved as a statue" (p. 175). See also *Behind the Sex of the God* by Carol Ochs. I am indebted to Elaine Pagels for drawing my attention to the parallel between these views of Genesis and certain Gnostic texts, particularly the Jewish Life of Adam and Eve, and the Gospel of Phillip.

23. Gen. 3:3–5.
24. Gen. 3:22.
25. For a review of the evidence for the aquatic ape theory of human evolution, see *ReVision* 18, no. 2 (Fall 1995). For a discussion of the expulsion from Eden in the light of this scenario, see my essay in that issue, "Mythological Traces of Aquatic Human Ancestry," pp. 44–48.
26. A text by the fourteenth-century Arabic alchemical philosopher Abul Kasim, quoted by Jung (*Psychology and Alchemy*, p. 348) alludes to this kind of reading of the story: "The prime matter . . . of the elixir is taken from a single tree which grows in the lands of the West. This is the tree of which whosoever eats, men and *jinn* [spirits] obey him. It is also the tree of which Adam (peace be upon him) was forbidden to eat, and when he ate thereof he was transformed from his angelic form to his human form."
27. The symbolic equation of tree and cross in the legend of the Holy Rood is discussed in Alan Watts, *Myth and Ritual in Christianity*.
28. From the "Turba Philosophorum," in C.G. Jung, *Alchemical Studies*, p. 305.
29. Jung, "The Philosophical Tree," *Alchemical Studies*, p. 303.
30. Jung, "The Philosophical Tree." On the basis of the alchemical art, Jung concluded that for women, the tree was most often imagined as emerging out of the head, a tree of the mind. For men, the tree is more often shown emerging out of the loins, a tree of generation.
31. *Through the Gateway of the Heart*, ed. Sophia Adamson, p. 11.
32. Jung, *Alchemical Studies*, p. 310. The tree as made of fire, which fits with the idea of the tree being related to the nervous system, is also found in the Indian traditions. See A. K. Coomaraswamy, "The Inverted Tree," in *Selected Papers of A. K. Coomaraswamy*, ed. Roger Lipsey. "The Tree is a fiery pillar as seen from below, a solar pillar as from above it is a Tree of Light" (p. 387).

Chapter 11: Journey to the Place of Vision and Power

1. Walt Whitman, *Leaves of Grass*, p. 80.
2. From the *Brihadaranyaka Upanishad*, in *The Principal Upanishads*, trans. S. Radhakrishnan, p. 274.
3. John 14:6; Matt. 25:14.
4. See Fritz Meier's essay, "The Transformation of Man in Mystical Islam," in *Man and Transformation*, ed. Joseph Campbell, p. 47.
5. From *The Sacred Pipe: Black Elk's Account of the Seven Rites of the Oglala Sioux*, recorded and edited by Joseph Epes Brown, pp. 58–59.
6. Mircea Eliade, *Shamanism: Archaic Techniques of Ecstasy*, p. 182.
7. R. D. Laing, *The Politics of Experience*, pp. 68–69.
8. Muhyiddin Ibn al'Arabi, *Journey to the Lord of Power*, p. 27.
9. *The Epic of Gilgamesh*, trans. N. K. Sandars, p. 94.
10. These journal entries, here and below, are quoted by permission from an unpublished autobiographical work by Marilee Stark.
11. For a deeply moving account of the Native American vision quest by two

people who have been instrumental in bringing that healing practice to thousands of contemporary individuals, see *The Roaring of the Sacred River* by Steven Foster and Meredith Little. For a brilliant literary treatment of the Australian walkabout, as well as other aspects of the aboriginal world, see *The Songlines* by Bruce Chatwin. The "year walk" is an initiatory practice of Basques that they enter into during their adolescence as a way of learning to relate to nature and overcome fear. I am indebted to Angeles Arrien, Basque anthropologist and folklorist, for providing information about this practice.

12. The classic account of this is Barbara Myerhoff, *Peyote Hunt: The Sacred Journey of the Huichol Indians.*

13. See Edwin Bernbaum, *The Way to Shambhala,* for an excellent discussion of this idea and the myths surrounding it.

14. Joseph Campbell, *The Hero with a Thousand Faces,* p. 58. Other interesting discussions of the threshold theme in mythology and shamanism are found in Joseph Henderson's *Thresholds of Initiation* and in Stephen Larsen's *The Shaman's Doorway.*

15. Marilee Stark; see note 10 above.

16. The passage is my translation from the German edition of Hildegard's book, *Wisse die Wege: Scivias,* p. 120. There exists also an English translation by Bruce Hozeski. See also my essay "The Mystical Symbolic Psychology of Hildegard von Bingen," in *ReVision* 11, no. 2 (Fall 1988): 3–12.

17. From Selected *Poems of Rainer Maria Rilke,* trans. Robert Bly, p. 177.

18. From *The Kabir Book,* versions by Robert Bly, p. 17.

19. *Zen Flesh, Zen Bones,* ed. Paul Reps, p. 88.

20. For an account of "lower world" journeys in traditional shamanism and in contemporary individuals learning the ancient methods, see Michael Harner, *The Way of the Shaman,* pp. 20–39. It is interesting to compare the shamanic experience of going "downward" in the altered state with the almost universal experience of downward movement when falling asleep. In the shamanic journey, one travels downward but stays awake. This approach has some similarities to what some have called the "waking dream" method of psychotherapy. See the book *Waking Dreams* by Mary Watkins for details on this approach.

21. Jonah 2:5–6.

22. Joan Halifax, *Shaman: The Wounded Healer,* p. 18.

23. For a poetic version of the myth of Inanna, see Diane Wolkstein and Samuel Noah Kramer, *Inanna: Queen of Heaven and Earth.* An in-depth discussion from a Jungian point of view is found in *Descent to the Goddess* by Sylvia Brinton Perera, which also focuses on the question of what aspect of the feminine psyche is represented by the death goddess Ereshkigal. The interpretation of the stripping of the ornaments at the seven gates, in terms of the yogic chakras, is based on this ritualistic element in the story: at the first gate, she must remove her crown (crown center); at the next, her ear-

rings (brain center); at the third, her necklace (throat center); then her breast ornaments (heart center); then ornaments from her hands and feet; then her abdominal girdle (abdominal center); and finally her pelvic girdle (generative or root center). See also the discussion of this myth in chapter 2.

24. For a review of parapsychology research on remote viewing and out-of-body experiences, see *Psi: Scientific Studies of the Psychic Realm* by Charles Tart.

25. See note 5 above.

26. Quoted in "The Dove and the Darkness in Ancient Byzantine Mysticism" by Jean Danielou, in *Man and Transformation*, ed. J. Campbell, pp. 277–278.

27. From *Selected Poems of Rainer Maria Rilke*, trans. Robert Bly, p. 13.

28. Mircea Eliade, *Shamanism: Archaic Techniques of Ecstasy*, p. 191.

29. *Tibet's Great Yogi Milarepa*, trans. W. Y. Evans-Wentz, p. 212.

30. *The Principal Upanishads*, ed. S. Radhakrishnan, p. 833.

31. Ps. 104:2–3.

32. *Treasury of Traditional Wisdom*, ed. Whitall Perry, p. 948.

33. H. A. Murray formulated the hypothesis of an "Icarus complex," which combines interest in fire, ascensionism, and urethral-phallic eroticism. This complex, according to Murray, may be an immature form of the "solar complex" and includes ambition, craving for immortality, and tendencies toward messianic enthusiasm. In Jung's psychology, it parallels the concept of ego-inflation. See *Endeavors in Psychology: Selections from the Personology of Henry A. Murray*, ed. Edwin S. Shneidman, pp. 535–556.

34. René Daumal, *Mount Analogue*, p. 156.

35. Farid ud-Din Attar, *The Conference of the Birds*, p. 131. The symbolism of the valleys to be traversed on the mystic's journey appears also in the writings of the nineteenth-century Persian founder of the Baha'i religion, Baha'Ullah (*The Seven Valleys and The Four Valleys*), as well as in the recorded talks and teachings of the nineteenth-century Indian saint Ramakrishna. One account is given in *The Face of Silence* by Dhan Gopal Mukerji.

36. Job 12:24.

37. Hos. 2:16–17.

38. See note 16 above.

39. See note 10 above.

40. T. S. Eliot, from "Little Gidding," *Four Quartets*.

Chapter 12: Returning to the Source

1. From Sengtsan, *Hsin Hsin Ming: Verses on the Faith-Mind*, trans. Richard B. Clark. Known also as the Third Chinese Zen Patriarch, Sengtsan (Japanese *Sosan*) lived in the sixth century C.E., a poor hermit monk.

2. J. M. Cohen and J-F. Phipps, *The Common Experience*, p. 158.

3. Used by permission from the author's files.

4. *The Gospel According to Thomas*, ed. A. Guillamont, p. 29.

5. D. T. Suzuki, "The Awakening of a New Consciousness in Zen," in *Man and Transformation*, ed. Joseph Campbell, p. 196.

6. *Zen Flesh, Zen Bones,* ed. Paul Reps, p. 103.

7. The Church of All Worlds, founded by Otter and Morning Glory Zell. See Margot Adler, *Drawing Down the Moon,* pp. 283–318.

8. *People* magazine, December 1982, p. 71.

9. Walter Kaufmann, "The Inevitability of Alienation," in *Alienation,* ed. Richard Schacht, pp. xv–lviii.

10. Ibid., p. lv.

11. Eph. 4:18.

12. Hildegard von Bingen, *Wisse die Wege: Scivias,* p. 120 ff. See also my essay "The Mystical Symbolic Psychology of Hildegard von Bingen," in *ReVision* 11, no. 2 (Fall 1988): 7

13. *The Nag Hammadi Library,* ed. James M. Robinson, p. 443.

14. Jacques Lacarrière, *The Gnostics,* pp. 26–29.

15. Philo Judaeus, "On the Confusion of Tongues," in *Treasury of Traditional Wisdom,* ed. Whitall Perry, p. 365.

16. For a discussion of *pravritti* and *nivritti,* see Judith M. Tyberg, *The Language of the Gods,* pp. 31–32, and Sri Krishna Prem, *The Yoga of the Bhagavat Gita,* especially chapter 16.

17. For etymologies of *evolution* and *involution,* see Eric Partridge, *Origins,* under "voluble."

18. David Bohm, "The Enfolding-Unfolding Universe," interview by Renée Weber, in *Revision* 1, no. 3/4 (Summer/Fall 1978): p. 24. See also Bohm's *Wholeness and the Implicate Order,* and the excellent review essay on the life work of David Bohm, "River of Truth," by William Keepin, in *ReVision* 16, no. 1 (Summer 1993): 32–46.

19. Arthur Young, *The Reflexive Universe,* p. 164.

20. Satprem, *Sri Aurobindo,* p. 301. At another place in the same work, Aurobindo is quoted: "We speak of the evolution of Life in Matter, the evolution of Mind in Matter; but evolution is a word which merely states the phenomenon without explaining it. For there seems to be no reason why Life should evolve out of material elements or Mind out of living form, unless we accept . . . that Life is already involved in Matter and Mind in Life because in essence Matter is a veiled form of Life, Life a form of veiled consciousness" (p. 304).

21. *The Nag Hammadi Library,* ed. James M. Robinson, p. 449.

22. See note 20, chapter 9.

23. William Bridges, "The Odyssey and the Myth of the Homeward Journey," in *Consciousness and Culture* 1, no. 1 (1977): 99–112.

24. C. G. Jung quotes the Arabic alchemist Kalid: "And Hermes said to his father: Father, I am afraid of the enemy in my house. And he said: my son, take a Corascene dog and an Armenian bitch, join them together, and they will beget a dog of a celestial hue. He will guard your friend, and he will guard you from your enemy, and he will help you wherever you may be, always being with you, in this world and the next" (*The Psychology of the*

Transference, p. 86 n). The process is also reminiscent of shamanic practices involving an animal ally.

25. The parable of the prodigal son is in Luke 15:11–32; the Syrian "Hymn of the Robe of Glory" is given in *The Wisdom of the Serpent*, ed. Joseph L. Henderson and Maud Oakes, pp. 153–160; a version called "Hymn of the Soul," extracted from the Acts of Thomas, is given in *The King's Son*, ed. Robert Cecil. This book, which is an anthology of writings on "Traditional Psychologies and Contemporary Thoughts on Man," includes a whole section entitled "Steps on the Road Home."

26. The Navaho prayer given in extract here, or versions similar to it, have been published in several places; this particular version was found by the author many years ago, on a trip through the Southwest, in a newspaper article on Navaho myth and religion.

BIBLIOGRAPHY

Adamson, Sophia, ed. *Through the Gateway of the Heart*. San Francisco: Four Trees Publications, 1985.

Adler, Margot. *Drawing Down the Moon*. Boston: Beacon Press, 1986.

Ammer, Christine. *It's Raining Cats and Dogs*. New York: Paragon House, 1989.

Arieti, Silvano. Creativity: *The Magic Synthesis*. New York: Basic Books, 1980.

Assagioli, Roberto. Psychosynthesis. New York: Viking Press, 1971.

Attar, Farid ud-Din. *The Conference of the Birds*. Boulder, CO: Shambhala, 1971.

Augros, Robert, and George Stanciu. *The New Biology: Discovering the Wisdom of Nature*. Boston: Shambhala New Science Library, 1988.

Augustine, Saint. *Saint Augustine: Confessions*. Edited by R. S. Pine-Coffin. New York: Penguin Books, 1961.

Aurobindo, Sri. *The Life Divine*, 2 vols. Pondicherry, India: Sri Aurobindo Ashram, 1977.

Baha'Ullah. *The Seven Valleys and the Four Valleys*. Wilmette, IL: Baha'i Publishing Trust, 1975.

Bakan, David. *The Duality of Human Existence*. Chicago: Rand McNally, 1966.

Baker, Ellsworth. *Man in the Trap*. New York: Macmillan, 1980.

Bateson, Gregory. *Mind and Nature*. New York: E. P. Dutton, 1979.

_____. *Steps Toward an Ecology of Mind*. New York: E. P. Dutton, 1979.

Beahrs, John O. *Unity and Multiplicity: Multilevel Consciousness of Self in Hypnosis, Psychiatric Disorder and Mental Health*. New York: Brunner/Mazel, 1982.

Becker, Ernest. *Escape from Evil*. New York: Free Press, 1975.

Bentov, Itzhak. *Stalking the Wild Pendulum*. New York: E. P. Dutton, 1977

Bernbaum, Edwin. *The Way to Shambhala*. Garden City, NY: Doubleday, Anchor Books, 1980.

Bettelheim, Bruno. *Freud and Man's Soul*. New York: Knopf, 1983.

Biederman, Hans. *Dictionary of Symbolism*. New York: Facts on File, 1992.

Blake, William. *The Marriage of Heaven and Hell*. Coral Gables, FL: University of Miami Press, 1968.

Bly, Robert. *The Kabir Book*. Boston: Beacon Press, 1971.

Boehme, Jacob. *The Forty Questions of the Soul and the Clavis*. Translated by John Sparrow. London: J. M. Watkins, 1911.

Bohm, David. *Wholeness and the Implicate Order*. London: Routledge & Kegan Paul, 1980.

Bolander, Karen. *Tree Drawings*. New York: Basic Books, 1977.

Boyd, James W. *Satan and Mara: Christian and Buddhist Symbols of Evil.* Leiden: Brill, 1975.

Bridges, William. *Transitions: Making Sense of Life's Changes.* Menlo Park, CA: Addison-Wesley, 1980.

Brown, Joseph Epes, ed. *The Sacred Pipe: Black Elk's Account of the Seven Rites of the Oglala Sioux.* New York: Viking Press, 1953.

Bucke, R. M. *Cosmic Consciousness.* New York: Bell Publishing, University Books, 1959.

Budge, Sir Wallis. *Egyptian Religion.* New York: Bell Publishing, 1959. (Originally published 1900.)

Burland, C. A. *The Arts of the Alchemists.* London: Weidenfeld & Nicholson, 1967.

Burr, Harold S. *The Fields of Life.* New York: Ballantine Books, 1972.

Campbell, Joseph. *The Hero with a Thousand Faces.* Cleveland, OH: World Publishing Co., 1956.

———, ed. *The Mysteries.* Papers from the Eranos Yearbooks, vol. 2; Bollingen Series, no. 30. Princeton, NJ: Princeton University Press, 1978.

———, ed. *Man and Transformation.* Papers from the Eranos Yearbooks, vol. 5; Bollingen Series, no. 30. Princeton, NJ: Princeton University Press, 1980.

Campbell, Robert J., ed. *Psychiatric Dictionary.* 5th ed. New York: Oxford University Press, 1981.

Capps, Walter H., and Wendy M. Wright, eds. *Silent Fire.* San Francisco: Harper & Row, 1978.

Capra, Fritjof. *The Turning Point.* New York: Simon & Schuster, 1982.

———. *The Tao of Physics.* 2nd ed. Boulder, CO: Shambhala, 1983.

Cavendish, Richard. *Visions of Heaven and Hell.* New York: Crown Publishers, 1977.

Cecil, Robert, ed. *The King's Son: Readings in the Traditional Psychologies and Contemporary Thoughts on Man.* London: Octagon Press, 1981.

Chatwin, Bruce. *The Songlines.* New York: Viking Penguin, 1987.

Chia, Mantak. *Awakening Healing Energy Through the Tao.* New York: Taoist Esoteric Yoga Foundation, 1981.

Chuang Tsu. *Chuang Tsu: The Inner Chapters.* Translated by Gia-Fu Feng and Jane English. New York: Random House, 1974.

Cirlot, J. E. *A Dictionary of Symbols.* New York: Philosophical Library, 1962.

Clark, Kenneth. *Animals and Men: Their Relationship as Reflected in Western Art from Prehistory to the Present.* New York: William Morrow, 1977.

Cohen, J. M., and J-F. Phipps. *The Common Experience.* Los Angeles: Tarcher, 1979.

Conze, Edward. *Buddhist Wisdom Books.* San Francisco: Harper & Row, 1958.

Cook, Roger. *The Tree of Life: Image for the Cosmos.* New York: Avon Books, 1974.

Coomaraswamy, A. K. *Hinduism and Buddhism.* Westport, CT: Greenwood Press, 1971.

_____. *Selected Papers of A. K. Coomaraswamy.* Vol. 1, *Traditional Art and Symbolism.* Vol. 2, Metaphysics. Edited by Roger Lipsey. Bollingen Series, no. 89. Princeton, NJ: Princeton University Press, 1977.

Cooper, J. C. *Symbolism: The Universal Language.* Willingborough, England: Aquarian Press, 1982.

Coudert, Allison. *Alchemy.* Boulder, CO: Shambhala, 1980.

Danielou, Alain. *Shiva and Dionysus.* New York: Inner Traditions International, 1984.

Daumal, René. *Mount Analogue.* New York: Viking Press, 1959.

Davis, Mikol, and Earle Lane. *Rainbows of Life: The Promise of Kirlian Photography.* New York: Harper & Row, 1978.

de Lubicz, Isha Schwaller. *Her-Bak: Egyptian Initiate.* New York: Inner Traditions International, 1978.

Delaney, Gayle. *Living Your Dreams.* San Francisco: Harper & Row, 1979.

Dement, William. *Some Must Watch While Some Must Sleep.* San Francisco: San Francisco Books, 1976.

Deutsch, Eliot. *Advaita Vedanta.* Honolulu: University of Hawaii Press, 1969.

Donahoe, James. *Dream Reality.* Oakland: Birch Press, 1979.

Dundes, Alan. *Life Is Like a Chicken Coop Ladder.* New York: Columbia University Press, 1984.

Dychtwald, Ken. *Bodymind.* Los Angeles: Tarcher, 1986.

Eckhart, Meister. *Meister Eckhart.* Translated by Raymond B. Blakney. New York: Harper & Row, 1941.

Edinger, Edward. *Ego and Archetype.* Baltimore: Penguin Books, 1972.

_____. *The Creation of Consciousness: Jung's Myth for Modern Man.* Toronto: Inner City Books, 1984.

_____. *Anatomy of the Psyche: Alchemical Symbolism in Psychotherapy.* La Salle, IL: Open Court Publishing, 1985.

Eliade, Mircea. *The Forge and the Crucible.* New York: Harper & Row, 1962.

_____. *The Two and the One.* New York: Harper & Row, 1965.

_____. *Images and Symbols.* New York: Sheed & Ward, 1969.

_____. *Yoga, Immortality, and Freedom.* Princeton, NJ: Princeton University Press, 1969.

_____. *Shamanism: Archaic Techniques of Ecstasy.* Princeton, NJ: Princeton University Press, 1972.

_____. *A History of Religious Ideas,* 3 vols. Chicago: University of Chicago Press, 1979.

_____. *Ordeal by Labyrinth.* Chicago: University of Chicago Press, 1982.

Eliot, T. S. *Four Quartets.* New York: Harcourt Brace Jovanovich, 1968.

Elkin, A. P. *Aboriginal Men of High Degree.* 2nd ed. New York: St. Martin's, 1977. Evans-Wentz, W. Y. *Tibetan Yoga and Secret Doctrines.* New York: Oxford University Press, 1958.

_____, ed. *The Tibetan Book of the Dead.* New York: Oxford University Press, 1960.

_____, trans. *Tibet's Great Yogi Milarepa.* New York: Oxford University Press,

1928.

Fadiman, James, and Donald Kewman. *Exploring Madness: Experience, Theory, and Research.* Monterey, CA: Brooks/Cole, 1973.

Ferguson, Marilyn. *The Aquarian Conspiracy.* Los Angeles: Tarcher, 1981.

Foster, Steven, and Meredith Little. *The Roaring of the Sacred River.* New York: Prentice-Hall, 1987.

Frankl, Victor. *Man's Search for Meaning.* New York: Washington Square Press, 1963.

Freemantle, Francesca, and Chogyam Trungpa, trans. *The Tibetan Book of the Dead.* Boulder, CO: Shambhala, 1975.

Freud, Sigmund. *Beyond the Pleasure Principle.* New York: Liveright Publishing, 1950.

_____. *General Psychological Theory.* Translated by J. Strachey. New York: Collier, 1963.

Fuller, Buckminster. *Synergetics.* New York: Macmillan, 1975.

Furst, Peter T. *Hallucinogens and Culture.* San Francisco: Chandler & Sharp, 1976.

Gabbard, Glen, and Stuart Twemlow. *With the Eyes of the Mind: An Empirical Analysis of Out-of-Body States.* New York: Praeger, 1984.

Gardner, Howard. *Art, Mind, and Brain.* New York: Basic Books, 1982.

Garfield, Patricia. *Creative Dreaming.* New York: Ballantine, 1974.

Gerber, Richard. *Vibrational Medicine.* Santa Fe, NM: Bear & Co., 1988.

Gimbutas, Marija *The Goddesses and Gods of Old Europe.* Berkeley: University of California Press, 1982.

_____. *The Language of the Goddess.* San Francisco: Harper & Row, 1989.

Godwin, Joscelyn. *Mystery Religions in the Ancient World.* San Francisco: Harper & Row, 1981.

Goleman, Daniel. *Varieties of Meditative Experience.* New York: E. P. Dutton, 1977.

_____. *Emotional Intelligence.* New York: Bantam Books, 1995.

Govinda, Lama Anagarika. *Foundations of Tibetan Mysticism.* London: Rider & Co., 1960.

Grant, Joan. *Winged Pharaoh.* New York: Berkeley Publishing Co., 1969.

Greenwell, Bonnie. *Energies of Transformation: A Guide to the Kundalini Process.* Cupertino, CA: Shakti River Press, 1990.

Gregory of Nyssa. *From Glory to Glory.* Translated and edited by Herbert Musurillo. Crestwood, NY: St. Vladimir's Seminary Press, 1979.

Groddeck, Georg. *The Book of the It.* New York: International University Press, 1976.

Grof, Stanislav. *Realms of the Human Unconscious.* New York: E. P. Dutton, 1976.

_____. *Beyond the Brain: Birth, Death and Transcendence in Psychotherapy.* Albany: State University of New York Press, 1985.

_____. *The Adventure of Self-Discovery.* Albany: State University of New

York Press, 1988.

Grof, Stanislav, and Christina Grof. *Beyond Death*. New York: Thames & Hudson, 1980.

Grof, Stanislav, and Joan Halifax. *The Human Encounter with Death*. New York: E. P. Dutton, 1977.

Guenther, Herbert V. *The Tantric View of Life*. Boulder, CO: Shambhala, 1972.

———, trans. *The Life and Teachings of Naropa*. New York: Oxford University Press, 1963.

Guillamont, A., ed. *The Gospel According to Thomas*. San Francisco: Harper & Row, 1984.

Haddick, Vern, ed. *Transcendence and Transformation: Writings from California Institute of Integral Studies*. New York: University Press of America, 1983.

Haich, Elizabeth. *Initiation*. Palo Alto, CA: The Seed Center, 1974.

Halifax, Joan. *Shaman: The Wounded Healer*. New York: Crossroad Publishing Co., 1982.

Harner, Michael. *The Way of the Shaman*. San Francisco: Harper & Row, 1980.

Hartmann, Franz. *Jacob Boehme: Life and Doctrines*. Blauvelt, NY: Multimedia, 1929.

Henderson, Joseph. *Thresholds of Initiation*. Middletown, CT: Wesleyan Press, 1967.

Henderson, Joseph L., and Maud Oakes. *The Wisdom of the Serpent: The Myths of Death, Rebirth and Resurrection*. New York: Collier Books, 1963.

Hendrickson, Robert. *Animal Crackers: A Bestial Lexicon*. New York: Viking Press/Penguin Books, 1983.

Herzog, Edgar. *Psyche and Death*. New York: G. P. Putnam, 1967.

Hilgard, Ernest. *Divided Consciousness*. New York: John Wiley & Sons, 1977.

Hillman, James, and Marie-Louise von Franz. *Lectures on Jung's Typology*. Dallas: Spring Publications, 1971.

Hixon, Lex. *Coming Home: The Experience of Enlightenment in Sacred Tradition*. Garden City, NY: Doubleday, Anchor Books, 1978.

Huxley, Aldous. *The Doors of Perception*. San Francisco: Harper & Row, 1970.

———. *Heaven and Hell*. San Francisco: Harper & Row, 1970.

———. *The Perennial Philosophy*. New York: Harper & Row, 1970.

Huxley, Francis. Dragon. New York: Collier Books, 1979.

Ibn al'Arabi, Muhyiddin. *Journey to the Lord of Power: A Sufi Manual on Retreat*. Translated by Rabia Terri Harris. New York: Inner Traditions International, 1981.

James, William. *Varieties of Religious Experience*. New York: New American Library, 1958.

Jantsch, Erich, and Conrad H. Waddington, eds. *Evolution and Consciousness: Human Systems in Transition*. Reading, MA: Addison-Wesley, 1976.

Johnson, Don. *The Protean Body*. New York: Harper & Row, 1977.

———. *Body*. Boston: Beacon Press, 1983.

Johnson, Raynor. *The Imprisoned Splendor.* New York: Harper & Row, 1954.

Jung, C. G. *The Collected Works.* Vol. 12, *Psychology and Alchemy.* Translated by R.F.C. Hull. London: Routledge & Kegan Paul, 1953.

_____. *The Collected Works.* Vol. 9, part 1, *The Archetypes and the Collective Unconscious.* Translated by R.F.C. Hull. Princeton, NJ: Princeton University Press, 1959.

_____. *The Collected Works.* Vol. 9, part 2, *Aion.* Translated by R.F.C. Hull. Princeton, NJ: Princeton University Press, 1959.

_____. *The Collected Works.* Vol. 10, *Civilization in Transition.* Translated by R.F.C. Hull. Princeton, NJ: Princeton University Press, 1964.

_____. *The Collected Works.* Vol. 16, *The Practice of Psychotherapy.* Translated by R.F.C. Hull. Princeton, NJ: Princeton University Press, 1966.

_____. *The Collected Works.* Vol. 13, *Alchemical Studies.* Translated by R.F.C. Hull. Princeton, NJ: Princeton University Press, 1967.

_____. *The Collected Works.* Vol. 16, *The Psychology of the Transference.* Translated by R.F.C. Hull. Princeton, NJ: Princeton University Press, 1969.

_____. *The Collected Works.* Vol. 8, *The Structure and Dynamics of the Psyche.* Translated by R.F.C. Hull. Princeton, NJ: Princeton University Press, 1969.

_____. *The Collected Works.* Vol. 14, *Mysterium Coniunctionis.* Translated by R.F.C. Hull. Princeton, NJ: Princeton University Press, 1970.

_____. *The Collected Works.* Vol. 6, *Psychological Types.* Translated by R.F.C. Hull. Princeton, NJ: Princeton University Press, 1971.

Karagulla, Shafica. *Breakthrough to Creativity.* Marina del Rey, CA: DeVorss, 1967.

Keleman, Stanley. *Living Your Dying.* New York: Random House, 1976.

_____. *Somatic Reality.* Berkeley, CA: Center Press, 1982.

Kesey, Ken. *One Flew Over the Cuckoo's Nest.* New York: Penguin, 1976.

Klonsky, Milton. *William Blake: The Seer and His Visions.* New York: Harmony Books, 1977.

Kluger, Rivkah Schärf. *The Archetypal Significance of Gilgamesh.* Einsiedeln, Switzerland: Daimon Verlag, 1991.

Koestler, Arthur. *The Act of Creation.* London: Pan Books, 1964.

Kramrisch, Stella. *The Presence of Siva.* Princeton, NJ: Princeton University Press.

Krishna, Gopi. *Kundalini: The Evolutionary Energy in Man.* Boulder, CO: Shambhala, 1971.

Krishnamurti, Jiddu. *The Flame of Attention.* San Francisco: Harper & Row, 1984.

LaBerge, Stephen. *Lucid Dreaming.* Los Angeles: Tarcher, 1985.

LaBerge, Stephen, and Howard Rheingold. *Exploring the World of Lucid Dreaming.* New York: Ballantine Books, 1990.

Lacarrière, Jacques. *The Gnostics.* New York: E. P. Dutton, 1977.

Laing, R. D. *Knots.* London: Tavistock, 1970.

_____. *The Divided Self.* New York: E. P. Dutton, 1977.

_____. *The Politics of Experience*. New York: Ballantine, 1978.

Lakoff, George, and Mark Johnson. *Metaphors We Live By*. Chicago: University of Chicago Press, 1980.

Lao Tsu. *Tao Te Ching*. Translated by D. C. Law. New York: Penguin Books, 1963.

_____. *Tao Te Ching*. Translated by Gia-Fu Feng and Jane English. New York: Vintage Books, 1972.

Larsen, Stephen. *The Shaman's Doorway*. New York: Harper Colophon Books, 1976.

Lauf, Detlef. *Secret Doctrines of the Tibetan Book of the Dead*. Boulder, CO: Shambhala, 1977.

Leach, Maria, ed. *Standard Dictionary of Folklore, Mythology, and Legend*. New York: Funk & Wagnall, 1972.

Leary, David, ed. *Metaphors in the History of Psychology*. New York: Cambridge University Press, 1990.

Leary, Timothy. *Flashbacks*. Los Angeles: Tarcher, 1983.

Leary, Timothy, Ralph Metzner, and Richard Alpert. *The Psychedelic Experience*. New York: University Press, 1964.

Lehrman, F., ed. *The Sacred Landscape*. Berkeley: Celestial Arts, 1988.

Lévi-Strauss, Claude. *The Savage Mind*. Chicago: University of Chicago Press, 1966.

Levine, Stephen. *Who Dies? An Investigation of Conscious Living and Conscious Dying*. Garden City, NY: Doubleday, Anchor Books, 1982.

Lifton, Robert J. *The Life of the Self*. New York: Simon & Schuster, 1976.

Lowen, Alexander. Bioenergetics. New York: Penguin, 1976.

Lynn, S. J., and J. W. Rhue, eds. *Dissociation: Clinical and Theoretical Perspectives*. New York: Guilford Press, 1994.

MacLaine, Shirley. *Out on a Limb*. New York: Bantam, 1983.

MacLean, Paul. *A Triune Concept of Brain and Behavior*. Clarence M. Hincks Memorial Lectures. Toronto: University of Toronto Press, 1973.

Maharshi, Ramana. *The Spiritual Teachings of Ramana Maharshi*. Foreword by C. G. Jung. Boulder, CO: Shambhala, 1972.

Mann, Edward. *Orgone, Reich, and Eros*. New York: Simon & Schuster, 1974.

Mann, John, and Lar Short. *The Body of Light*. New York: Globe Press Books, 1990.

Markley, O. W., et. al *Changing Images of Man*. Edited by the Center for the Study of Social Policy—SRI International, and O. W. Markley. Elmsford, NY: Pergamon Press, 1981.

Mead, G.R.S. *The Doctrine of the Subtle Body in the Western Tradition*. Wheaton, IL: Theosophical Publishing House, 1919.

Metzner, Ralph. *Know Your Type: Maps of Identity*. Garden City, NY: Doubleday, 1979.

_____. *Maps of Consciousness*. New York: Macmillan, Collier Books, 1971.

_____. *The Well of Remembrance: Rediscovering the Earth Wisdom Mythol-*

tive Christianity. Ithaca, NY: Cornell University Press, 1977.

———. *Satan: The Early Christian Tradition.* Ithaca, NY: Cornell University Press, 1981.

Russell, Peter. *The Global Brain Awakens.* Palo Alto, CA: Global Brain, 1995.

Russell, Walter. *The Secret of Light.* New York: W. Russell, 1947.

Saint John of the Cross. *The Poems of St. John of the Cross.* Translated by J. F. Nims. Chicago: University of Chicago Press, 1959.

Sandars, N. K., trans. *The Epic of Gilgamesh.* New York: Penguin Books, 1960.

Sannella, Lee. *Kundalini: Psychosis or Transcendence?* San Francisco: H. S. Dakin Co., 1976.

Satprem. *Sri Aurobindo, or the Adventure of Consciousness.* San Francisco: Harper & Row, 1968.

———. *The Mind of the Cells: Willed Mutation of Our Species.* New York: Institute for Evolutionary Research, 1982.

Schacht, Richard. *Alienation.* Garden City, NY: Doubleday, Anchor Books, 1970.

Sengstan. *Hsin Hsin Ming.* Translated by Richard B. Clarke. Buffalo, NY: White Pine Press, 1984.

Sharaf, Myron. *Fury on Earth: A Biography of Wilhelm Reich.* New York: St. Martin's Press, 1983.

Sheldrake, Rupert. *A New Science of Life.* Los Angeles: Tarcher, 1981.

———. *The Presence of the Past: Morphic Resonance and the Habits of Nature.* New York: Times Books, 1988.

———. *The Rebirth of Nature: The Greening of Science and God.* New York: Bantam Books, 1991.

Shepard, Paul. *Thinking Animals: Animals and the Development of Human Intelligence.* New York: Viking Press, 1978.

———. *Nature and Madness.* San Francisco: Sierra Club Books, 1982.

———. *The Others: How Animals Made Us Human.* Washington, DC: Island Press, 1996.

———. *Traces of an Omnivore.* Washington, DC: Island Press, 1996.

Stevens, Anthony. *Archetypes: A Natural History of the Self.* New York: Quill, 1983.

Stone, Merlin. *When God Was a Woman.* New York: Harcourt Brace Jovanovich, 1976.

Suzuki, Shunryu. *Zen Mind, Beginner's Mind.* Tokyo: Weatherhill, 1970.

Swedenborg, Emanuel. *Heaven and Hell.* Translated by Sadataro Suzuki. London: Swedenborg Society, 1908.

Swimme, Brian, and Thomas Berry. *The Universe Story.* San Francisco: HarperSanFrancisco, 1992.

Tart, Charles, ed. *Altered States of Consciousness.* New York: John Wiley & Sons, 1969.

———. *Transpersonal Psychologies.* New York: Harper & Row, 1975.

———. *Psi: Scientific Studies of the Psychic Realm.* New York: E. P. Dutton,

1977.

_____ . *Waking Up: Overcoming Obstacles to Human Potential*. Boston: Shambhala New Science, 1986.

_____ . *Open Mind, Discriminating Mind: Reflections on Human Possibilities*. San Francisco: Harper & Row, 1989.

Taylor, C. W., and F. Barron, eds. *Scientific Creativity: Its Recognition and Development*. New York: John Wiley & Sons, 1966.

Tedlock, Dennis, trans. *Popul Vuh*. New York: Simon & Schuster, 1985.

Teilhard de Chardin, Pierre. *The Phenomenon of Man*. San Francisco: Harper & Row, 1965.

Thomas, Lewis. *The Lives of a Cell*. New York: Penguin Books, 1974.

_____ . *Late Night Thoughts on Listening to Mahler's Ninth Symphony*. New York: Viking Press, 1980.

Thompson, William Irwin. *The Time Falling Bodies Take to Light*. New York: St. Martin's Press, 1981.

Thurman, Robert, trans. *The Tibetan Book of the Dead*. New York: Bantam Books, 1994.

Toffler, Alvin. *The Third Wave*. New York: Bantam, 1981.

Tompkins, Peter, and Christopher Bird. *The Secret Life of Plants*. New York: Harper & Row, 1973.

Trismosin, Solomon. *Splendor Solis*. Translated by Joscelyn Godwin. Edinburgh: Magnum Opus Hermetic Sourceworks, 1981.

Tyberg, Judith M. *The Language of the Gods*. Los Angeles: East-West Cultural Center, 1970.

Underhill, Evelyn. *Mysticism*. New York: New American Library, 1955.

von Bingen, Hildegard. *Wisse die Wege: Scivias*. Salzburg: Otto Mueller Verlag, 1954.

_____ . *Scivias*. Translated by Bruce Hozeski. Santa Fe, NM: Bear & Co., 1986.

von Franz, Marie-Louise. *Projection and Re-Collection in Jungian Psychology*. La Salle, IL: Open Court, 1980.

_____ . *Shadow and Evil in Fairy Tales*. Irving, TX: Spring Publications, 1980.

Wade, Jenny. *Changes of Mind: A Holonomic Theory of the Evolution of Consciousness*. Albany: State University of New York Press, 1995.

Waite, A. E., ed. *The Hermetic Museum*, 2 vols. 1893. Reprint, New York: Samuel Weiser, 1983.

Wasson, R. Gordon. *Soma: Divine Mushroom of Immortality*. New York: Harcourt Brace Jovanovich, n.d.

Wasson, R. Gordon, Carl A. P. Ruck, and Albert Hofmann. *The Road to Eleusis: Unveiling the Secret of the Mysteries*. New York: Harcourt Brace Jovanovich, 1978.

Watkins, Mary. *Waking Dreams*. New York: Harper & Row, 1976.

Watts, Alan. *Myth and Ritual in Christianity*. Boston: Beacon Press, 1968.

Weil, Andrew. *Natural Health, Natural Medicine*. Boston: Houghton-Mifflin, 1990.

Wheelwright, Phillip. *Metaphor and Reality*. Bloomington: Indiana University

Press, 1962.

White, John, ed. *Kundalini, Evolution, and Enlightenment*. Garden City, NY: Doubleday, Anchor Books, 1979.

White, Stewart Edward. *The Unobstructed Universe*. New York: Dutton & Co., 1940.

Whitman, Walt. *Leaves of Grass*. New York: Random House, 1892.

Wilber, Ken. *The Atman Project*. Wheaton, IL: Theosophical Publishing House, 1980.

_____. *Eye to Eye*. Garden City, NY: Doubleday, Anchor Books, 1983.

_____. *A Sociable God*. New York: McGraw-Hill, 1983.

Wilhelm, Richard, ed. and trans. *The Secret of the Golden Flower*. New York: Harcourt, Brace & World, 1981.

Wolkstein, Diane, and Samuel Noah Kramer. *Inanna: Queen of Heaven and Earth*. New York: Harper & Row, 1983.

Yogananda, Paramahansa. *Autobiography of a Yogi*. Los Angeles: Self-Realization Fellowship, 1973.

Young, Arthur. *The Reflexive Universe*. New York: Seymour Lawrence, 1976.

INDEX

ABOUT THE AUTHOR

RALPH METZNER, PhD, (1936-2019) was a recognized pioneer in psychological, philosophical, and cross-cultural studies of consciousness. He obtained his PhD in Clinical Psychology at Harvard University and collaborated with Timothy Leary and Richard Alpert in studies of psychedelics during the 1960s, co-authoring *The Psychedelic Experience* and editing *The Psychedelic Review*. He was a psychotherapist in private practice in the San Francisco Bay Area and Professor Emeritus at the California Institute of Integral Studies in San Francisco, where he taught consciousness studies and personality transformations for 30 years. Author of over 100 scientific papers and scholarly essays, he published more than 20 books on psychology, psychedelics, and European mythology. His most recent works include *Allies for Awakening: Guidelines for Productive and Safe Experiences with Entheogens* (2015), *Ecology of Consciousness: The Alchemy of Personal, Collective and Planetary Transformation* (2017), and *Searching for the Philosophers' Stone: Encounters with Mystics, Scientists, and Healers* (2018). Ralph was a resident of Sonoma for 30 years where he lived with his wife, Cathy Coleman; stepson, Elias Jacobson; and daughter, Sophia Metzner.